THE
CIVILIZATION
OF
CHINA

THE
CIVILIZATION
OF
CHINA

*From the Formative Period to the
Coming of the West*

TRANSLATIONS AND INTRODUCTIONS BY

DUN J. LI

Charles Scribner's Sons   New York

Library of Congress Cataloging in Publication Data

Li, Dun Jen, 1920–   comp.
    The civilization of China.

    1. China—Civilization—Addresses, essays, lectures.
I. Title.
DS721.L54347   915.1'03'08   74–8326
ISBN 0–684–13940–5
ISBN 0–684–13943–X (pbk)

1 3 5 7 9 11 13 15 17 19 H / C 20 18 16 14 12 10 8 6 4 2
1 3 5 7 9 11 13 15 17 19 H / P 20 18 16 14 12 10 8 6 4 2

Printed in the United States of America

Contents

CHAPTER 4
Disintegration and Amalgamation

CHAPTER 5
Sui and T'ang

CHAPTER 6
The Two Sungs (1)

CHAPTER 7

The Two Sungs (2)

CHAPTER 8

Yüan

CHAPTER 9

Ming

CHAPTER 10

Ch'ing

Preface

This book, an anthology of Chinese history that covers a period from ancient times to approximately 1800, describes the indigenous civilization before the Western impact. Its purpose is to provide a bird's-eye view of traditional China through the use of translated materials.

The book is organized chronologically. Each chapter, which corresponds to a major period in Chinese history, has two distinctive parts: an introduction of my own and the translated documents relating to the period under discussion. The introduction is meant, first, to give a general background of the selections, and second, to familiarize the reader with some of the basic sources covering the period. The selections, being the translated documents from these basic sources, were chosen to accentuate the predominant characteristics of that period. The Sung dynasty, for instance, is well known for its achievements in philosophy; the second chapter covering that dynasty, therefore, has four selections on philosophy. Since the abuse of power by eunuchs reached a high point during the Ming dynasty, it seems logical that a selection on eunuchs should be included in the chapter covering the Ming.

All the selections in this book are my own translations. In selecting materials to translate, I tried to avoid any that had already been rendered into English, including my own previous translations. With the exception of the four selections in chapter 2 ("The Philosophers"), which, being well known, must have been translated into English before, all the selections, as far as I know, appear in the English language for the first time. In the case of these four selections, I hope the reader will find my versions less confusing and easier to read than any previous ones.

Because of the basic differences between Chinese and English, especially between archaic Chinese (in which most selections in this book were written) and modern English, translation from one to the other poses enormous problems. Judged by its final product, a translation of this kind may fall into one of the following categories: incomprehensibility, comprehensibility, readability, or stylistic grace. Insistence on literal translation will in most cases make the final product either idiotic (such as the translation of *shui-hu* ["marsh"] as "water margin") or totally incomprehensible (such as the translation of *lao hsiao-chieh* ["spinster"] as "old little sister"), and too often has a masterpiece of Chinese literature been transformed into the incoherent chatter of a three-year-old child. Completely rewriting the original to achieve stylistic grace, on the other hand, cannot be characterized as translation. A translation from Chinese to English, therefore, has to be judged on a scale that ranges from the lower end of comprehensibility to the higher end of readability. As this author has learned from years of experience, making the translation fairly attractive, either from Chinese to English or the other way around, involves not only the reordering of phrases and sentences but also, sometimes, extensive editing of the original. It is admittedly difficult to reproduce the beauty of the original, but a translator serves neither the author nor the reader if his product is linguistically offensive.

A literary work, large or small, summarizes the author's indebtedness to all those who, directly or indirectly, have guided or influenced him in one way or another. In preparing this book two names repeatedly came to my mind. One was Master Lu, a white-haired, stern-faced man who taught me Chinese and every other subject that a school child was supposed to learn between the ages of five and nine. Every day he opened his school at 6 A.M. and closed it at 4 P.M. and would not release his charges for either breakfast or lunch until they had done what he regarded as satisfactory work. The other was Master Ch'a, my first English teacher in middle school. Master Ch'a learned English by memorizing his English-Chinese dictionary and, as far as I can recall, never left our village for a single day in his life. He had no difficulty with words that could be found in his dictionary, but he had to improvise whenever an idiom or a slang word appeared. He was ingenious enough to interpret "So long" to mean "We have talked so long that it is time to say good-bye," but he was totally baffled when he encountered a sentence such as "It rains cats and dogs." "Maybe the American sky is different," he explained and then laughed uncontrollably. Master Lu died when I was still in China and Master Ch'a, presumably, is still living somewhere in mainland China. To these two gentlemen and to all others who have taught me at one time or another I wish to dedicate this book.

The William Paterson College of New Jersey   Dun J. Li
Wayne, New Jersey
June 1974

CHAPTER

1

The Formative Period

LIKE many other peoples with a long history, the Chinese have their own legends explaining their beginning as a nation and their advance toward a civilization. Before the development of archaeology as an exact science in modern times, they relied almost exclusively on written records for an understanding of their remote past, but these records, written long after the alleged events had taken place, tended to be sparse in detail and conflicting in content. Important innovations in the beginning of a civilized life, such as marriage and family, agriculture and commerce, were attributed to a few culture heroes, when in fact they could not but have been products of a long evolutionary process (selection 1). Nevertheless, legends served a useful purpose, since they forged a group consciousness among those who believed in them, and this group consciousness, based upon a shared historical background and the prospect of a common destiny for the future, marked the beginning of a nation. In forging a national consciousness, it mattered little how much truth or falsehood these legends contained.

Legends tended to multiply with the passage of time, and writers of succeeding generations were apt to read into them contemporary beliefs and to refine them accordingly. Filial piety, for instance, was a much-emphasized virtue in a later period and the culture heroes in ancient legends, from the viewpoint of contemporary writers, could not be truly great without possessing it in abundance. Thus Shun, a "good emperor" of China's remote past, was described as not only a model ruler but also an unusually pious son (selection 2).

Among the written records of China's remote past, perhaps none is more remarkable than the *Book of Odes (Shih ching)*.

The book, consisting of folk songs, political poems, and religious hymns, gives us firsthand information about Chinese life some one thousand years before the Christian era. Particularly valuable are the folk songs that describe the hopes and frustrations, as well as the daily routine, of people in North China. For example, the author of one of these folk songs took a close look at the life of the peasants around him and recorded it; the result has become one of the most important and reliable documents on the social and economic history of ancient China (selection 3). Even today the *Book of Odes* remains a gold mine; those who wish to dig can always find some nuggets.

Beginning in the sixth century B.C., or the time of Confucius (551–479 B.C.), books began to multiply, partly because of the Confucian veneration for the written word. Confucius himself was said to have written the *Spring and Autumn Annals (Ch'un ch'iu)*, a chronology of his native state of Lu, but modern historians have serious doubts about this alleged authorship. More interesting are three subsequent books that elaborate on the chronological entries of the *Spring and Autumn Annals:* namely, *Commentaries of Tso (Tso chuan), Commentaries of Kung-yang (Kung-yang chuan)*, and *Commentaries of Ku-liang (Ku-liang chuan)*. Compared with the chronology on which they are commentaries, these three books are much more descriptive; yet, according to the modern standards we are used to, they could still be criticized for being too fragmentary in details and too moralistic in tone (selection 4). Nevertheless they are the major sources dealing with this period, namely, the Spring and Autumn period (722–481 B.C.).

From the point of view of a lay reader, a later book dealing with a subsequent period is much more satisfactory. *Documents of the Warring States (Chan-kuo ts'e)* contains chapters corresponding to the various states then dividing China, instead of being arranged in chronological order. Its author, while describing war and peace and the numerous ways leading to them, did not fail to give space to the literarily more engaging but politically less consequential events that have proved to be universally appealing. It is the presence of these events that has enabled this book to charm Chinese readers for more than two thousand years (selection 5).

The value of the *Documents of the Warring States* as a source of historical information was recognized early. In the second century B.C., for instance, Ssu-ma Ch'ien used it extensively in writing his own book, *Historical Records (Shih chi)*. He, of course, also used many other sources, most of which, unfortunately, have been permanently lost. Whatever sources he used, it is nearly impossible to exaggerate his contribution to historiography. Had it not been for his masterpiece, an enormous gap of historical knowledge would have resulted and we would not know, for instance, the events that led to the unification of China in 221 B.C. Like many historians of our own time, Ssu-ma Ch'ien tended to stress the dramatic and the spectacular, especially events of a tragic nature. The implication is that had the events he described ended other than the way they did, as could easily have happened, the course of history would have been entirely different (selection 6). While it is debatable whether the movement of history really hinges upon certain key points, this approach to writing history does make more interesting reading.

(1)

Anonymous / *Culture Heroes*[1]

Having observed heavenly and earthly phenomena and drawn inspiration from far and near, including from birds and beasts, Pao-hsi, a king of ancient times, first drew the Eight Diagrams. The purpose of the Eight Diagrams was twofold: to communicate with the unknown and to express, in visible terms, the laws that underlay every object and phenomenon on earth. Pao-hsi taught people to use ropes to make nets, thus enabling them to hunt and fish more efficiently.

After Pao-hsi's death, Shen-nung succeeded him as the ruler of China. Having convinced his subjects of the benefit of agriculture, he taught them to make plows and plowshares from wood in the forest. He gathered people at noon for the purpose of trade, so they could part with the goods they did not want in order to obtain the goods which they needed. Everyone became better off as a result of this process.

After Shen-nung's death, he was succeeded, successively, by Huang-ti, Yao, and Shun as the ruler of China. These rulers taught their subjects the principle of change which, when mastered, would enable them not only to live a full life but also to enjoy it thoroughly, since the principle of change is ordained by Heaven itself. Change must occur when the existing way is no longer adequate, and only through change can a new workable way be found. As long as it works, the existing way lasts. Heaven protects those who change with the change of circumstances. Huang-ti, Yao, and Shun, by following this principle, ruled China successfully, without doing anything dramatic or spectacular.

These rulers taught people to fashion wood to make boats and oars, so goods could be exchanged between different parts of China. They also taught people to harness horses and oxen, so men and goods could be transported to distant areas. They instructed people to strengthen their doors and to hire watchmen to beat rattles at night, in order to ward off thieves and robbers. To pound husks from the grain, they taught people to sharpen wood to make a pestle and to dig a hole in the ground to serve as a mortar. They also taught people to use wood to make bow and arrows, so they would be feared by those who intended to harm them.

In remote times people lived in caves in the wilderness. The sages of a later period taught them to build houses, complete with beams and pillars, so they could protect themselves from the harsh elements.

In remote times people wrapped their dead with straw before burying them in the wilderness. The dead body was not sealed in a casket; nor was a tree planted on the grave site. They did not even observe a mourning period. The sages changed all this in a later period. Not only was a coffin required, but the coffin with the dead man in it also had to be housed in a brick vault.

In remote times people made knots with ropes as a means of communication. The sages of a later period taught people to communicate with one another through the use of written words. As a result of the invention of a written language, not only did the government become more efficient, but the people also became better governed.

Notes

1. The source of this selection, namely, *Appendix to the Book of Changes (Yi hsi-tz'u)*, was attributed to King Wen of Chou (Chou Wen-wang) of the twelfth century B.C. More likely it was written in a later period by an anonymous author or authors.

(2)
Ssu-ma Ch'ien / *Good Emperors*[1]

Huang-ti ("Yellow Emperor")[2] was the son of Shao-tien. His surname was Kung-sun; his personal name was Hsien-yüan. Born with supernatural intellect, he was able to speak when only two months old. At the age of fifteen, he had mastered every subject there was to be known. At the age of twenty, he was widely known for his integrity and character, as well as his brilliance as a learned man.

Huang-ti lived at a time when the rule of Shen-nung had declined. The regional lords fought among themselves, while oppressing their own people at home. Because Shen-nung could not bring them to account, Huang-ti trained himself in the art of warfare and sent his armed forces against those who had refused to pledge their allegiance to the king. As a result of his efforts, all the regional lords came to the king's court to pay their respects, with the exception of Ch'ih-yu, who was too powerful to be brought to his senses.

Meanwhile another regional lord, namely Yen-ti, also harbored the thought of invading and annexing the territories of other regional lords. These regional lords, to seek protection, pledged their allegiance to Huang-ti. To prepare himself for the forthcoming confrontation with Yen-ti, Huang-ti taught his people the cultivation of various crops in accordance with the change of seasons, comforted them and built up their morale, and continued to train his army until every soldier of his was as strong as a bear and as ferocious as a tiger. In the wilderness of Panch'ien [modern Hopeh province], Huang-ti decisively defeated Yen-ti.

Ch'ih-yu, however, was still in revolt and refused to obey the

order of the king [Shen-nung]. Gathering troops from other regional lords together with his own, Huang-ti fought Ch'ih-yu in
the wilderness of Cholu [modern Hopeh province]. He captured
his opponent and subsequently executed him. After this victory,
all the regional lords acclaimed Huang-ti, instead of Shen-nung,
as the Son of Heaven.

Emperor Yao,[3] whose personal name was Fang-hsün, was by all
counts an extraordinary person. He was as loving as Heaven itself
and as all-knowing as if he were a god. He was like the sun that
illuminates; he was like the clouds that bring beneficial rain. He
was wealthy and yet unconceited, noble and yet unpretentious.
Customarily he wore a yellow hat and a black robe. When traveling, he rode in a vermilion carriage pulled by white horses.

As a man of noble character, Yao was able to induce others to
do good themselves. First he brought harmony among members
of his own clan and then expanded this harmony to the relationship of all the people within his jurisdiction. When, finally, all of
his subjects had become wise and enlightened enough, he promoted harmony and friendship among all the nations. . . .

One day Yao addressed his vassals as follows: "A great flood has
occurred that has swept away men and animals. Our people have
suffered greatly. Whom, pray, would you recommend to control
the raging water?" Upon hearing the recommendation of Kun,
Yao objected. "Kun has disobeyed my order by harming innocent
people," he explained.

"There is no one else knowledgeable enough to undertake the
task," said the vassals. "Let him proceed, and we shall find out
soon." Yao accepted the recommendation and charged Kun with
the responsibility of taming the flood. Kun worked on water
control for nine years, but he did not succeed.

"Oh, my vassals everywhere," said Yao on another occasion, "I
have been occupying this post for seventy years. Will one of you
consent to succeed me?"

"We are not virtuous enough to succeed you, sir," the vassals
replied unanimously.

"In that case," said Yao, "will you recommend someone who
is virtuous enough? It matters not whether he is a relative of
yours or an obscure commoner who has succeeded thus far in
hiding his true worth."

"We have heard of an unmarried commoner named Shun," the
vassals responded.

"Will you tell me more about this man?" asked Yao. "Why do you think that he is good enough to succeed me?"

"He is the eldest son of a blind man," the vassals replied. "He has a stubborn father, a meddlesome mother, and an egotistic brother. Yet he is as dutiful toward his parents as he is protective toward his younger brother. The family, consequently, is well managed and harmonious. It has not done anything wrong."

To find out how good Shun really was, Yao married him to his two daughters. After the marriage, Shun brought his two wives to Kueijui [modern Shansi province] where they were taught womanly virtues. Greatly pleased with Shun's management of his household, Yao charged him with the responsibility of supervising the five family officials, whose duty it was to maintain harmony in family relationships throughout the empire. As the five officials performed well under the new leadership, Shun was appointed the lord chancellor of all officials. Acting in this capacity, he was able not only to bring order and dignity to the court but also to win respect from all of Yao's vassals. Subsequently Yao sent him to high mountains, deep forests, winding rivers, and treacherous swamps. In each case Shun was able to find his way out, despite wicked winds and thunderous storms. Yao was finally convinced that Shun, indeed, was the new sage destined to succeed him. . . .

In the seventieth year of his reign, Yao met Shun for the first time. In the ninetieth year of his reign, he abdicated on the latter's behalf. He died eight years later.[4]

Shun, whose personal name was Ch'ung-hua, was the first born son of a blind man named Ku-sou. Upon the death of his mother, his father remarried and subsequently had another son named Hsiang. Hsiang, unfortunately, turned out to be a conceited, egotistic person. Consistently biased in favor of his wife and second son, Ku-sou was brutal toward his first born. Shun, nevertheless, received without complaint whatever punishment his father chose to impose upon him. Whenever he sensed that his father was about to kill him, however, he simply ran away from him. At all times he served his father, stepmother, and half brother with great diligence, despite the way they treated him.

Though a native of Yi, Shun had at various times worked as a farmer in Lishan, as a fisherman in Leitse, as a potter in Hopin, as an artisan in Shouch'iu, and as a merchant in Fuhsia.[5]

At home his father, stepmother, and half brother continued to harbor the thought of killing him. They had a difficult time finding an excuse, however, since Shun had always been careful and obedient. One day, while Shun was painting the top of the family barn in observance of an order from his father, his father set fire underneath. Shun used two wide-rimmed bamboo hats as a parachute and landed on the ground without being killed. Another time, while digging a well deep underneath the ground as ordered by his father, he saw rocks and earth coming down from the opening of the well. Fortunately, having sensed in advance that his father and half brother would use the well digging as a means of killing him, he had taken the precaution of digging a connecting tunnel to a neighboring well, through the opening of which he later emerged unharmed. Thinking that Shun had been buried alive inside the well, Hsiang was greatly pleased with his work and asked his parents to divide the family properties with him on the ground that he, instead of his father, was primarily responsible for Shun's "timely" death. The family properties were then divided; Hsiang took all the livestock, leaving the farm to his parents.

Returning home from the well, Shun proceeded to his own room, where he found Hsiang playing his lute. Hsiang, shocked to see a lively Shun, said sheepishly, "I was greatly worried about what might have happened to you."

"In that case," Shun replied, "let us act more like brothers from now on." From then on, Shun was even more pious toward his parents and more considerate toward his half brother.

Shun became widely known as a pious son when he was twenty years old. Ten years later he was recommended to Yao. At the age of fifty he assumed the role of acting emperor. Eight years later, Yao died. Two years after Yao's death, Shun formally acquired the imperial title.[6]

Yü, whose personal name was Wen-ming, was the son of Kun. . . . During the time of Emperor Yao there was a great flood that destroyed men and properties and caused enormous sufferings to all the people. When Yao sought an expert in water control, his vassals recommended Kun, saying that Kun was most knowledgeable in this matter. Kun worked for nine years without succeeding in taming the flood; Yao, consequently, sought a different man and found him in Shun. When Shun, as the acting emperor, made an inspection tour of the empire and found the water as ravaging as it had been before, he ordered the execution of Kun at a place called Yüshan [modern Kiangsu province], an execution that was hailed by all the people as a correct measure. After Kun's death, Shun appointed Kun's son Yü the superintendent of water control. Hopefully Yü would complete the work that his father had failed to do.

Grieved by the fact that his father suffered capital punishment on account of his inability to tame the flood, Yü was determined to succeed. He taxed his brain and toiled with his body to find the best means available. For thirteen years he worked intensely, so intensely that he did not once enter his own house when he passed by it. He ate and dressed simply, so the expenses thus saved could be used for the worship of gods and spirits, whose blessing he sought. He lived in a crude dwelling, so the expenses thus saved could be used for the construction of ditches and canals. Traveling on land by vehicles, on water by boats, in swamps by sleighs, and in mountains by slings, he worked all year round in the nine provinces of China, always carrying with him a plumb line, a compass, and a square. . . . [7]

Upon Yü's triumph over the great flood, Emperor Shun, in recognition of his service, bestowed upon him a black tablet made of jade. Simultaneously he announced to the world that the enormous task of taming the great flood had been successfully completed. A new era of peace and prosperity thus began. . . .

Seventeen years after Yü had been recommended to Heaven as the next emperor, Emperor Shun died. Yü observed a mourning period of three years and then went to Yangch'eng [modern Honan province] for retirement. The regional lords of China, instead of going to the capital to pledge their allegiance to Shun's son Shang-chün, came to Yangch'eng to pay their homage to Yü. Yü assumed the imperial title and called his regime Hsia. [8]

Notes

1. Ssu-ma Ch'ien was the royal historian during the reign of Han Wu-ti (r. 140–87 B.C.). This selection, taken from the *Historical Records*, is the first systematic account of the "good emperors" of China's remote past. Source: *Shih chi*, rolls 1 and 2.

2. According to China's traditional historians, Huang-ti lived in the twenty-seventh century B.C.

3. Yao was supposed to have lived in the twenty-fourth century B.C.

4. Among China's traditional historians there is a difference in opinion as to how old Yao was when he died: 116, 117, or 118 years old.

5. Yi was located in modern Hopeh province; Lishan and Hopin, in modern Shansi province; Leitse, Shouch'iu, and Fuhsia, in modern Shantung province.

6. Traditional historians in China place this event in 2255 B.C.

7. This was followed by a detailed account of the construction of canals, dikes, and dams all over China.

8. Traditional historians in China place this event in 2205 B.C.

(3)
Anonymous / *In the Seventh Month*[1]

In the seventh month the Antares moves westward. I shall receive new clothes soon, in the ninth month.

In the eleventh month the wind is cold. In the twelfth month the wind is bitter. Without new clothes, how can I pass through the winter?

In the third month I repair the plow. In the fourth month I plow the field. My wife and children bring me food; together we eat in the southern field. The lord's steward passes by, smiling his approval.

In the seventh month the Antares moves westward. I shall receive new clothes soon, in the ninth month.

The sun shines warmly in the spring; everywhere one hears the oriole sing. Carrying a deep basket, my daughter goes to the mulberry grove. The leaves are moist and tender, to be plucked for the silkworms at home.

Days in the spring move lazily; a multitude of silkworms crawl on the straw. "All this saddens me greatly. Oh, heavens! When can I join the lad I love?"

In the seventh month the Antares moves westward. In the eighth month I cut straw and reeds. I bundle leaves and branches. To reach distant branches, I climb the tree with an ax.

In the seventh month the tailor birds sing. In the eighth month I weave silk. I dye it black, yellow, and flashing red. I shall make clothes for the lord.

In the fourth month the grass grows beautiful and long. In the fifth month the cicada starts to sing. In the eighth month I collect harvests. In the tenth month trees shed their leaves.

In the first month I hunt foxes for their skin. With the skin I shall make winter clothing for the lord. In the second month I learn martial arts, being drilled with other peasants. I have acquired a litter of piglets; I shall present the fattened ones to the lord.

In the fifth month the centipede stirs. In the sixth month the cricket acquires its wings. It stays in the field in the seventh month, but comes to my house in the eighth. In the ninth month I find it inside my room. It goes into hiding underneath my bed in the tenth.

As winter comes closer, mice are smoked out from their hidings; walls are plastered to cover holes and crevices. I caulk doors and windows, especially those facing the north. "Oh, my wife and children, by the New Year you will have a new house."

I eat plums and scallions in the sixth month, and melons and peas in the seventh. In the eighth month I peel dates; in the tenth month I receive rice. Using rice I make spring wine; I shall present it to the lord on the anniversary of his birth.

I eat melons in the seventh month and empty gourds to make vessels in the eighth. In the ninth month I make hemp fiber and collect edible seeds and plants. For firewood I bring home dead trees. Oh, heavens! A peasant has to live!

In the tenth month I rebuild the vegetable garden and make it a threshing floor. In the tenth month I store the crops: millet, hemp, wheat, and melon seeds.

Having finished working at home, I must report to the lord. I cut straw by day; in the evening I twist it into ropes. I must hurry to repair the lord's barn; before long it will be spring when I cultivate his field.

In the second month I hew out ice; in the third month I store it in a shady, cold place. In the fourth month the lord tastes the ice in his temple, where he offers scallions as tribute and lambs as sacrifice.

Frost begins to gather in the ninth month, when the air

becomes cold. In the tenth month the threshing floor is swept clear and clean, as the day of celebration has finally arrived. Two jars of spirits are opened; lambs are slaughtered for this important occasion. To the lord's mansion we all go. Raising our cups high, we shout aloud, "Long live the lord!"

Notes

1. This is one of the oldest folk songs in Chinese history, attributed to the people of Pin (modern Shensi province) who sang the praise of Kung-liu, a prince who governed them in the eighteenth century B.C. Most likely it was written in a later period, in the eleventh or tenth century B.C., when Chou feudalism was in its prime. Source: "The Folk Songs of Pin" *(Pin feng)* in the *Book of Odes,* roll 13.

(4)
Tso Ch'iu-ming / *Prince Ch'ung-erh*[1]

As a refugee from his own state,[2] Prince Ch'ung-erh escaped to Puch'eng.[3] When the people of Puch'eng proposed to defend the city against the Tsin army that had come to arrest him, the prince voiced strong objections. "I received a livelihood as well as my very life from my father, the duke," said the prince. "Because of his assistance, I was able to have supporters of my own. Since a crime would be committed if I choose to resist him, I shall flee instead."

Prince Ch'ung-erh fled to Ti,[4] accompanied by Hu Yen, Chao Ts'ui, Tien Chieh, Wei Wu-tzu, Ssu-k'ung Chi-tzu, and others. It was during his stay at Ti that the Ti people invaded Ch'iang-chiu-ju and captured from its chieftain two of his daughters, namely, Shu-wei and Chi-wei. The prince took Chi-wei, the younger of the two sisters, and gave Shu-wei to Chao Ts'ui. Later Chi-wei gave birth to Pai-t'iao and Shu-liu, and Shu-wei became the mother of Chao Tun.[5] Having stayed at Ti for a period of time, Prince Ch'ung-erh planned to move to the state of Ch'i. "If I do not return at the end of twenty-five years," he said to Chi-wei, "you are free to marry somebody else."

"I shall be dead by then," Chi-wei replied. "I shall wait for you, no matter how long it takes."

On his way to Ch'i, Prince Ch'ung-erh passed through the state of Wei, where its ruler, Duke Wen, refused to receive him. In Wulu whereto he had been banished by the duke, the prince requested food from a native. Instead of food, the native presented him with a lump of earth. The prince, furious at the insult, was about to whip the native when he was stopped by Hu Yen. "This lump of earth is a gift from Heaven," said Hu Yen. He saluted the native, respectfully took the lump of earth, and placed it in a carriage.[6]

In the state of Ch'i, Prince Ch'ung-erh was received most cordially by its ruler, Duke Huan [Ch'i Huan-kung, 686–643 B.C.]. The duke married him to Chiang, one of his relatives, and presented him with expensive gifts, including twenty carriages. As the prince loved the easy life and refused to leave Ch'i, his followers, dismayed at his lack of ambition, gathered under a mulberry tree and tried to find a way to persuade him to change his mind. They did not realize that a servant girl, who was plucking mulberry leaves on the top of the tree, had heard everything they discussed. The servant girl informed Chiang, her mistress, of the plot which, if successfully carried out, would take the prince away from his wife. But Chiang, instead of thanking her for this information, ordered her to be killed immediately.

"I have heard that you are entertaining a great ambition of your own," said Chiang to the prince. "The person who happened to have learned about it has been killed by me."

"I have no such ambition," the prince replied.

"Be gone, my lord husband," said Chiang. "Nothing in the world can kill the manliness of man more effectively than an easy, carefree life."

Shortly afterward, Chiang and Hu Yen formed a plot whereby Prince Ch'ung-erh was made dead drunk before he was shipped away from Ch'i without his knowledge. When he finally awoke, the prince was so furious that he chased Hu Yen with a spear.

Having arrived at the state of Ts'ao, Prince Ch'ung-erh, while taking a bath, was subjected to the humiliation of being watched at close range. Duke Kung, the ruler of Ts'ao, had heard that the prince's ribs were joined and was determined to verify this rumor himself. "As far as I have been able to observe," said Hsi Fu-chien's wife,[7] "Prince Ch'ung-erh's followers are all men of the greatest ability. They will someday succeed in bringing their master to his native state and installing him as its ruler. Since Tsin is a powerful state, its new ruler will doubtless punish those states that have been less than kind to him. In view of what Duke Kung has done, Ts'ao will be the first among his targets of vengeance. You, my husband, should disassociate yourself from the official position before it is too late." Acting upon his wife's advice, Hsi Fu-chien presented Prince Ch'ung-erh with delicacies and a piece of jade. The prince accepted the delicacies, but returned the jade.

When Prince Ch'ung-erh arrived at the state of Sung, Duke Hsiang, its ruler, presented him with twenty carriages as a gift.

Upon his arrival at Cheng, however, Duke Wen, its ruler, decided not to receive him. Shu-chan, his minister, protested. "What Heaven has ordained," he said, "no man can change. Prince Ch'ung-erh possesses three advantages, indicating perhaps that he has been designated by Heaven to become the ruler of his state. It is for this reason that I implore you to be considerate toward him. First, if both parents bear the same surname, their offspring will not multiply. The prince's mother was named Hu Chi, indicating that she bore no relation whatsoever to the prince's father in blood. Second, the state of Tsin is in chaos while the prince is traveling abroad. This indicates that Heaven has designated no one except him to restore order in that state. Third, he has as his advisers three of the most outstanding men in China who will, in due course, help him to fulfill his ambitions. Besides, Tsin and Cheng are brotherly states and have the obligation of receiving each other's children. This obligation becomes all the more compelling when we take into consideration what Heaven has clearly revealed to men." Duke Wen did not follow this advice; Prince Ch'ung-erh, consequently, left Cheng for the state of Ch'u.

In a banquet honoring Prince Ch'ung-erh, the king of Ch'u asked his guest how he would repay him for the hospitality that had been extended to him, once he returned to his native state of Tsin. "The state of Ch'u has all it needs in terms of men and wealth," the prince replied. "I cannot think of anything to repay you, since Tsin is inferior to Ch'u in this regard."

"Nevertheless, think of something," the king of Ch'u insisted.

"If, with your blessing, I am indeed returned to my state, I shall order my army to withdraw by thirty miles when it meets yours on the battlefield. If you choose to continue to advance despite my withdrawal, I shall do my very best to defeat you."[8]

General Tzu-yü proposed that Prince Ch'ung-erh be killed in view of his impudent remarks, but the king declined. "The prince from Tsin is lofty in ambition and yet frugal in personal life," said the king. "He is refined and courteous. As for his followers, they are as serious as they are broad-minded. They are a loyal, able group. The present ruler in Tsin,[9] on the other hand, has no real support of his own and is in fact detested by people at home and abroad. I have heard that the clan of Chi, from which the prince comes, descends directly from T'ang Shu,[10] though its power and influence have since declined. Is it possible that Prince Ch'ung-erh has been designated by Heaven to revive it? As Heaven wills, man obeys. Those who oppose the will of Heaven will incur its wrath and bring on themselves the greatest misfortunes." Having said this, the king ordered that Prince Ch'ung-erh be escorted with courtesy to the state of Ch'in.

While in Ch'in, Duke Mu, its ruler, married Prince Ch'ung-erh to five of his relatives, including Huai-ying. One day Huai-ying presented the prince with water and towel for the latter to wash his hands. The prince, after washing but before drying his hands, waved Huai-ying away, causing water to sprinkle on Huai-ying's clothes. Huai-ying was furious. "Ch'in and Tsin are states of equal footing," said she; "how dare you insult me?" Frightened, the prince surrendered himself and pleaded for mercy, in such a humble manner as if he were her prisoner of war.

One day, when Duke Mu intimated his intention to give a banquet in the prince's honor, Hu Yen suggested that Chao Ts'ui, instead of himself, should accompany the prince. "Ts'ui is more cultured than I am," he explained. At the banquet the prince recited "Water in the River," and the duke responded with "The Sixth Month."[11] "Let Ch'ung-erh show his gratitude by saluting the duke for the favor he has received," said Chao Ts'ui. Prince Ch'ung-erh descended the steps and kowtowed. Duke Mu, to express his own modesty and appreciation, came down one step to waive this extreme form of salutation. "Since his lordship has granted Ch'ung-erh the unusual privilege of supporting the king,"[12] said Chao Ts'ui, "how could Ch'ung-erh not kowtow to show his gratitude?"

In the second month of the twenty-fourth year during the reign of Duke Hsi of Lu [636 B.C.],[13] the Ch'in forces reached

Hsün.[14] Shortly afterward, Prince Ch'ung-erh entered the state of Tsin. No resistance was encountered when he arrived at the capital, Ch'üwo [modern Shansi province]. On the morning of the next day he worshiped at his ancestral temple, Wukung.

Notes

1. This selection was taken from *Commentaries of Tso*, allegedly written by Tso Ch'iu-ming, who lived in the sixth century B.C. It describes the wanderings of Prince Ch'ung-erh in various parts of China for a period of nineteen years (655–636 B.C.) before he returned to his native state to become Duke Wen of Tsin (d. 629 B.C.). His assumption of power marked the beginning of Tsin as the most powerful state in North China. Source: *Tso chuan*, the twenty-third and twenty-fourth years of Duke Hsi of Lu (637–636 B.C.).

2. Duke Hsien of Tsin (d. 650 B.C.), the prince's father and a psychopathic case in his advanced age, had wanted to kill all his sons by his first wives in order to designate as his successor a son by his second wife. He had forced his first-born son, Prince Ch'ung-erh's elder brother, to commit suicide. Prince Ch'ung-erh himself barely escaped death.

3. Puch'eng was located in modern Shensi province. The event occurred in 655 B.C.

4. A non-Chinese tribe located in northern Shensi.

5. Interracial marriages between Chinese and non-Chinese, especially among aristocratic families, were very common at this time. The offspring, almost without exception, identified himself or herself with his or her father's side, whether Chinese or non-Chinese.

6. A lump of earth, in Hu Yen's mind, resembled land. Its presentation by this native was an omen that Prince Ch'ung-erh would eventually return to his native state and become its rightful ruler.

7. Hsi Fu-chien was a minister in the state of Ts'ao.

8. Later, in 632 B.C., the two sides did meet in one of the most important battles of this period, namely, the Battle of Ch'engpu. Keeping his promise, Tsin Wen-kung (formerly Prince Ch'ung-erh) ordered his troops to withdraw by thirty miles when they were brought face to face with the Ch'u army on the battlefield. General Tzu-yü of Ch'u, mistaking this withdrawal for an indication of weakness, kept pushing forward, until he and his army were totally surrounded. The victory Tsin won in this battle marked the beginning of its hegemony in North China.

9. Duke Hui of Tsin (d. 636 B.C.), Prince Ch'ung-erh's younger brother. Duke Hui had tried, but failed, to kill Prince Ch'ung-erh.

10. A feudal prince investitured in Shensi by King Ch'eng of Chou (d. 1115 B.C.) in the twelfth century B.C.

11. Both poems come from the *Book of Odes*. The main theme of "Water in the River" *(Ho shui)* is that all water will eventually end in the sea. The prince, in this case, was comparing Duke Mu with the sea which was deep and wide enough to receive water from all rivers, one of which resembled himself. The

poem "The Sixth Month" *(Liu yüeh)* describes the unswerving effort of Yin Chi-fu, the prime minister who served under King Hsüan of Chou (r. 827–782 B.C.), to bring under the king's control feudatories that were in rebellion. Duke Mu recited this particular poem for the purpose of indicating to Prince Ch'ung-erh that he would do his part to return the prince to his native state where he would be installed as its rightful ruler.

12. This was an indirect way of saying that Duke Mu had made the promise of installing Ch'ung-erh as the ruler of Tsin, since the prince, obviously, would not be in a position to support the king of Chou (Chou Hsiang-wang, r. 651–619 B.C.) if he were not the ruler of Tsin. Actually the king had little or no power over his nominal subordinates, such as the dukes of Ch'in or Tsin, who could indeed do whatever they pleased. The principle of supporting the king, though often invoked, was merely a perfunctory gesture.

13. The *Commentaries of Tso*, like the *Spring and Autumn Annals*, follows the chronology of Lu, the home state of Confucius.

14. A city on the border between Ch'in and Tsin.

(5)
Anonymous / *Feng Hsüan*[1]

In the state of Ch'i there was a man named Feng Hsüan who, having no means of support, intimated to Prince Meng-ch'ang [d. 289 B.C.], through an intermediary, that he would like to be one of the prince's household guests.

"Is there anything you would particularly like to do?" asked the prince when Feng Hsüan was brought before him.

"No," Feng Hsüan replied.

"Do you have any special ability?"

"No."

Prince Meng-ch'ang laughed. Nevertheless he accepted Feng Hsüan as one of his household guests.

The prince's servants, having sensed that the prince did not think too highly of this man, fed him low-quality food. This continued for a few days.

One day the servants found Feng Hsüan leaning against a column and singing aloud, while beating his sword for rhythm. "Oh, sword—my long sword!" he sang. "Shouldn't you and I return home? How can a meal be a meal without fish?" Upon hearing his complaint from the servants, the prince said that he should be provided with the same kind of food as his other guests received.

A few days later, the servants heard Feng Hsüan beating his sword and singing again. "Oh, sword—my long sword! Shouldn't you and I return home? How can a man move around without a carriage?" The servants laughed at his impudence, but nevertheless reported his complaint to the prince. "Give him a carriage," said the prince. From then on, Feng Hsüan was listed as the prince's most honored guest.

Riding the carriage and raising his sword high, Feng Hsüan visited many of his friends. "The prince really treats me like a guest," he told them.

However, it was not long before he complained again. "Oh, sword—my long sword!" he sang while beating his sword. "Shouldn't you and I return home? How can a man be a man when he cannot support his family?" All the servants detested him when they heard this song. They considered him a greedy man whose greed had no limit. The prince, nevertheless, asked Feng Hsüan whether he had any relatives; the reply was that he had an old mother. "Let his mother be adequately supplied with food and other necessities," the prince ordered. "Make sure that she will not lack anything." From then on, Feng Hsüan did not sing again.

One day the prince showed some account books to his household guests and inquired whether any of them had accounting experience, since he needed someone to go to his fief Hsüeh to collect debts for him.

"I can do this for you," Feng Hsüan volunteered.

"Who is this gentleman?" asked the prince.

"This is the same person who used to sing 'Return Home with My Long Sword,'" the servants replied.

"I am sorry that I have not been able to see you as often I should have," the prince smiled. "I have been busy with state affairs that are extremely troublesome; they worry me a great deal. The matter is not helped by my own lack of ability and foresight. Taking into consideration the fact that I have not been very considerate and may indeed have offended you, are you still willing to collect debts for me?"

"Yes, I am," Feng Hsüan replied.

The servants prepared a carriage, plus other traveling conveniences, for the trip. The prince handed to Feng Hsüan the promissory notes that had been long overdue.

"What should I buy with the money that I shall collect?" asked Feng Hsüan, who had gone to the prince to say good-bye.

"Buy things that I do not have in my house," the prince replied.

Arriving at Hsüeh, Feng Hsüan ordered local officials to identify all the debtors and bring all of them to meet him. When they arrived, he announced, on his own authority and in violation of his instructions, that the prince had decided to cancel all the debts they owed him. Having said this, he burned all the promissory notes. "Long live the prince!" they shouted.

Returning to Ch'i, Feng Hsüan sought audience with the prince early in the morning. The prince was so happily surprised with the speedy completion of his mission that he dressed formally to receive him.

"Have you collected all the debts?" the prince inquired. "How were you able to do this so quickly?"

"Yes, I have collected all the debts for you," Feng Hsüan replied.

"What did you buy with the money?"

"You, sir, told me to buy things that you do not have in your house," said Feng Hsüan. "As I look around, there is nothing you really lack. You have all kinds of treasures inside your house, and you have stables full of racing horses and game hounds. All around you there are beautiful women who serve you as concubines and servants. If there is one thing you lack, it is love. I have bought love for you."

"How did you buy love?"

"Let me explain," said Feng Hsüan. "Today you have this small fief of yours called Hsüeh. Instead of loving and protecting your subjects as you should, you exploit them by charging them high interest. I, therefore, canceled all the debts and burned all the promissory notes on my own authority. I told the Hsüeh people that I had been authorized by you to do this; they were so overjoyed that they shouted aloud, 'Long live the prince!' I have indeed bought you love, love from all of your subjects."

The prince was not very happy with the answer. "What can I say?" the prince remarked. "You should go home and take a rest."

One year later, the king of Ch'i[2] dismissed Prince Meng-ch'ang from his post on the ground that he did not dare to retain as his prime minister the prime minister of his predecessor. Having been dismissed from his post, Prince Meng-ch'ang had no other choice but to return to his fief Hsüeh. For a whole day the people of Hsüeh, having heard about the arrival of their prince, traveled miles to welcome him, including old men, old women, and small children. Turning to Feng Hsüan, the prince said happily, "Now I know what you meant when you said that you had bought love for me."

Notes

1. *Documents of the Warring States*, from which this selection is taken, was written by an anonymous author or authors who lived in the third century B.C. The extant version was edited by Liu Hsiang in the first century B.C. Source: *Chan-kuo ts'e*, roll 11.

2. King Min of Ch'i (Ch'i Min-wang), who ascended the throne in 300 B.C.

(6)

Ssu-ma Ch'ien / *Ching K'o the Assassin*[1]

We know little about Ching K'o's childhood except that he was born in Wei.[2] When history began to take notice of him, he, as an adult, had traveled in several states and eventually settled in Chich'eng [modern Hopeh province], capital of the state of Yen.

In Chich'eng Ching K'o was said to have had two friends: a dog butcher[3] whose name has been lost to posterity and a musician named Kao Chien-li who specialized in the playing of the *chu*.[4] All three were addicted to drinking; not a single day passed that they were not found dead drunk in the street. Whenever intoxicated, Ching K'o would sing to the accompaniment of Kao Chien-li's *chu*. Then they would laugh or cry as they pleased, in a totally uninhibited manner as if nobody else in the world had ever existed.

There was, however, another aspect of Ching K'o's personality. He loved to read, and to those few who knew him well he was a serious man with deep convictions. He could indeed count as his friends many prominent men in the states he had visited. In Yen, for instance, he was befriended by T'ien Kuang, an elderly scholar then in retirement, who regarded Ching K'o as an extraordinary man, one of the most unusual he had ever met.

It was during Ching K'o's stay at Yen that an event of enormous importance concerning the fate of that state began to unfold. Tan, the crown prince of Yen, had recently escaped from the state of Ch'in where he had hitherto served as a hostage.[5] Previously, when he was a hostage in the state of Chao, Cheng,[6] a Ch'in prince who was actually born in Chao, befriended him; it was not surprising that upon Cheng's ascension to the throne as king of Ch'in he should request Tan's transfer to Ch'in as his hostage. The old friendship, however, could not be renewed under the new circumstances; in fact, the king of Ch'in had treated Tan so badly that the latter, full of resentment and anger, returned to his own state without his host's knowledge. Once home, Tan sought ways of revenge against his former friend and now deadly enemy. Yet, how could Yen, a small and weak state, fight against the mighty Ch'in?

Meanwhile the state of Ch'in had not been idle. Almost daily it sent its troops eastward to annex territories, the territories of such states as Ch'i, Ch'u, Han, Chao, and Wei. It would be a matter of time before these troops reached the Yen border. The king of Yen and his ministers were greatly alarmed, including Tan, the crown prince, who sought advice from his teacher-adviser Ch'ü Wu.

"Now that the Ch'in state has acquired territories in practically every part of China," Ch'ü Wu replied, "it has been able to subject Han, Chao, and Wei to constant intimidation. Geographically speaking, it has always had greater advantages. Fortified in the north by Kanch'ien and Kuk'ou,[7] it enjoys the agricultural wealth of the Ching-Wei Plain in the south.[8] Protected by dangerous passes to its left and the Lung-Shu Mountains[9] to its right, it controls the rich resources of Pa-Han.[10] Its population is large; the confidence of its leaders is great. If it so chooses, it has enough men under arms to invade all the areas south of the Great Wall[11] and north of the Yi River [modern Hopeh province], the fate of which, in that case, will become highly uncertain. Why should you be so obsessed with a past slight as to offend a person whom you can least afford to offend?"

"Nevertheless, there must be something we can do," said Tan. "It will take time," Ch'ü Wu replied.

Not long afterward, the Ch'in general Fan Yü-ch'i, having been accused of committing a crime of treason against the king of Ch'in, escaped to Yen to avoid punishment. Tan, feeling sorry for him, took him under his wing. "This cannot be done," Ch'ü Wu protested. "The king of Ch'in, a brutal and revengeful man, has been angry with the state of Yen for a long time and has been in fact our constant source of fear. What will happen to us when he finds out where General Fan is hiding? Your action can be compared to placing a piece of meat on the path of a hungry tiger —the disaster is imminent. Even if Kuan Chung and Yen P'ing[12] were living among us today, they could not save us. My advice is to send General Fan to live among the Hsiung-nu[13] so as to eliminate any excuse the king of Ch'in might use to intimidate us. Meanwhile we should seek an alliance with Han, Chao, and Wei to our west and Ch'i and Ch'u to our south, and a peace treaty with the Hsiung-nu in the north. Only then may we be able to extricate ourselves from the danger we are in."

"Wise as your strategy is," said Tan, "I am not certain about its practicality, since it will take a long time to materialize. Furthermore, General Fan sought my assistance at a time when he could not be safe anywhere else. If I abandon a man to whom I have shown compassion and cast him away to the Hsiung-nu for fear of the powerful Ch'in, what would the world think of me? I would rather die than do something like this. I beg you to think more thoroughly and give me better advice."

"To seek security while performing dangerous deeds, namely, to foster disaster in the name of creating good fortunes, is, in my opinion, a shallow strategy carrying with it grave consequences," Ch'ü Wu replied. "It is like dangling a feather on top of a burning flame—the feather will quickly disappear. Knowing only too well the vulturous behavior of the brutal Ch'in, what else could I say? May I suggest that you speak with Mr. T'ien Kuang who, as a resident of Yen, has long been known for his wisdom and courage."

"Will you please introduce me to him?" asked the crown prince.

"Respectfully I will," Ch'ü Wu replied.

Ch'ü Wu paid a visit to Mr. T'ien and informed him of the

crown prince's wish to meet him. Mr. T'ien, accepting the invitation, repaired to the crown prince's palace where he was most cordially received. Once seated, the crown prince dismissed all the attendants and inquired, "May I be guided by your wisdom, sir, now that the states of Yen and Ch'in cannot live peacefully together?"

"I have heard that a unicorn can run a thousand *li* [about three hundred miles] per day during its prime but is unable to keep pace with a worn-out horse when it becomes old," Mr. T'ien replied. "Whatever reputation I have was earned during my younger days and has nothing to do with me at this moment. Being a tired and exhausted man, what is there for me to say in the realm of national affairs? However, there is a man named Ching K'o."

"Will you, sir, introduce me to Ching K'o?" asked the crown prince.

Having replied affirmatively, T'ien Kuang proceeded to leave. The crown prince escorted him to the door and then cautioned him that the conversation they had had concerned the vital interest of the state and that under no circumstances should he reveal it to others. T'ien Kuang raised his head and smiled, answering yes.

Being old, T'ien Kuang walked with halting and uncertain steps; it took him a long time to reach Ching K'o's residence. "Few people in Yen do not know that you and I have been great friends," said T'ien Kuang. "The crown prince learned about the reputation I had during my younger days; he had no idea that I could no longer do the kinds of things I used to be able to do. He told me that the states of Yen and Ch'in could not live peacefully together and generously sought my advice. I took the liberty of mentioning your name, knowing that being a good friend you would not mind my doing so. I shall appreciate your making a trip to the crown prince's palace."

Once assured that Ching K'o would make the trip, T'ien Kuang proceeded as follows: "I have heard that a gentleman's conduct should be above suspicion at all times. When the crown prince advised me to keep an absolute secret the conversation I had with him on grounds of national security, he indeed subjected me to suspicion. Please proceed to the crown prince's palace immediately and inform him that T'ien Kuang is dead and that a

dead man cannot reveal any secrets." Upon finishing these remarks, T'ien Kuang slashed his own throat.

Ching K'o met with the crown prince and informed him of
T'ien Kuang's death and the remarks he had made before his
death. The crown prince collapsed to the floor on both of his
knees, sobbing for a long time before he could speak. "When I
asked Mr. T'ien to keep a secret, I merely wished to safeguard
the successful completion of a proposed deed. It was not my
intention that he should use this drastic method to seal the secret." Finally regaining his composure, the crown prince seated
the visitor, knelt down before him, and proceeded to speak as
follows:

"Paying no heed to my own lack of character, the late Mr. T'ien
was generous enough to arrange my meeting with you, before
whom I can pour out what I have on my mind. This indicates
perhaps that Heaven has shown its mercy on the state of Yen and
has decided not to abandon me. As you know, the greed of the
Ch'in state is unlimited, and it will not be satisfied until all of
China is brought under its control and all the Chinese become its
subjects. Now that the king of Han has been captured and his
territories annexed [230 B.C.], the Ch'in state is proceeding to
invade Ch'u to its south and Chao to its north. At this moment
General Wang Chien, at the head of several hundred thousand
troops, is pushing toward Chang-Yeh[14] while another general, Li
Hsin, is proceeding northward to attack Taiyuan and Yünchung
[both in modern Shansi province]. It is unlikely that the state of
Chao can last long. Once Chao is eliminated, the state of Yen will
be next in line. Yen is a small, weak country and has been ravaged
by war time and again. It cannot successfully resist Ch'in even if
it could mobilize all its resources; nor can it succeed in making
alliances with other states that, being fearful of Ch'in, will refuse
to cooperate.

"There is only one way, in my judgment, to escape this
dilemma," the crown prince continued. "If we can find a brave
man to serve as envoy to bear expensive gifts to the Ch'in state,
the king of Ch'in, being so greedy as he always is, will doubtless
receive him. During the audience, the envoy will seize the king
and then demand the return of all the territories which he has
unjustifiably taken from other states, in the same manner as Ts'ao
Mei once did successfully in front of Duke Huan of Ch'i.[15] If the

king refuses to comply with the demand, the envoy will then kill him. The death of the king will doubtless be followed by civil strife in the capital, which will in turn generate suspicion and dissension between the central government on one hand and the generals on the other, namely, the generals who command large concentrations of troops abroad. Only then can we make a successful approach to other states to form a grand alliance against the Ch'in state which, in that case, will certainly be defeated. This is the plan dearest to me, even though I do not know whom I can trust with this important mission. Will you, sir, kindly consider?"

After a long silence, Ching K'o thanked the crown prince for the confidence he had in him but added that he was not certain whether he was the right man to shoulder this heavy responsibility. Once again the crown prince fell upon his knees and pleaded. Finally Ching K'o agreed.

The crown prince appointed Ching K'o as his senior adviser and housed him in one of the most luxurious residences in town. Almost daily he went to visit him, bringing with him delicacies and expensive curios, only occasionally interrupted by fine carriages and beautiful women.

A long time passed. Yet Ching K'o gave no indication when he would make the trip. Meanwhile General Wang Chien had decisively defeated the state of Chao, captured its king, and annexed all of its territories [228 B.C.]. The Ch'in army continued to move northward; in fact, its vanguards had already reached the southern border of the Yen state.

Frightened, the crown prince went to see Ching K'o again. "Now that the Ch'in army will pass across the Yi River[16] any day, it will not be long before I lose the privilege of entertaining you as my guest," said the prince.

"You have stated what I myself wish to discuss with you," Ching K'o replied. "There is one obstacle, however. How can we make the king of Ch'in trust me enough to let me come close to him? It is reliably reported that the king of Ch'in will reward anyone with one thousand pieces of gold and a fief of ten thousand households if he can bring General Fan to him, dead or alive. I beg Your Excellency to lend me the head of General Fan and the map of Tuk'ang[17] of Yen to be presented to the king of Ch'in as a tribute. The king, being pleased with what I have to present, will doubtless receive me. Only then can I repay the favor which Your Excellency has so generously bestowed upon me."

The crown prince was not pleased with Ching K'o's request. "General Fan, a gentleman of the finest character, came here to seek my protection when he was poor and desperate," he said. "How can I betray him in order to satisfy a selfish desire of mine? I beg you to think of some other method."

Knowing that the crown prince was too compassionate a person to kill Fan Yü-ch'i, Ching K'o decided to see the general himself. "There is no question as to how nicely the king of Ch'in has treated you," said the visitor sarcastically. "He has not only put to death all your relatives, including your parents, but also attempted to purchase your head with one thousand pieces of gold and a fief of ten thousand households. Are you not going to do something about this?"

Fan Yü-ch'i raised his head and sighed; tears began to stream down from his eyes. "I feel pain in the marrow of my bones whenever I think of the misfortune that has fallen upon me," he replied. "But there is nothing I can do."

"Yes, there is," said Ching K'o. "One word from you will not only enable you to seek revenge against the king of Ch'in but also free the Yen state from the precarious situation it is presently in."

"What is it?" General Fan stepped forward and asked the question most earnestly.

"I wish to borrow your head to be presented to the king of Ch'in as a tribute," said Ching K'o calmly. "When the king of Ch'in is informed of what I have to present, he will be much pleased and agree to receive me. Then, with my left hand holding his arm, I can put a sword right through his chest. At that moment not only your grievances but also those of the Yen state will be fully avenged. Will you kindly consider this proposal?"

Fan Yü-ch'i rolled up his right sleeve and then grabbed the bared arm with his left hand.[18] "Day or night I have not for a moment forgotten my hatred and anger," said he. "I am glad that you have shown me the most effective way to seek revenge." Without further ado, he unsheathed a sword and cut off his own head.

The death of General Fan quickly brought to the scene the crown prince, who bent over the dead body and sobbed aloud.

Since the dead man obviously could not be restored to life, the crown prince agreed to Ching K'o's proposal and gave the instruction that General Fan's head be carefully preserved. A search was then made for the finest sword money could buy; when it was found, it happened to belong to Madame Hsü of Chao who agreed to part with it for a consideration of one hundred gold pieces. After the sword was coated with deadly poison, its effectiveness was tested on men[19] who died instantly, as soon as the point of the blade touched the skin and drew a small amount of blood. The crown prince appointed as Ching K'o's deputy a boy named Ch'in Wu-yang who, though only thirteen years old, had a solid record of homicide and was reported to be so ferocious that he could scare people to death simply by staring at them. But Ching K'o had in mind a deputy of his own choice who, living far away, had not arrived. Consequently he was not yet ready to make the trip.

As Ching K'o waited for his man to arrive, the crown prince thought that he might have changed his mind regarding the trip. "We are quickly running out of time," said the crown prince. "If you do not object, I would like to dispatch Ch'in Wu-yang first."

Suddenly Ching K'o became angry. "Do you understand that the person you are proposing to send to Ch'in is merely a boy?" he scolded. "Is he supposed to complete his mission successfully with a single sword while surrounded by powerful and unpredictable enemies? Now that you have accused me of deliberately delaying the trip, I am bidding you farewell even though my chosen companion has not yet arrived."

The day when Ching K'o was scheduled to leave, the crown prince and a few of his friends, who had been informed of the purpose of this trip, were all dressed in white as the occasion demanded and they escorted him all the way to the Yi River. On the river bank Kao Chien-li played a sad melody with his *chu*, and Ching K'o responded to it with a song. All present, overwhelmed by the occasion and the song, found tears in their eyes. The song ended with the following words:

> The mournful soughing of the wind;
> The frozen coldness of the Yi River—
> A man is leaving;
> Return he never will.

Suddenly Kao Chien-li changed his music: it now conveyed a strong sense of controlled anger and noble courage, instead of melancholy or sadness. Amid this music Ching K'o mounted his carriage and drove away, without even once turning his head back.

Arriving at Ch'in, Ching K'o presented one thousand pieces of gold to Meng Chia, a favorite minister of the king's. Meng Chia, thus bribed, reported to the king as follows: "The king of Yen, being fully convinced of the futility of resisting Your Majesty's might, has decided to surrender his country to the Ch'in state. His only condition is that he should be allowed to serve Your Majesty in a new capacity as governor, with salaries appropriate to that position, in the hope that he will continually be able to preserve his ancestors' temple and to worship therein. Being too frightened to make the presentation himself, he has ordered the execution of Fan Yü-ch'i as Your Majesty would have desired and dispatched an envoy to speak on his behalf. The envoy has in his possession not only the head of Fan Yü-ch'i but also the map of Tuk'ang and is now awaiting Your Majesty's pleasure. He will obey whatever order Your Majesty chooses to issue."

Overwhelmed with joy, the king of Ch'in ordered the reception of Ching K'o in the Hsienyang Palace, amid pomp and ceremony as the happy occasion demanded. The procedure called for the presentation of Fan Yü-ch'i's head by Ching K'o, to be immediately followed by Ch'in Wu-yang's presentation of the map. Ching K'o presented the head, which had been sealed in a box, in laudable dignity and a most commendable manner. However, when it was time to present the map, Wu-yang, while ascending the steps toward the throne, became frightened and lost his composure. His behavior, naturally, puzzled and surprised many ministers in the audience. "I beg Your Majesty's indulgence," Ching K'o smiled, "to forgive a man who, reared in the barbarian land of the north, has for the first time been given the privilege of being presented to the Son of Heaven. He is trembling with fear because he is so overwhelmed by that privilege. Will Your Majesty be generous enough to allow him to complete the presentation?"

"Will you hand over the map to me?" said the king to Ching K'o.

Ching K'o took the box that contained the map from Wu-yang's trembling hands and presented it to the king. The king opened the box and pulled out the map slowly. Then suddenly, at the end of the map, he saw the point of a shining blade. In a quick motion Ching K'o grabbed the king's right arm with his left hand and, simultaneously, pulled out the blade from the box. The king instinctively leaned back and struggled to stand up; in the process he managed to tear off the sleeve by which Ching K'o held him. As soon as he was free, the king tried to unsheathe his sword but failed in his attempt, since the sword was too long to be dislodged in a moment of panic.[20] He sprang to his feet and began to run, until he reached a huge bronze column. Around the column he continued to run, with Ching K'o in hot pursuit. Meanwhile all the ministers present, taken aback by the unexpected event, watched helplessly in total confusion.

According to the Ch'in law, no minister or attendant was allowed to carry a weapon in the king's presence; and all the imperial guards, without the king's specific order, were forbidden to present themselves in the audience hall. The attempted assassination occurred so suddenly that the king, being constantly pursued, had become too panicky to issue the required order. Meanwhile the chase went on around the column. Occasionally, when Ching K'o came too close, the king tried to fend him off with his own hands.

The chase finally ended when Hsia Wu-ch'i, the royal physician, threw his medicine bag in the direction of Ching K'o and hit the latter on the head. "Use your sword, king; use your sword!" the ministers cried aloud while Ching K'o was temporarily immobilized. The king unsheathed his sword and struck Ching K'o on his left thigh. Revived by the pain, Ching K'o raised his sword and plunged forward, only to miss his target and meet head-on with the bronze column. This gave the king the opportunity to strike back, inflicting eight wounds altogether. Lying against the column in a heap and knowing that there was no more he could do, Ching K'o laughed and cursed. "Do you know why I have failed?" he yelled at the king with all the energy he was still able to gather. "I failed because I wanted to capture you alive and force you to sign a peace treaty with the state of Yen. Only in this way can I repay the favor which the crown prince of Yen has so generously bestowed upon me." A moment later Ching K'o was killed by the king's attendants.

It took a long time for the king to recover from the shock. When the time arrived for dispensing rewards, he singled out Hsia Wu-ch'i for praise. "The royal physician loves me," he said. For this love the royal physician received two hundred pieces of gold, though other ministers and attendants also obtained various amounts.

Furious over the attempted assassination, the king of Ch'in dispatched more troops to Chao and ordered General Wang Chien to launch an all-out invasion of the Yen state. In the tenth month General Wang captured Chich'eng, and the king of Yen, together with his crown prince, moved his best troops to the area east of the Liao River[21] where he intended to make a last stand. Meanwhile the Ch'in forces, under General Li Hsin, were pushing relentlessly toward the north. Not knowing what to do under the circumstances, the king of Yen found himself receiving all kinds of advice, including some from Chia, king of Tai,[22] which read in part as follows: "The reason for Ch'in's relentless attack against Yen is its hatred for Crown Prince Tan. If you kill the crown prince and present his head to the king of Ch'in as a tribute, the Ch'in forces will lift the siege and your country will then be preserved."

Incredible though this suggestion may seem, the king of Yen was eventually compelled by the prospect of total disaster to follow it, after the crown prince had been decisively defeated by Li Hsin, lost all of his army, and escaped to Yenshui [southern Manchuria] for hiding purposes. To Yenshui the king sent an executioner who subsequently brought back the head of the crown prince. Unfortunately the death of the crown prince and the king's intention to present his head to Ch'in as a tribute did not reduce in the slightest the pressure of the Ch'in forces which, in fact, had intensified their efforts. It took five more years, however, before Ch'in finally conquered Yen and captured its king [222 B.C.]. One year later, the Ch'in state eliminated the remainder of its rivals and brought all of China within one jurisdiction. From then on the king of Ch'in was known as Ch'in Shih Huang-ti, or First Emperor of the Ch'in dynasty.

The termination of Yen as a state meant, among other things, that all the retainers and guests of Crown Prince Tan dispersed as wanted fugitives all over China, including Kao Chien-li who, having changed his name, found employment as a bartender in

Sungtzu [modern Hopeh province]. Kao did not like his new occupation: the hours were long, the work too tedious. One day, hearing a guest of his employer play the *chu*, he commented freely on which part he liked and which part he did not. Those who heard him reported his comments to the employer who was greatly annoyed as a result. "Who does this coolie think he is? A musician?" Nevertheless the employer was willing to give Kao an opportunity to prove himself. Kao was summoned to play; hardly had he struck a few notes before all the guests were immensely impressed. By then he had decided not to live incognito forever. He excused himself, changed into the clothes he used to wear, dressed up his appearance, and took from a case the *chu* which he had not played for a long time. As soon as he reappeared, the guests were surprised to see a new man, the equal of any of them, and came to greet him in the most endearing manner. Kao Chien-li began to play and sing simultaneously: the melody and the lyrics were so moving and the execution was so beautiful and precise that they drew tears from all of the guests.

Kao Chien-li's reputation as a musician eventually reached the emperor, namely Shih Huang-ti, who summoned him for a performance. Someone mentioned that the musician was a former retainer of Tan, a wanted fugitive, but the emperor, having great respect for Kao's talent, decreed that the musician's life should be spared, though he must be blinded for life. The performance proved to be better than any the emperor had ever heard. The emperor, thoroughly delighted, called upon Kao to perform again and again. In one performance Kao Chien-li moved as close as possible to the emperor and, without anybody's knowledge, put a piece of heavy lead inside his *chu*. Slowly he inched forward as he continued to play. Then, when he felt he was close enough, he suddenly raised the *chu* above his head and threw it, with all his energy, toward the emperor. Unfortunately for him, the *chu* missed its target. He was executed shortly afterward.

For the rest of his life the emperor never again received a person from any of his conquered territories.

Notes

1. *Shih chi*, roll 86. As for the author, see pp. 71–73.
2. An area that occupied what is now eastern Honan and southern Hopeh.
3. This seems to indicate that during this period of Chinese history (third

century B.C.) dog eating was a common practice, especially among the low-income people.

4. *Chu*, an ancient Chinese musical instrument similar to the lute, has long been lost. According to a contemporary description, it had a narrow neck and roundish shoulder, with five, thirteen, or sometimes twenty-one strings. When playing, the musician used his right hand to beat the strings with a bamboo stick while controlling the notes with his left hand.

5. During the period of Warring States (403–221 B.C.) it was customary for the king of one state to send one of his sons to another state as a hostage. The purpose was to guarantee nonaggression or friendship with that state. Needless to say, this method of maintaining friendly relations rarely worked.

6. Cheng, later known as Ch'in Shih Huang-ti, was then a hostage at Chao on behalf of his own state, Ch'in.

7. Both are located in northern Shensi.

8. Both the Ching and the Wei Rivers are located in southern Shensi.

9. Mountain ranges that stretch from southwestern Shensi to northwestern Szechuan.

10. Szechuan and southern Shensi.

11. During the period of Warring States, each of the northern states built its own Great Wall to protect itself from the nomads farther to the north.

12. Kuan Chung was the chief minister of Ch'i in the seventh century B.C.; Yen P'ing served in the same capacity in Ch'i in the sixth century B.C. Both were famous for their statesmanship and wisdom.

13. A nomadic tribe to the north of China.

14. An area that covers northeastern Honan and southern Hopeh.

15. In 681 B.C. Ts'ao Mei, a general from the state of Lu, seized Duke Huan of Ch'i and threatened him with a knife while the latter was attending an interstate conference. The general demanded the return of all the territories that Ch'i had conquered at Lu's expense and released the duke only after the latter had promised that he would comply with the demand. The territories were later returned.

16. The boundary between Chao and Yen.

17. A fertile valley in modern Hopeh province where the capital of Yen was located.

18. An ancient way of showing determination.

19. Presumably convicted criminals.

20. Ancient Chinese wore swords on their backs.

21. Southern Manchuria.

22. After Ch'in's conquest of Chao, the Chao loyalists installed Crown Prince Chia as king of Tai. Later Tai, like its predecessor Chao, was conquered by Ch'in.

CHAPTER
2

The Philosophers

THE ancient Chinese saying that "the more an author suffers, the better his work will be" *(wen ch'iung erh hou kung)* may or may not be true, but there is some truth in the statement that the quantity of literature increases with each worsening of times. In 771 B.C. the West Chou dynasty was terminated by a barbarian invasion, and the era of the Three Dynasties (Hsia, Shang, and West Chou), which had always been remembered with great pride, finally came to an end. The five centuries after 771 B.C. were among the worst of times in the sense that political disintegration continued; wars were fought constantly, and people of all classes suffered as a result. Yet these five centuries were also among the best of times. The technology of iron smelting, which was discovered during this period, not only increased agricultural production but also facilitated the opening up of virgin fields, especially in South China. The decline of Chou feudalism and its eventual demise increased the tempo of social changes and speeded up social mobility. New cities sprang up all over the country, and scholars and merchants traveled regularly between them, to seek fame or wealth and often both. All these developments were of enormous importance to the continuous shaping of China as a nation and they paved the way for the eventual unification of China. Yet, from a modern man's viewpoint, none of these developments was more important than the proliferation of literature during this period.

The importance of this literature lies more in its practical impact than in its ideological content. From an ideological point of view, one may argue that the authors of this literature, with some exceptions, were merely advocates of common sense (good government, personal ethics, and so on), and even these few exceptions who had adventured metaphysically did not develop their themes to their ultimate conclusions. With the possible exception of the Dialecticians *(Ming chia)*, who were denounced by their contemporaries for having engaged in such "trifles" as "argument for argument's sake," the writers of this period regarded themselves as savers of man and his world rather than philosophers per se. Each was conducting a crusade of his own, and his philosophy, or whatever one may call it, was merely a means to usher in a new era when "all men are brothers." This overwhelming concern with "learning for the purpose of utilization" *(hsüeh yi chih yung)* prevented ideological presentation from following its own logical course, and a philosophical insight, whenever it occurred, was often sidetracked to provide rationalization for such mundane necessities as "conscientious rulers and loyal subjects" instead of being developed further. But this criticism, though valid from a modern man's point of view, was never raised by the writers of this period since to them no branch of learning, including philosophy, could justify its existence without being related in some way to the actual conduct of life. Wisely or not, they set the patterns for centuries of Chinese philosophers to follow.

From the point of view of practical impact, none of the philosophies developed during this period was more important than Confucianism, which for more than two thousand years was the official ideology sponsored by practically all the Chinese regimes. Confucius (551–479 B.C.), founder of this school, believed that philosophy was something to live by rather than to be written about and prided himself on having "related" *(shu)* rather than "written" *(tso)* anything in particular. Yet Confucian literature multiplied despite Confucius. First, a large amount of literature that had existed long before the time of Confucius and had been regarded as the common heritage of all Chinese was claimed by the Confucians as exclusively their own and was often referred to by them as "books of ancient kings" or "sayings of great sages," even though some of this literature, such as the folk songs in the *Book of Odes* (selection 3), have nothing to do with either kings or sages. Second, as the ideological battle continued throughout this period, the Confucians, in order to fight their war more effectively, had to manufacture new weapons. One of the new weapons was the *Doctrine of the Mean (Chung yung)*, which quoted Confucius copiously and was attributed to Tzu-ssu, a grandson of Confucius's, in an ill-concealed attempt to make these direct quotations sound creditable. Why was this book not attributed to Li, Confucius's son? Well, Li was regarded by all who knew him, including his own father, as a hopeless prospect who could not be expected to read any books, let alone write one. In the long run, however, it really does not make any difference whether a particular book is forged or genuine, insofar as the shaping of religious or philosophical tradition is concerned, as long as the adherents of this tradition think that it is genuine or, knowing that it is forged, nevertheless believe that its contents conform to their own thinking as to what that religion or philosophy should be. Otherwise there would not have been such a thing as religious or philosophical tradition. Thus the *Doctrine of the Mean,* whoever its author happens to be, has become one of the *Four Books* that supposedly summarize the cream of Confucian knowledge.

This does not mean that historians should not make an attempt to differentiate the original sources from the lesser ones. From the viewpoint of both tradition and historical accuracy, the most important of the *Four Books* is the *Analects of Confucius (Lun-yü)* which was composed shortly after the death of Confucius. Traditionally it was the first read and most quoted of the Confucian sources, despite its small volume; historically it was the only book that describes Confucius as he was, without ostentation, embellishment, or rationalization. Its lack of logic or system, its declaratory rather than analytical statements, and the inconsistency of its contents all argue well for its authenticity, since any forger worth his salt could easily have avoided these "obvious shortcomings." In its typically fragmentary manner, the book covers practically every subject, from the position of the Polar Star to a gentleman's code (selection 7).

Unfortunately, works similar to the *Analects* do not exist for other philosophers of this period, and consequently we know less about them. Lao-tzu, the alleged founder of the Taoist school of philosophy, was a mystic figure who, many historians contend, never even existed. The *Book of Taoist Virtue (Tao-te ching)* that bears his name was a later creation, perhaps of the fourth century B.C. Chuang Chou (ca. 368–288 B.C.), the second most important man in the Taoist tradition and certainly one of the most imaginative of all philosophers of ancient China, said a great deal about himself in his writing; but, in view of the most unlikely places into which his creative mind could venture, one is not certain whether the stories he told about himself are apocryphal or historical. The *Book of Chuang-tzu*, as Chuang Chou's work is entitled, contains, in its present version, thirty-three essays, seven of which have been identified as his own writing, while the rest, numbering twenty-six, were penned by either his disciples or some other Taoist sympathizers, none of whom could positively be identified. One of the most original of these essays is *Autumn Flood* (*Ch'iu shui*, selection 8) which examines the relativity of values and its application to human affairs. It summarizes some of the best Taoist ideas.

By and large the laissez-faire attitude of the Taoists toward life and man was more an exception than a rule, and many other philosophers of this period, believing in man's capacity to improve himself and his environment, took a more positive approach. The most positive among them was a man named Mo Ti (ca. 468–378 B.C.) who advocated universal love—to love all the people in the world to the same extent as one loved oneself (selection 9). Though Moism, as the teachings of Mo Ti are called, rivaled Confucianism as one of the two most popular schools of thought at one time, its influence steadily declined after the fourth century B.C. until, by the second century B.C., Ssu-ma Ch'ien had little to say about either Moism or Mo Ti when he wrote his universal history. "Mo Ti, an official of the Sung state and an expert in defense, advocated thrift," stated the Grand Historian. "Some say that he was a contemporary of Confucius, while others say that he lived one generation after Confucius." These two sentences constitute the complete coverage of one of the greatest men of ancient China by the Father of History in China! One reason for this lack of interest in Moism during the past millennia is that during the time of chaos and war when Confucianism inevitably lost much of its influence, people most naturally turned to Taoism—the antithesis of Confucianism—for solace and comfort, rather than to Moism which required even more involvement with this world than Confucianism. Not until modern times did Moism arouse new interest, perhaps because of its similarity to some Christian concepts.

Whether he is a Confucian, Taoist, or Moist, a person assumes the basic goodness of man and the likelihood of his continued improvement. A Legalist, on the other hand, regards all men as inherently evil and all exhortations to do good as self-defeating and useless. Man's salvation, therefore, lies not in his improvement as an ethical being, which cannot be achieved in any case, but in the manipulation, by an omnipotent but impartial authority, of his natural instinct for the advance of his own self-interest. The advance of self-interest can take either a negative or a positive form, namely, either the avoidance of pain or the enhancement of pleasure. Reward and punishment, as the means of providing pleasure and inflicting pain, respectively, are most effective in persuading or forcing an individual to do what society demands of him, for the benefit of society as well as his own good. What society encourages or prohibits is described in great detail in a set of rules called the law, to be enforced impartially by an omnipotent authority called the king. The king, having achieved power and wealth in the most absolute terms and having therefore no more interest to advance except the preservation of his own position, can represent the interest of society better than any individual or group of individuals. The maintenance of the king's authority, or the necessity of preventing it from being undermined, precedes all other considerations, since the king's authority is indeed the collective authority of society as a whole. Thus a Legalist, by following his own argument, becomes an ardent supporter of absolutism.

The most eloquent spokesman for Legalism was Han Fei (d. 233 B.C.) who, according to Ssu-ma Ch'ien, stuttered as a young man and decided to offset this defect by concentrating on writing. Two of his essays found their way to the king of Ch'in, later known as Ch'in Shih Huang-ti. After reading them, the king was immensely impressed, saying that he could die without regret if somehow he could meet the author of these two essays. In one of them (A Private Complaint, or Ku fen) the author warns the king against the prospect of conspiracy to usurp his authority by what the author calls power brokers and suggests that only a Legalist, who owes no loyalty except to the king and can easily be dismissed if he fails to perform, should be entrusted with a position of authority (selection 10). It is no wonder that the king liked the essay and wanted very much to meet its author.

(7)
Confucius / *A Gentleman's Code*[1]

Confucius says, A gentleman does not specialize.

Confucius says, A gentleman practices what he teaches.

Confucius says, A gentleman, fair and impartial to all, does not form his own clique. A small man is fair and impartial only to those who belong to his clique.

Confucius says, One only brings harm to oneself by indulging in ideological extremes.

Confucius says, A gentleman does not compete for the sake of competition. In the archery contest, for instance, the competitors salute one another before ascending the platform to shoot and drink to each other's health after the shooting. They compete, but they compete as gentlemen.

Confucius says, Praying to Heaven does not help a man who has offended Heaven by his own deeds.

Confucius says, Having no preconceived ideas, a gentleman views things with total impartiality. He does what he believes is right.

Confucius says, A gentleman loves virtue; a small man loves material gains. A gentleman thinks of the consequence of his proposed deed; a small man thinks of only the benefit that he can obtain as a result of his proposed deed.

Confucius says, A gentleman is not concerned about his lack of position; he is concerned about his lack of virtue. He is not concerned about whether other people know him; he is concerned about whether he has in himself something worthy of knowing.

Confucius says, A gentleman understands what is right; a small man understands what is profitable.

Confucius says, Tso Ch'iu-ming[2] despises a man who maintains a pleasant and polite appearance but is insincere inside. So do I. Tso Ch'iu-ming despises a man who camouflages inner hatred with outward friendliness. So do I.

Confucius says, A gentleman is slow in words, but quick in action.

Confucius says, Yen Hui [a disciple of Confucius] is a virtuous man indeed! He lives in a poor neighborhood and has no worldly possessions except a basket of food and a gourd of water. Others worry about him; yet he is as happy and contented as he can possibly be. Yen Hui is a virtuous man indeed!

Confucius says, To know what is good is not enough; you have to love it. To love goodness is not enough; you have to rejoice in doing it.

Confucius says, If I can no longer act properly, if I stop learning, if I cannot perform a good deed when the opportunity presents itself, or if I cannot correct a fault after it has been pointed out to me, I shall be very concerned indeed.

Confucius fished with a hook instead of a net. He shot birds in flight; he did not catch them in their nests.

Confucius says, There is such a thing as overthrift; there is such a thing as overspending. But it is better to be overthrifty than to be overspending.

Confucius says, A gentleman is at peace with himself; a small man always worries.

Confucius says, Even if a man is as talented as Duke Chou [a famous statesman of the twelfth century B.C.], his talent is useless if he is conceited and miserly.

Confucius says, To be rich and famous among the corrupted is as shameful as to be poor and anonymous among the honest.

Confucius says, I feel sorry for a man who is unconventional and yet dishonest, misinformed and yet rash, stupid and yet untrustworthy.

Confucius had none of the following faults: prejudice, stubbornness, false pride, or self-righteousness.

Confucius says, I have not met a man who loves virtue more than sex.

Confucius says, Only in winter do you realize that pines do not shed their leaves.[3]

Confucius did not leave the conference hall when informed that his stable had been burned down. "Is anybody hurt?" he asked. He did not inquire about the horses.

Confucius says, Excess is as bad as deficiency.

Confucius says, Can he be regarded as a gentleman who preaches honesty in a most serious manner and yet acts dishonestly?

Confucius says, A gentleman does not worry or fear. Having done nothing that he can be ashamed of, why should he worry or fear?

Confucius says, A gentleman assists others in doing good and prevents them from doing evil. A small man does the opposite.

Confucius says, A gentleman can be compared to wind, and all other people can be compared to grass. The grass bends toward whichever direction the wind blows.

Confucius says, If you feel that your friend has done something wrong, tell him exactly how you feel and try to guide him in a different direction. Stop your persuasion if he insists on his own ways. You should by no means bring insult to yourself.

Confucius says, A gentleman makes friends through common interest in culture and maintains the friendship by putting into practice the principle of love.

Confucius says, An honest man can inspire others to be honest. A dishonest man cannot make others honest even though he has issued the strictest orders.

Confucius says, A gentleman is friendly toward those with whom he disagrees; a small man quarrels with those with whom he agrees.

Confucius says, A good man is a person loved by good men but hated by bad men.

Confucius says, A gentleman is easy to please as a person but difficult to please on matters of principle. A small man is difficult to please as a person but easy to please on matters of principle.

Confucius says, A gentleman is too generous to be prideful; a small man is too proud to be generous.

Confucius says, A gentleman may occasionally violate the principle of love. A small man never believes the principle of love.

Confucius says, A gentleman and a small man stand at the same distance from goodness. The former moves toward it; the latter moves away from it.

Confucius says, A gentleman does not indulge in ungentlemanly thought.

Confucius says, A gentleman is slow in making promises but quick in carrying them out.

Confucius says, A gentleman is too kindhearted to worry, too knowledgeable to be confused, and too courageous to be afraid.

Confucius says, Be not concerned whether other people know you; be concerned whether you have something worthy of knowing.

Someone asked Confucius whether it was right to recompense injury with kindness. Confucius replied: "With what are you going to recompense kindness if you recompense injury with kindness? It is more correct to recompense injury with honesty and to recompense kindness with kindness."

Confucius says, To refuse to speak to a man who is willing to listen is to lose the man, but to speak to a man who refuses to listen is a waste of words. A wise man does not lose any man or waste any words.

Confucius says, Criticizing oneself more severely than criticizing others is a sure way to keep away complaints.

Confucius says, I have no use for those who spend most of their time in showing off their cleverness without uttering one word on serious matters.

Confucius says, The essence of a gentleman is integrity which, when expressed outwardly, becomes proper conduct. This integrity is accompanied by honesty within and humility without.

Confucius says, A gentleman is concerned about his lack of ability; he is not concerned about other people's ignorance of his ability.

Confucius says, A gentleman is afraid that upon his death people might not have anything memorable to say about him.

Confucius says, A gentleman finds happiness within himself, while a small man finds happiness only in other people's approval of him.

Confucius says, A gentleman has too much self-respect to be argumentative and too much goodwill for all to form his own clique.

Confucius says, A gentleman does not recommend a man on account of his articulateness; nor will he refuse to recommend a man because of it.

Confucius says, Sophistry corrodes the goodness of man. A man who is not forbearing on small matters cannot be trusted with important tasks.

Confucius says, If a man is detested by all, find out why this is so. If a man is liked by all, find out why this is so.

Confucius says, A fault becomes a fault only when it is repeated.

Confucius says, A gentleman is more concerned about the principle he adheres to than the kind of food he has to eat. He is more concerned about learning than any kind of material reward he might receive as a result of his learning. He prefers principle to wealth.

Confucius says, A gentleman is small in small matters and great in great matters. A small man is great in small matters and small in great matters.

Confucius says, A gentleman adheres to righteousness steadfastly, paying no attention to trifles.

Confucius says, A man can be helped by three kinds of friends: the frank and outspoken, the understanding, and the well informed. A man can be harmed by three kinds of friends: the pleasant but dishonest, the flexible but unprincipled, and the articulate but sycophantic.

Confucius says, There are three kinds of pleasure that benefit a man: pleasure in listening to ceremonial music, pleasure in speaking of the goodness of others, and pleasure in having friends of principle. There are three kinds of pleasure that harm a man: pleasure in listening to licentious music, pleasure in engaging in aimless wanderings, and pleasure in eating without restraint.

Confucius says, When speaking with a gentleman, one should be careful not to commit any of the following errors: brashness, secretiveness, and blindness. Brashness occurs when one begins to speak of oneself without being requested to do so. Secretiveness results when one refuses to speak about oneself after having been requested to do so. A man is blind if he keeps talking about himself after others have lost interest in listening to him.

Confucius says, A gentleman should be warned against three things. As a youngster when his vitality has not yet been stabilized, he should be warned against sexual indulgence. As an adult when his vitality has reached its maximum, he should be warned against combativeness. As an old man whose vitality has already declined, he should be warned against acquisitiveness.

Confucius says, A gentleman must keep the following thoughts in mind: to see clearly, to listen carefully, to be warm and pleasant, to maintain a respectful attitude, to speak honestly, to conduct himself in a serious manner, to ask questions whenever in doubt, to foresee the harmful consequence of his own anger, and to be mindful of the principle of righteousness whenever confronted with the prospect of material gains. Avoid evil as if it were boiling water.

Confucius says, To cover up internal weakness with a stern, terrifying appearance characterizes a small man. He can be compared to a petty thief who, having practiced his profession, acts in a dignified manner to avoid suspicion.

Confucius says, A gentleman has in mind the performance of righteous deeds; he has nothing to do with bravery if the action involved is not righteous. A small man is like a bandit: the braver he is, the worse he will be.

Confucius says, A gentleman detests a person who speaks ill of others in their absence, scandalizes his superiors in order to make himself look superior, acts rashly in the name of bravery, or stubbornly maintains a position that he knows is wrong.

Confucius says, He who does not know the wishes of Heaven is not a gentleman.

Notes

1. Passages in this translation are arranged in the order they originally appeared in *Lun-yü.*
2. See p. 18.
3. Only in adversity can a man's true worth be known.

(8)
Chuang Chou / *Autumn Flood*[1]

Autumn flood arrived in time, and hundreds of streams poured their swollen contents into the River. Water covered the banks as well as the islets; viewed from a distance, a horse might be mistaken for an ox, and vice versa. The River God was overjoyed, saying to himself that there had never been a beautiful sight like this. Floating eastward in the direction of the current, he eventually reached the North Sea where the ocean began. The vast expanse of water extended as far as his eyes could see and seemed to have no end. Immensely impressed, he heralded the God of the North Sea, sighed, and spoke as follows: "A popular saying has it that a great man considers himself the greatest until he sees somebody greater, and I have never realized, until now, that this saying is equally applicable to me. I used to doubt the sincerity of those who belittle the wisdom of Confucius and the self-sacrifice of Pai-yi,[2] but now I believe them. As I look at your enormous dimension, I realize that had I not had the opportunity of meeting you, I would have continued to commit the error of unjustified arrogance, thus making myself a laughingstock to all men of knowledge."

Hearing these remarks, the God of the North Sea responded as follows: "A frog in the well, confined by four walls, cannot be expected to understand the meaning of the sea. Nor can a summer insect, compelled by nature to live in a warm season, be made to appreciate the coldness of ice. Is it really surprising that a narrow-minded scholar, shackled by conventions, cannot comprehend the significance of Tao? Now that you have emerged from the narrow confines of valleys and gorges and for the first time witnessed the vastness of the sea, maybe I can speak with you on the large issues of the universe, since obviously you, by now, have been convinced of your own lack of knowledge. As you know, all water ends in the sea. The sea, being as vast as it is, does not expand or shrink regardless of summer or winter, flood or drought. How different it is from the rivers where water rises or falls at nature's mercy! Yet, as God of the North Sea, I am not proud or arrogant in the least because, compared with Heaven and Earth between which I reside, I am merely a small pebble or tiny plant, hardly noticeable in a mountain range. As a product of the *yin* and the *yang*,[3] I realize that the universe is infinitely vast and that I have not seen everything myself. Compared with the universe, the world as we know it is like a small depression in a huge swamp. Compared with the world, China as we know it is like one kernel of grain in a giant granary. There are a multitude of creatures, and man is only one of them. Even in China which itself is a speck in the universe, man constitutes merely one of the countless things it contains. In short, against the numerous things that exist, man is no more than the tip of a hair underneath the stomach of a horse. The statesmanship of the Five Emperors,[4] the contention among the Three Kings,[5] the concern of compassionate men, and the toil of able scholars—all this, in fact, is much ado about nothing. Likewise, the fame Pai-yi earned on account of his refusal to inherit the crown and the wisdom attributed to Confucius on account of his extensive learning—both indicate nothing other than the egotism of the persons concerned. Both men are no better than you the River God who, only a short time ago, thought that he had more water under his command than anybody else."

"Is it correct to assume that the universe is greater than the tip of a hair that forms part of the universe?" asked the River God.

"No," the God of the North Sea replied. "Anything, large or small, is infinite in its capacity and eternal in its span of time; it changes without following specific rules and begins and ends at random. A wise man, having observed the far and the near, and having been convinced of the validity of this truism, does not regard the small as less valuable and the large as more worthy. He knows that capacity, in things large or small, is infinite by definition. This is true today, as it has been true all the time. Since satisfaction can be obtained from things small as well as from those that are large, a wise man does not feel lonely when he is alone; nor does he desire to accumulate for the sake of accumulation, even though accumulation to him may require only a minimum amount of effort. Knowing the infinity of time and the endless cycle of waxing and waning, he is neither overjoyed when he gains, nor crestfallen when he loses. Knowing that changes occur at random and that the speed of changes defies the calculation of man, he neither rejoices at the creation of life nor regards its ending as a great calamity. He lets nothing in the past cloud his judgment as to when or how a thing will begin or end. What a man knows is infinitely smaller than what he does not know; the time he has before his birth is infinitely longer than the time when he is living. How can he not be confused and eventually suffer defeat when he attempts to utilize his infinitesimal capacity to master the maximum that has no end? He is as incapable of knowing the outward limit of the tip of a hair as he is of knowing the dimension of the universe."

"Is it correct to say that the minutest has no form and that the infinite has no boundary?" the River God asked again.

"From the viewpoint of the minutest, anything else is infinitely large," the God of the North Sea replied. "From the viewpoint of the infinite, anything else is so small as to be obscure. The minutest is the smallest in 'small,' just as the infinite is the largest in 'large.' Each, understandably, looks at the other from its own prejudicial point of view. The concepts of 'fine' and 'coarse' are dependent on the existence of form since, in a state of formlessness, the thing involved can no longer be divided on a quantitative basis. Nor can quantity be used to express the concept of boundlessness since numbers are by definition limited in scope. Thus, what can be expressed in words has to be something coarse in nature; the fineness of any object can only be understood, impervious to verbal expression. If a thing is not subject to expression in words or understanding through reasoning, the concept of 'coarse' or 'fine' is no longer applicable.

"A true man, whatever he does, has no intention of either harming or benefiting others, not because of any conscientious effort to have no such intention, but because of the absence of such an intention a priori. He does not compete for material gains; nor does he decline to accept them when they come his way without any effort of his own. He does not look down upon those socially below; nor does he look up to those socially above. He does not rely on others' assistance, whatever he has to do; he lives by his own labor. He does not follow convention; nor does he conscientiously try to be different. He raises no objection when others move in a direction different from his; he neither praises nor condemns sycophants. Rank and salary, however great, cannot make him do what he does not want to do; nor does he regard as an insult condemnation by others. He knows that the concepts of right and wrong are only relative and that 'great' and 'small' are merely in the eyes of the beholder. A man of Tao seeks neither fame nor notoriety, since perfection resides in the absence of neither gains nor losses. A true man has no self; he is above and beyond any quantitative analysis."

"From the external as well as the internal point of view, what is the criterion for judging an object's worth, namely, good or bad, great or small?" asked the River God.

"There is no such thing as a good or bad object from the viewpoint of a man of Tao," the God of the North Sea replied. "From the viewpoint of the object, however, naturally it considers itself better than any other object. From the viewpoint of the world at large, the value of an object depends upon the way the world views the object, independent of its inherent worth. Speaking of the concepts of 'great' and 'small' in a qualitative rather than a quantitative sense, you will find greatness in every object, however small, if you emphasize that part of the object that is uniquely great. By the same token, you will find smallness in every object, however great, if you emphasize that part of the object that is uniquely small. Therefore, the whole universe can be viewed as no larger than the kernel of a grain; conversely, the tip of a hair can be regarded as a gigantic mountain. In short, 'great' and 'small' have no permanency of their own and are in fact relative terms. If you look at an object from the viewpoint of its utility to man, you will find utility in every object, if the objective utility of that object happens to coincide with your own subjective utility. On the other hand, there is no utility in any object if the objective utility of the object does not meet your subjective demand. 'East' and 'west' indicate two opposite directions; but 'east' could not have existed without 'west,' and vice versa. The same can be said about utility or nonutility, or right and wrong. Every object has its 'right' element if that element is what you are looking for. Likewise, every object has its 'wrong' element if that element happens to be the one you deplore.

"Yao and Shun were hailed as most intelligent and selfless when they abdicated in favor of the most virtuous men instead of their sons.[6] Yet, when King K'uai did likewise, his kingdom was almost exterminated.[7] T'ang and Wu fought for the throne and won;[8] Pai Kung, on the other hand, precipitated his own death by attempting the same thing.[9] What is right in one case becomes wrong in another; virtue becomes vice and vice becomes virtue in accordance with the change of time or circumstances. A battering ram can be used to storm a fortress but is completely useless for plugging a small hole. A fleet horse can run a thousand *li*[10] a day but is inferior to a cat in its capacity to catch mice. A bat is sharp enough to spot a tiny insect at night but is so blind during daytime that it cannot even see a mountain. Those who believe that right can exist without the existence of wrong, or that peace can exist without the existence of war, are forever condemned to ignorance. Can Heaven exist without the existence of Earth? Can the *yang* exist without the existence of the *yin?* The answer to these questions is rather obvious. Those who answer otherwise are either fools or think other people are. History shows that the Five Emperors and the Three Dynasties did not succeed one another by following a specific rule: those who rose in the wrong time, fought against the trend, and consequently suffered defeat were called pretentious usurpers, while those who rose in the right time, fought with the trend, and consequently succeeded were hailed as men of principles. Hold your tongue, River God! How can I expect you to know the difference between 'good' and 'bad,' or 'great' and 'small'?"

"What should I do, or not do?" asked the River God. "Now that

I have recognized the futility of either advance or retreat, what will become of me?"

"From the viewpoint of a man of Tao, 'good' may be 'bad,' and 'bad' may be 'good,' " the God of the North Sea replied. "Set your will free, so your actions can conform to the principle of Tao. 'Few' may be 'many,' and 'many' may be 'few.' Follow no specific rules in the conduct of your life, so you yourself will not deviate from the principle of Tao. Be as serious as a wise king who shows no favoritism for anyone; be as detached as the Earth God who grants favor only to the deserving. Your mind should be as broad as the universe that knows no division or boundary and be so self-sufficient that it sustains everything in the world without any outward means of support. View all things with total impartiality, since they are equal regardless of whether they are short or long. Nothing in the universe is permanent, as everything lives only long enough to die. Only Tao, having no beginning or end, lasts forever. Even form waxes and wanes—there is no permanence about it either. The past cannot be relied on to guide the present, as time speeds by only in one direction and never reverses itself. The endless cycle of expansion and contraction, growth and decay, beginning and end, is the rule of all existences and the reason underlying all the objects and things in the universe. Life can be likened to a fleet horse galloping at full speed—it changes constantly and continuously, in every fraction of a second. What should you do? What should you not do? It really does not make any difference, since you will change, imperceptibly and inevitably, despite yourself."

"For what reason, then, is Tao so valuable?" asked the River God.

"To understand Tao, one must know the reason underlying all existences," the God of the North Sea replied. "To know the reason underlying all existences, one must be a master of the constant change of circumstances. He who has mastered the constant change of circumstances will not allow things outside of himself to afflict his inner mind. A man of perfect virtue is immune from burning by fire or drowning by water; cold and heat cannot torment him, nor can the wildest beasts cause him any harm. I am not saying that you should prove your virtue by exposing yourself to any of the ordeals mentioned; what I mean is that knowing where safety or danger is, you keep yourself away from danger and journey instead to the area of safety. It is only in this sense that nothing in the world can harm you. It has been said that Heaven forms the core of reality, while man is only one of its outward manifestations. Once you know that true virtue lies in Heaven rather than in man and that man's actions should be in conformity with the wishes of Heaven, you should proceed to act in accordance with this knowledge. Acting constantly upon this knowledge, you become virtuous yourself and can do whatever you please. You have returned to the essential and can speak for the first time about the absolute."

"What do you mean by Heaven and man?"

"That a horse or ox has four legs is the work of Heaven; putting a halter on a horse's head or piercing a hole through an ox's nose is the doing of man. In summary, do not use human effort to destroy Heavenly creations; do not allow the temporary to override the permanent; do not sacrifice perennial interest for ephemeral advantage. Only by carefully observing these rules and never violating them will you return to the essence."

Notes

1. The Chinese original appears in *Chuang-tzu,* essay 17.

2. Pai-yi was the eldest son of a petty prince in the twelfth century B.C. Upon his father's death, he left the principality voluntarily so that his brother Shu-ch'i, instead of himself, could inherit the principality. See *Shih chi,* roll 61.

3. The two opposite but complementary forces whose interactions create the universe and everything in it.

4. According to Ssu-ma Ch'ien, the Five Emperors were Huang-ti ("Yellow Emperor," d. 2698? B.C.), Chuan-hsü (2513–2435? B.C.), Ti-k'u, T'ang-yao (or Yao, 2357–2255? B.C.), and Yü-shun (or Shun, 2255–2205? B.C.). See *Shih chi,* roll 1.

5. The Three Kings were Yü (founder of the Hsia dynasty, d. 2205? B.C.), T'ang (founder of the Shang dynasty, d. 1754? B.C.), and Wu (founder of the Chou dynasty, d. 1116 B.C.).

6. See pp. 8–11.

7. In 316 B.C. King K'uai of Yen abdicated in favor of his prime minister Tzu-chih who had the reputation of being virtuous. P'ing, the crown prince, revolted, entailing a civil war that witnessed the deaths of hundreds of thousands. Two years later, the state of Ch'i intervened, captured the Yen capital, and killed both King K'uai and Tzu-chih. P'ing was installed as King Chao of Yen (Yen Chao-wang) in 312 B.C. See *Shih chi,* roll 34.

8. See footnote 5.

9. Pai Kung, a grandson of King P'ing of Ch'u, revolted against King Hui, his uncle, in 479 B.C. Defeated, he committed suicide by hanging himself. See *Tso chuan,* the sixteenth year of Duke Ai.

10. Approximately 330 miles.

(9)
Mo Ti / *Universal Love*[1]

"For a man of love, the most important concern is to promote benefits for all men and to eliminate all that is harmful to them," said Mo Ti.

"Of all the things that harm man, what is the worst?" asked an inquirer.

"The worst is for strong countries to attack weak countries, powerful families to undermine the less powerful ones—in short, anything that involves the strong oppressing the weak, the majority bullying the minority, the cunning playing tricks upon the honest, or the socially superior trampling upon the socially inferior is bad for all men. Bad people, after all, do exist in this world, including kings who are not benevolent, ministers who are not loyal, fathers who are not loving, and sons who choose not to perform their filial duties. Ordinary folks who kill or injure one another at other people's command, with knives, poison, water, or fire, deserve equal condemnation. The question may be asked, Where does this deplorable state of affairs originate? Does it originate in love? Of course not. It originates in the presence of bad men. Why are these men bad? Are their actions motivated by universal concern for other people's well-being or partial obsession with their own interest? Partial obsession with their own interest, of course. From the above discussion we have to conclude that partiality, instead of universality, is the real cause of all that afflicts this world.

"Master Mo[2] once said that he who criticizes others must offer alternatives of his own. Failure to do so would be like the replacement of water by water or fire by fire which, besides not making any sense at all, clearly indicates the unreliability of the critic's criticism. Master Mo, offering an alternative of his own, suggests the replacement of partiality by universality."

"But how?" asked the inquirer.

"If one state regards all other states as if they were its own, it would not launch attacks against them," replied Mo Ti. "If it regards their cities as if they were its own, it would not try to capture these cities. Likewise, if one family regards all other families as if they were its own, it would not try to undermine these families. Is it good or bad for the world that states stop attacking one another and individuals and families stop undermining or robbing one another? Surely it is good. Where does this good originate? In the existence of bad men? Of course not. It orginates in the love for our fellow men. When you speak of love for our fellow men, do you have in mind universality or partiality? Universality, of course. From the above discussion we have to conclude that universality, instead of partiality, is the true source of human benefit. That is why Master Mo says, 'Universality is the correct road.'

"Having proven that universality is the source of all the good and partiality the source of all the evil in the world, we can now appreciate the validity of Master Mo's saying that universality, instead of partiality, is the correct road, keeping in mind the statement I made previously, namely, that for a man of love the most important concern is to promote benefits for all men and to eliminate all that is harmful to them. Once we decide to travel on this road, those of us who are endowed with higher intelligence or more physical strength will have the obligation to help those less well endowed. Likewise, those of us who have learned the right way of doing things will have the obligation to teach others about it. As an example showing how the strong can help the weak, widows and widowers must receive adequate means of support so they can live out their natural span of life, and orphans must have others looking after them so they can grow to become independent adults. Since universality is obviously advantageous, I cannot understand why so many people continue to criticize it."

"It is doubtless true that many people continue to criticize it," said the inquirer. "They are saying that even though universality is sound from a theoretical point of view, it cannot really be put into practice."

"If it cannot be put into practice," replied Mo Ti, "even I would have no part in it. How can a good thing, if it is really good, not be put into practice? Let us look at both sides of the question. Suppose there are two men, one of whom believes in partiality, while the other believes in universality. The first man says, 'How can I consider my friend's welfare in the same way I consider mine, and how can I give my friend's relatives the same attention as I give to my own?' He, consequently, will not feed his friend when he is hungry, will not clothe him when he suffers from cold, will not attend to his needs when he is sick, and will not bury him when he dies. The second man, who believes in universality, does the opposite. He says, 'I have heard that a superior man considers his friends' welfare in the same way he considers his own and gives his friend's relatives the same attention as he does his own.' He, consequently, will feed his friend when he is hungry, clothe him when he suffers from cold, attend to his needs when he is sick, and bury him when he dies. He believes in universality, and he puts it into practice. In short, both men practice what they believe in, and their words and deeds are in total agreement with each other.

"Suppose there is a third man who is about to go to war where life and death are extremely uncertain or who is about to make a long trip to such places as Pa, Yüeh, Ch'i, and Ching[3] and does not know when he will be able to return. What would he do under the circumstances? Would he entrust the care of his family to the first man who believes and practices the principle of partiality, or to the second man who believes and practices the principle of universality? I am sure that, facing these alternatives, even the most stupid man or woman, including a person who does not believe in the principle of universality, will choose the second man, namely, the man who believes and practices the principle of universality. Thus, whatever a person may say about the impracticability of universality, he will choose universality, instead of partiality, whenever he has the opportunity, thus contradicting his own assertion that universality is impractical. I, for one, cannot understand why people still criticize it when they are fully aware of its advantage."

"It is doubtless true that many people continue to criticize it," said the inquirer. "They are saying that even though the principle of universality may be used as a basis for selecting friends, it cannot be used as a basis for selecting a ruler."

"Let us look at the issue from both sides," said Mo Ti. "Suppose there are two rulers, one of whom believes and practices the principle of universality, while the other does not. The second ruler, who believes and practices the principle of partiality, says, 'How can I possibly have the same consideration for my subjects as I have for myself? This certainly demands too much from human nature. Furthermore, life is too short for me to indulge in such sentimentalities.' He, consequently, will not feed his subjects when they are hungry, will not clothe them when they suffer from cold, will not attend to their needs when they are sick, and will not bury them when they die. In short, he believes and practices the principle of partiality. The first ruler, the ruler who believes and practices the principle of universality, does the opposite. He says, 'I have heard that an enlightened ruler places the welfare of his subjects above his own. Only by doing this can he be regarded as an enlightened ruler.' He, consequently, will feed his subjects when they are hungry, clothe them when they suffer from cold, attend to their needs when they are sick, and bury them when they die. In short, he believes and practices the principle of universality.

"These two rulers are diametrically opposed in their beliefs, and each is absolutely sincere in carrying out his own belief. Now we would like to ask this question: 'In a year of the plague when countless people, despite their hard labor, suffer from cold and hunger and die in the ditches, which of these two rulers would you like to be your own, the ruler who believes and practices the principle of universality, or the ruler who does not?' I am sure that facing these alternatives, even the most stupid man or woman, including a person who does not believe in the principle of universality, will choose the ruler who believes and carries out the principle of universality. Thus, whatever a person may say about the impracticability of universality, he will choose universality, instead of partiality, whenever he has the opportunity, thus contradicting his own assertion that universality is impractical. I, for one, cannot understand why people still criticize it when they are fully aware of its advantage."

"It is doubtless true that many people continue to criticize it," said the inquirer. "They are saying that even though the principle of universality is in total agreement with the principle of love and righteousness, it is nevertheless difficult to practice it. Its implementation can be compared to carrying the T'ai Mountain[4] with one hand while trying to leap over a river. Everyone would like to practice the principle of universality, but it simply cannot be done."

"It is true that no one has been able to carry the T'ai Mountain with one hand while trying to leap over a river," said Mo Ti. "But the principle of universal love and mutual benefit was indeed put into practice by six of our ancient sage kings."[5]

"How do you know that these ancient sage kings put this principle into practice?" asked the inquirer.

"I of course did not personally witness the implementation of this principle, since I live at a different time from these ancient sage kings," Mo Ti replied. "Nevertheless its implementation was recorded on bamboo and silk and inscribed on metal and stone, so posterity would have no doubt at all that it was indeed implemented. For instance, the Great Oath[6] says, 'King Wen is like the sun and the moon whose light shines brightly in all the four quarters of the Western Land.'[7] This statement indicates that King Wen's love was so broad in scope that it was like the light of the sun and the moon which shone everywhere without discrimination or partiality. This is King Wen's principle of universality, which Master Mo has adopted for himself. A similar idea can also be found in the Oath of Yü.[8] In this document Yü says, 'All of you listen to me carefully! It is not I, a humble man of insignificance, who wish to be engaged in war; it is the Yumiao[9] who deserve punishment by Heaven. I shall lead you, princes of various nations, in a military campaign against them.' From this statement we know that in conducting a military campaign against the Miao, Yü was not motivated by fame, wealth, or personal amusement; his purpose was to promote benefits for all men and to eliminate all that was harmful to them. This is Yü's principle of universality, which Master Mo has adopted for himself.

"A similar idea can be also found in the Speech of T'ang.[10] In this document T'ang says, 'Lü,[11] your humble and insignificant servant, respectfully offers this black beast as sacrifice and reports to Heaven and Earth as follows: "This year we have a serious drought that pains me greatly. I do not know any sins of mine that have aroused the wrath of Heaven and Earth. To the best of my knowledge, I have not failed to promote goodness and suppress evil. In fact, I have carried out the wishes of Heaven as I understand them. If any of my subjects has committed a wrong, let Heaven punish me. If I have committed any wrong, please do not punish my subjects." ' This prayer indicates that powerful though he was as the Son of Heaven and wealthy though he was as the owner of all of China, T'ang did not hesitate to offer his own body as a sacrifice if somehow he could persuade the Heavenly Lord and other deities to be more merciful toward his subjects. This is T'ang's principle of universality, which Master Mo has adopted for himself.

"Lastly, a similar idea can be also found in the Odes of Chou.[12] It says, 'How vast and magnificent is the way of the king that contains no bias or prejudice! How equitable and honest is the way of the king that contains no prejudice or bias! It is as straight as a dart and as smooth as a whetstone. A gentleman travels on it, and a small man admires it from a distance.' It can be concluded from this quotation that my advocacy of universality is not just an exercise in phraseology; the principle of universality was indeed carried out in ancient times, by such monarchs as King Wen and King Wu who dispensed favors in accordance with the principle of equity: they rewarded the virtuous and punished the wicked without showing any favoritism for their brothers or other relatives. This is the principle of universality of King Wen and King Wu, which Master Mo has adopted for himself. I, for one, cannot understand why people still criticize it when they are fully aware of its advantage."

"It is doubtless true that people continue to criticize it," said the inquirer. "They are saying that this principle may not be advantageous to parents, since it violates the principle of filial piety."

"Let us look at the issue from the viewpoint of a dutiful son," said Mo Ti. "In searching for the best way to serve his parents, does he wish people outside of his family to love and care for his parents or to hate and harm them? He wishes other people to love and care for his parents, of course. How does he achieve this purpose? The way to achieve this purpose is to love and care for other people's parents, so these people, in return for what he has done, will love and care for his parents. As a devoted son, he does not have any choice, since to love and care for other people's parents is the only way to make other people love and care for his parents. Are the dutiful sons in the world so stupid that they cannot see this obvious point?

"To develop this point further, let us look at some of our ancient writings. In the Greater Odes[13] the author says, 'As words are returned, so is kindness. Give me a peach; a plum thou shalt receive.' This indicates that those who love will be loved in return and those who hate will indeed be hated. I, for one, cannot understand why people in the world wish to criticize the principle of love. Is it too difficult to practice? There are things in the world much more difficult, but they have been put into practice. Here are a few examples.

"Formerly, King Ling of Ching[14] loved slender waists, and throughout his reign many people chose not to eat more than a spoonful of rice each meal in order to have smaller waistlines. Being so weak, they could not stand up without the assistance of a cane and could not walk without the support of a wall. Strenuous dieting is a most difficult thing to do; yet the people of Ching did it. In less than one generation they changed their ways in order to ingratiate themselves with their king. Formerly Kouchien, the king of Yüeh,[15] emphasized the importance of bravery and trained his men for three years to be brave. Yet he was not certain whether they had indeed become brave. One day he set some ships on fire, and beat drums as an order for his soldiers to advance. One after another the soldiers went, and a countless number of them died either in water or in fire. They chose not to retreat long after the drumming had stopped. The soldiers of Yüeh were fearless indeed! To choose to die by fire is a most difficult thing to do; yet the people of Yüeh did it. In less than one generation they changed their ways in order to ingratiate themselves with their king. Formerly, Duke Wen of Tsin[16] loved the wearing of rustic clothing; consequently all his ministers, during his reign, contented themselves with robes made of the coarsest material, jackets made of sheepskin, hats made of raw silk, and shoes made of unprocessed hemp. In this way they presented themselves before the duke, in or outside his court. To appear as a rustic is a most difficult thing for a gentleman to do; yet the ministers of Tsin did it. In less than one generation they changed their ways in order to ingratiate themselves with their ruler.

"All the examples elaborated above—strenuous dieting, dying by fire, and gentlemen wearing rustic clothing—are difficult things to do, but people have been known to do them. In less than one generation they changed their ways in order to ingratiate themselves with their superiors. The principle of love and mutual benefit is as easy to carry out as it is advantageous. The only obstacle to its implementation is, in my judgment, the lack of official support. If the rulers of this country express confidence in it and promote it by rewarding those who practice it while punishing those who do not, I believe that the people will embrace it like fire's natural tendency to shoot upward and water's natural tendency to move downward, until the whole country will adopt and carry it out. For the principle of universality is the way of the sage kings, the foundation of safety for all the nobility, and the guarantee of a satisfactory livelihood for all the people in the world. A gentleman who has examined it carefully and carried it out thoroughly will be benevolent if he is a king, loyal if he is a subject, loving if he is a father, dutiful if he is a son, considerate if he is an elder brother, and respectful if he is a younger brother. Since no gentleman in his right mind would not wish to be benevolent if he were a king, loyal if he were a subject, loving if he were a father, dutiful if he were a son, considerate if he were an elder brother, and respectful if he were a younger brother, it is obvious that the principle of universality can easily be carried out. For this principle is the way of the sage kings that can bring the greatest benefit to all the people in the world."

Notes

1. The Chinese original appears in "Universal Love, Part 3," *(Chien ai hsia) Mei-tzu*, roll 16.
2. The author refers to himself.
3. Modern Szechuan, Chekiang, Shantung, and Hupeh provinces, respectively.
4. The highest mountain in Shantung province.
5. The Chinese text says "six of our ancient sage kings," but only four names are given. "Six" could have been a typographical error for "four."
6. The Great Oath *(T'ai shih)*, a chapter in the *Book of History*, was said to have been written by King Wu of Chou, in the year he began his military campaign against Cheo, last ruler of the Shang dynasty.
7. King Wen was the father of King Wu. Before conquering the Shang regime, Chou's home base was modern Shensi province, located in the western part of China.
8. Originally a chapter in the *Book of History*, the Oath of Yü *(Yü shih)* has since been lost. Yü was the founder of the Hsia dynasty.
9. An ancient name for Miao.
10. The present version of the *Book of History* has a chapter entitled *T'ang kao* or T'ang's Command, instead of *T'ang shui* or T'ang's Speech. It is believed that they are really the same thing. T'ang was the founder of the Shang dynasty.
11. T'ang's personal name.
12. Part of the Odes of Chou *(Chou shih)*, as quoted here, appears in the *Book of Odes*, while the other part can be found in the *Hung fan* ("Grand Model") section of the *Book of History*.
13. The Greater Odes, or *Ta ya*, is part of the *Book of Odes*.

14. Ching is the same as Ch'u, modern Hupeh province.
15. Modern Chekiang province.
16. See pp. 14–18.

(10)
Han Fei / *A Private Complaint*[1]

The possession of sound judgment, together with foresight, characterizes a man of learning and skill; it enables him to unmask selfish dealings before they materialize. The possession of undisputed integrity, plus an unbending will, likewise characterizes an able Legalist; it enables him to forestall conspiratorial designs before they actually occur.

The duty of a minister is to administer men and events in strict observance of the law; he is not appointed by, and certainly should not be responsible to, a power broker. A power broker is a man who acts arbitrarily in violation of the authority entrusted to him, exercises power for the advancement of his self-interest, appropriates public funds for the enrichment of private coffers, and yet somehow manages to continue to enjoy the king's confidence and thus stay in power. He will be out of power, however, as soon as a man of learning and skill, or an able Legalist, is entrusted with a position of authority, since a man of learning and skill can easily unmask his selfish dealings, while an able Legalist, as stated previously, can forestall conspiratorial designs before they actually occur. Besides, both owe no loyalty except to the king to whom they are absolutely obedient. Not surprisingly, a power broker and an able Legalist have always been implacable enemies.

As long as a power broker remains in power, however, he will be supported by public officials within and foreign states without. Foreign states will continue to praise him because they realize that without his assistance they cannot obtain what they want from the state that he represents. At home public officials will have no choice but to serve continually as his private tools because they realize that without his assistance they cannot complete the work assigned to them and thus win recognition and reward which they believe are their due. Even officials in the Inner Court will find it advisable to hide his misdeeds because they realize that without his assistance they cannot stay in the king's favor very long. Learned scholars will quote him constantly and speak of him in glorious terms because they realize that failure to do so will result in the reduction of salaries and stipends or some other form of humiliation. With the support of these four groups—foreign states, public officials, officials in the Inner Court, and learned scholars—a power broker has no difficulty in covering up his outrageous behavior and traitorous deeds. Outwardly the king's loyal minister, he is most disloyal in the sense that he recommends to and appoints for him only those officials who, like himself, are actually the king's enemies. Meanwhile, the king is prevented by these four groups from seeing the truth himself. As time goes on, the king becomes weaker and weaker, while the power of the power broker continues to increase.

It is true that a power broker comes to power on account of the king's affection for and confidence in him—the kind of affection and confidence that tend to increase as the king becomes more and more used to him. Once in power, he enhances his influence by thinking the way the king would think, namely, by sharing, or pretending to share, the king's likes and dislikes. As ranks and titles continue to be showered on him, he forms his own clique and builds his own following and has the whole nation constantly eulogizing him. How can a Legalist, however able he is, approach the king under these circumstances, since he is neither a beloved relative of the power broker nor one of his favorite followers? Besides, he advocates a government by law, the direct opposite of the kind of government based upon personal relations which is cherished by all kings. How can he, a man of inferior position who has no clique or following behind him, compete with those whom the king loves and trusts? How can he, arguing against the king's wishes, compete with those who understand and serve well every one of the king's little whims? How can he, as a commoner who occupies no official position, compete with the members of the nobility who have great power at their command? How can he, as one individual, argue successfully against the whole nation? Besides the overwhelming odds against him, he has the additional disadvantage of being presented to the king once in years, while a power broker can see the king anytime during the day and argue his case without being contradicted. Under the circumstances how is it possible for the king to appreciate his talent and ability and to be awakened to the failings of those who supposedly serve him?

It is easy to see the dangerous situation a Legalist is in when we take into consideration the fact that he and a power broker are implacable enemies and yet the chance of success in his fight against the latter is practically nonexistent. A power broker can easily sentence him to death, if some excuse can be found to make him appear guilty. If no legal excuse can be found, he can nevertheless be done away with through some secret arrangement. Thus a Legalist, by believing in the sanctity of the law and voicing sound but unpopular ideas, ends up with his own death: either by public execution or through private murder. Meanwhile, those who form cliques to deceive the king or argue speciously to advance their own selfish interests will win the trust and support of a power broker who rewards them with position and wealth if they have military deeds to their credit or artificially builds their reputations abroad in order to enhance their position at home if, unfortunately, they have no military deeds to speak of. Given the kinds of rewards a power broker can dispense, those who wish to be rewarded will come to his door instead of that of the king. As long as the king does what a power broker would like him to do, namely, punish the innocent and reward the unworthy, who, among the Legalists, would wish to risk his life to speak candidly on the issue at stake? How, under the circumstances, can we expect evil and conspiratorial ministers to resign voluntarily for the common good? As public power that is vested in the king slowly diminishes, private power in the hands of powerful ministers will continue to increase.

We know that a foreign country, however wealthy or strong it is, cannot be useful to the king of China, since China cannot extend her jurisdiction far beyond her own border. A king of China has lost his country and in fact has no more to do with it than he has with a foreign country if he is blind and foolish enough to allow his ministers to take over the power of the state. To examine the parallel further, we find the situation even worse than it appears on the surface since a foreign country does not, after all, belong to him, while China does. When people say that the state of Ch'i has disappeared, they do not mean that its cities or territories have disappeared from the face of the earth; they mean that the house of Lü has been replaced by the house of T'ien as the royal family of that state.[2] Likewise, when people say that the state of Tsin has disappeared, they do not mean that its cities or territories have been destroyed; they mean that the power of the royal house of Chi has been taken over by the Six Families.[3] Once a power broker is on the verge of taking over the power of the state, the king must be totally blind if he allows the trend to continue without making some attempt to repossess what is legally his own. A man who suffers the same disease a dead man has suffered will not survive; a man who does the same thing the doomed have done will be doomed too. Similarly, if a king allows events to develop in the same manner as they did develop at one time in the states of Ch'i and Tsin, he cannot possibly hope to preserve his kingdom.

The difficulties that a Legalist encounters are the same regardless of the size of the states involved, large or small. Surrounded by those who are less than wise, a king is in fact seeking wisdom from fools whenever he consults them on the worth of others who are truly wise. Surrounded by those who are less than virtuous, he is in fact discussing virtue with thieves whenever he consults them on the conduct of others who are truly virtuous. In the former case, a fool's standard is used to measure wisdom; in the latter case, a thief's rule is employed to gauge moral worth. Since a savant no more wishes to be judged by fools than a saint wishes to be judged by thieves, it is unlikely that the king will ever have the opportunity to be awakened to the fact that he has continually been deceived by those whom he trusts.

A man of integrity is expected to follow two paths in his entry into officialdom: the purity of character for the virtuous and the abundance of knowledge for the wise. Being pure in character and abundant in knowledge, he, when allowed to serve as an official, will not distort the law to advance the private ends of any individual, however powerful he is. He has nothing to offer except his loyal service when those in power are primarily interested in bribes. Knowing what he is, these men in power want to make sure that he will never have the opportunity of being presented to the king. As soon as he seeks an audience, they slander and scandalize him; his erudition is subject to ridicule and his immaculateness to smearing. How can the king be informed of the true state of affairs when all men of integrity are kept away from him? When good men are not rewarded and bad men not punished, only the most incompetent and the most corrupt can be found to serve the king.

In summary, all countries, large or small, suffer one defect in common, namely, the surrounding of the king by unworthy personnel. They are called powerful ministers in large countries and personal retainers in smaller states. The fact that they continue to enjoy power is indicative of their unredeemed guilt as well as the lack of good judgment on the part of the king. The unpleasant reality that every king must face is that his interests and the interests of his ministers are not always the same and are in fact mutually exclusive in most cases. The king's interests lie in the employment of officials in accordance with ability, granting ranks and titles in accordance with performance, and the appointment to specific positions in accordance with the ownership of special skills. A minister's interests, on the other hand, are better served when a person appointed as an official, or an official promoted to a higher position, is a member of his clique, regardless of whether he is competent, deserving, principled, or otherwise. He does not mind the loss of territories to foreign countries as long as he himself can become more wealthy in the process; nor does he object to the continuous increase of his own power at the expense of that of the king. Eventually he takes over the kingdom, de jure as well as de facto; he becomes the king, and the king becomes his subject. To reward his accomplices, he grants them land and titles. A process of deception and self-service is climaxed in the coronation of a thief.

One cannot fail to notice that whenever power changes hands from one king to the next in line, no more than two out of every ten power brokers can still maintain their former positions, for the new king is aware, as the old king was not, of the serious crimes that these power brokers have committed against the crown. Of all the crimes committed by a minister against the crown, deception is among the worst, for which he should rightfully be sentenced to death. Since a wise man is farsighted enough not to risk his life by engaging in deception and since a virtuous man, because of his integrity, opposes deception as a matter of principle, neither of them will join a power broker's private clique. The followers of a power broker, consequently, are among the worst elements in society: they are either too stupid to know what is involved or too corrupt to keep themselves away from conspiracy. With a following like this, a power broker can continue to deceive the king, while amassing a large fortune for himself in the process. Meanwhile, the members of his clique exploit and oppress the people all over the country. Whenever an issue arises, they all voice the same opinion and advance the same argument as if they shared one mouth. How in the world can the king ever find out the truth? Individually or jointly, they bring more danger to the nation and more humiliation to the king. Is any crime more serious than this? A king who is unable to see a power broker's scheme has committed a most serious error indeed. How can the nation be preserved under a circumstance like this?

Notes

1. The Chinese original appears in *Han-fei-tzu*, roll 4.

2. The state of Ch'i was established as a feudatory of Lü Shang in the twelfth century B.C. In 672 B.C. a petty prince named T'ien Wan (formerly known as Ch'en Wan) emigrated from Ch'en to Ch'i and was appointed by Duke Huan of Ch'i as his minister of public works. For the next two centuries the house of T'ien continued to enhance its own power at the expense of the house of Lü until eventually, in 386 B.C., it was formally recognized as the royal house of Ch'i. See *Shih chi*, roll 46.

3. The state of Tsin was a feudatory established in the twelfth century B.C., and its first ruler, T'ang Shu, was a member of the Chi family and a younger son of King Wu of Chou (Chou Wu-wang). Beginning in the middle decades of the sixth century B.C. the power of the state gradually fell into the hands of the so-called Six Ministerial Families *(Liu ch'ing)*, namely, Han, Chao, Wei, Fan, Chung-hsing, and Chih. Three of the families (Han, Chao, and Wei) eventually partitioned the state of Tsin among themselves. This event, which occurred in 403 B.C., marked the beginning of the Warring States period. See *Shih chi*, roll 39.

CHAPTER

3

The Grand Unifications

"AFTER I die," said Ssu-ma T'an on his deathbed while holding his son's hand, "you will be appointed Grand Historian to succeed me. As the Grand Historian, do not forget to do what I myself have failed to do. There are three stages in the fulfillment of one's obligations as a dutiful son. The first stage is honoring one's parents; the second stage is performing loyal services to the king. Neither of the two, however, is more important than the third, namely, building a great name for posterity to remember and for all of one's forebears to be proud of."

The above event, which occurred in 110 B.C., provided Ssu-ma Ch'ien (b. 145 B.C.) with the impetus to write a history that was destined to bring him eternal fame. One year later, he was appointed Grand Historian as his father had predicted and earnestly began collecting materials for the work he had in mind. Toward the end of 99 B.C. his work was suddenly interrupted. Earlier, in the fall of that year, a general named Li Ling (d. 74 B.C.), in command of five thousand infantrymen, was ordered by Emperor Han Wu-ti (r. 140–87 B.C.) to march deep into the nomadic territory to the north to fight against an old Chinese enemy called the Hsiung-nu. After the first news arrived that General Li had won one victory after another against overwhelming odds, the emperor and his ministers celebrated. Then the bolt struck. All but four hundred men of the expeditionary forces had been annihilated by the enemy; most unforgivably, General Li, the commander, had chosen to be captured alive instead of commiting suicide as the honor of the nation had dictated. Facing an angry and irreconcilable emperor, all the ministers voiced strong condemnation of the general, all, that is, except Ssu-ma Ch'ien who testified that Li, being a man of high principle, must have chosen to spare his own life for the purpose of redeeming himself in the future. For this "unforgivable" crime of defending a "traitor," Ssu-ma Ch'ien was punished by castration, a punishment next only to the death sentence in severity according to popular opinion.

Had Ssu-ma Ch'ien followed the popular dictate that a gentleman should commit suicide rather than subject himself to humiliation, especially a humiliation of such nature as castration, we would not have the *Shih chi,* or *Historical Records,* one of the greatest works China has ever produced. One suspects that throughout the ordeal he constantly had in mind his father's last instruction as quoted above. "Knowing what I had to accomplish," he wrote in a letter to a friend, "I went through the worst punishments without anger or fear." The work was finally completed in 91 B.C., eighteen years after it had been begun and eight years after his personal tragedy. "It would then be kept in a famous mountain," said the Grand Historian, "waiting for those who, understanding its value, would distribute it in all of the large cities." It was not kept in a "famous mountain" for long, however. Twenty years after its author's death, the book was widely read and praised by China's intellectual elite. For the next two millennia no Chinese could be regarded as truly learned without reading the Grand Historian's masterpiece.

In terms of historiography two things need to be said about the *Shih chi.* First, it was the first universal history of China, tracing the nation's past from its legendary beginning to approximately 100 B.C. Second, Ssu-ma Ch'ien developed in his book a new structure or organization that was to be followed by all future dynastic historians. The book is divided into five distinct parts: twelve royal biographies *(pen-chi),* some of which are actually dynastic histories in brief, ten chronological charts *(nien piao),* eight treatises *(shu),* thirty biographies of aristocratic families *(shih chia),* and seventy ordinary biographies *(lieh chuan)*—altogether 130 individual items, each of which, in the fashion of those ancient days, was inscribed on one roll of silk. Hence we say, even in modern times, that the *Shih chi* contains 130 rolls and identify its contents by referring to its roll number, instead of its pages, a concept that did not exist before the invention of printing.

The *Shih chi* ended in 100 B.C., and other historians must pick up from there and carry on. Early in the first century A.D. a man named Pan Piao (d. A.D. 54) decided to take the task upon himself. Described by his contemporaries as "serious" and "contemplative," he praised Ssu-ma Ch'ien's work but nevertheless had some strong reservations. "The work covers too wide an area to be detailed in each subject and involves too many schools of philosophy to sustain a central theme," he wrote. "It seems that the author was more interested in displaying his erudition than in rendering sound judgment. Furthermore, he elevates Taoism at the expense of Confucianism in his treatise on philosophy, glorifies wealth and downgrades moral values in his treatise on economics. Finally, by speaking favorably of the unorthodox and the adventurous in his treatment of the knights-errant, he is in fact casting doubt on the sound principle of rectitude." This criticism must be viewed against the background of universal acceptance of Confucianism as the only way of a good life in the first century A.D., whereas in the second century B.C., when Ssu-ma Ch'ien lived, Confucianism had just begun to emerge as the leading school of thought. It is true that Ssu-ma T'an lauded Taoism in an essay contained in his son's book, but elsewhere the book is eminently fair in its treatment of Confucianism.

Pan Piao did not finish his work, as he died at the comparatively young age of fifty-one. Fortunately he was survived by two sons and one daughter, each of whom was as brilliant as their father had ever been. Pan Ch'ao (d. A.D. 102), the younger son, later made history by bringing all of central Asia under Chinese control. Pan Ku (A.D. 32–92), the elder son, was more of an introvert, destined to pursue an academic rather than a political and military career. In A.D. 58 or thereabouts, he began to concentrate on completing what his father had left. Twenty years later, the *Han shu,* or *History of the Han,* was completed and won instant recognition as a great masterpiece. "There was not a learned man who did not read it," commented Fan Yeh (398–445) who, early in the fifth century, wrote the *Hou Han shu,* or *History of the Later Han,* as a successor to Pan Ku's work. Having completed the major project of his life, Pan Ku spent much of his time writing poetry and, for a short period, even served as an aide-de-camp under General Tou Hsien (A.D. 92) during the latter's military campaign against the Hsiung-nu. The general's death was followed by Pan Ku's own political oblivion, and his political enemies lost no time throwing him into jail where he died at the age of sixty.

In the manuscripts Pan Ku left behind it was found that he had intended to write one treatise on astronomy and compose eight chronological charts, but somehow he was never able to complete them. Pan Chao (d. ca. A.D. 105), his younger sister and an outstanding scholar in her own right, was summoned by the reigning emperor Han Ho-ti (r. 89–105) to the court to complete the unfinished work. The treatise on astronomy and the chronological charts were completed in due course, and the *Han shu,* consisting of twelve royal biographies, eight chronological charts, ten treatises, and seventy ordinary biographies, finally reached its present form.

Outstanding though they are, both the *Shih chi* and the *Han shu* (and, for that matter, all the dynastic histories that followed) contain obvious shortcomings. The most annoying, from a modern historian's point of view, is the cavalier attitude toward the identification of sources. For instance, Ssu-ma Ch'ien copied *ad verbum* long passages from the *Documents of the Warring States* without identifying their source or bothering to mention the fact that they were not his own words. Pan Ku likewise copied Ssu-ma Ch'ien extensively, often without changing a word. In modern days we would have to call this kind of behavior plagiarism, one of the worst sins a writer can commit. Apparently plagiarism was not regarded as a sin in ancient times. Once a book was circulated, it immediately became public property; there were no such things as copyrights to safeguard what we today consider an author's legitimate right to his work. In fact, an author honored a dead or living colleague by copying him, confidently expecting that a reader would know the source he copied, since his colleague's work was also in circulation. This expectation was of course not always justified.

The use of long quotations, sometimes in the form of an essay that contains several thousand Chinese characters, stemmed from the desire to let the person described speak for himself without undue interference from others, including his biographer. This is especially true if the person described was a man of letters. In the "Biography of Tung Chung-shu" (*Han shu,* roll 56), for instance, we find the distribution of Chinese characters roughly as follows:

Number of characters describing Tung's life	574
Number of characters in general comments	159
Number of characters leading to quotations	54
Number of characters in quotations	6,600
Total number of characters in the biography	7,387

The bulk of the biography consists of three of Tung Chung-shu's lengthy memorials that are of enormous importance to the study of Chinese philosophy in general and Confucianism in particular. It has so little to say about Tung Chung-shu's personal life that we do not even know in what year he was born or died. This certainly is not the way a modern historian would write a biography.

Nevertheless, because of this unique way of writing history, many important documents (imperial decrees, memorials, essays, poems, and letters) that could have been easily scattered and lost have been preserved in toto for posterity, as they are contained in the prestigious and widely read dynastic histories. All selections in this chapter are translated and excerpted from the *Shih chi*, the *Han shu*, and the *Hou Han shu*, the three major sources that cover the Ch'in-Han period (221 B.C.–A.D. 220). Their backgrounds are briefly described as follows:

Chia Yi (201–168 B.C.), the author of "The Evil of the Ch'in" (*Ko Ch'in lun; Shih chi*, roll 6), won national recognition as a prodigious scholar in his late teens and was invited by Emperor Han Wen-ti (r. 179–157 B.C.) to serve as an "imperial professor" *(po-shih)* while still in his early twenties. The author's evaluation of the Ch'in regime set the tune for centuries of Chinese scholars to follow; they found little with which to quarrel in the basic theme contained in this short essay.

Chu-fu Yen (d. 127 or 126 B.C.), like Chia Yi before him, advocated breaking up large feudatories to increase the imperial power at Ch'angan. His proposal, submitted to Emperor Han Wu-ti in 127 B.C. and translated here as "The Advisability of Dividing Large Feudatories into Small Ones" (*Han shu*, roll 64a), was readily accepted and quickly carried out, but he himself had to be sacrificed in order to appease the angry lords.

Tung Chung-shu, a Confucian scholar whose name has been mentioned earlier, was primarily known for his advocacy of "The

Harmony between Heaven and Man" (*Han shu*, roll 56). Though enjoying great prestige and influence throughout his life, he never used his position to acquire private wealth, on the grounds that a gentleman who received salaries for his own support should not compete with common people for making profit. This empathy with the underprivileged can be found in practically all of his writings, one of which, in the form of a memorial submitted to Emperor Han Wu-ti, is here translated as "The Plight of the Peasantry" (*Han shu*, roll 24a).

The plight of the peasantry that continued to accelerate throughout the first century B.C. precipitated the economic reforms that were conducted by Wang Mang (d. A.D. 23) during the first two decades of the Christian era. Besides the nationalization of land and its distribution among the peasantry, the reformer also introduced several other measures, one of which was the market stabilization program. This program, described by Pan Ku in *Han shu*, roll 24b, appears here as selection 15.

Pan Chao, Pan Ku's younger sister, was reported to have authored her own book that consisted of sixteen rolls. Unfortunately, aside from the treatise on astronomy and the eight chronological charts mentioned earlier, the extant work that can be clearly identified as hers is a short discourse, "The Seven Feminine Virtues" (*Hou Han shu*, roll 114). It is interesting to see today how a Chinese woman in the first century A.D., regarded by historians as one of China's greatest women of letters, viewed woman's role in a man-dominated society.

(11)

Chia Yi/ *The Evil of the Ch'in*[1]

Why did the nation not make any protest and in fact readily accept him after he, Shih Huang-ti [d. 210 B.C.], had conquered all the rival states, unified China, assumed the title of emperor, and proceeded to enjoy all that the nation could offer? To answer this question, we must take into consideration the fact that before the unification China had not had a common sovereign for a long time—the royal house of Chou had long declined and even the Five Autocrats[1] had, one after another, disappeared from the scene. There was no central authority that compelled loyalty and obedience from every Chinese; consequently, different states fought among themselves. The strong attacked the weak; the numerous ravaged the few. Wars were incessant, entailing enormous sufferings to all people concerned. After the Ch'in state had unified China and Shih Huang-ti assumed the title of emperor, for the first time in a long period a center of authority was reestablished, to which all Chinese, hopefully, could look for the protection of their lives. It is no wonder that they should most humbly support the new regime. Whether the Ch'in regime could continue to advance to greater achievement, or, for that matter, maintain itself as a viable going concern, depended very much upon its ability to preserve the goodwill that the people had for it at this time.

But Ch'in Shih Huang-ti did not choose to preserve this goodwill. For the new emperor was an extremely selfish, avaricious man, constantly indulging in an unsurpassed but unjustifiable egotism and shutting out outside advice. He did not trust the ministers who had performed well for him; nor did he attempt to endear himself to his subjects. He deliberately undermined institutional authority and replaced it with a private dictatorship of his own. He banned literature not to his liking and revised the penal code to make it so draconian as to be inhuman. He placed might above right and set a most regretable example by making naked power—and naked power alone—the arbitrator of world affairs. He did not realize that there was a world of difference between the way a country was conquered and the way it should be governed. While the application of naked power may be necessary to the conquest of a country, the attainment of peace and prosperity requires the adoption of policies that conform to the wishes of the governed. The mistake Shih Huang-ti made was that he used the method of conquering a country to govern a country and consequently antagonized the nation as a whole. Isolated from the people from whom he had no support, he and his regime could not survive long. Had he chosen to learn from history, especially that part of history dealing with the decline of the Shang dynasty and its replacement by the Chou regime, and adopted policies in conformity with what he had learned, the regime he established would not have collapsed as fast as it later did, however mediocre his successors might be. He was the very opposite of the Three Kings[2] who not only established a great name for themselves but also, because of the adoption of wise policies, enabled their respective regimes to last a long, long time.

When Shih Huang-ti died and his son Erh-shih ascended the throne,[3] the nation looked forward to a change of policies with great expectation. Having suffered the insufferable, people of all walks of life wanted some relief from their government: some food for those who had little to eat and some clothing for those who suffered from cold. Since their demand was small and could easily be met, what a wonderful opportunity the new emperor had to make himself a ruler of love and compassion and thus win the unswerving loyalty of all of his subjects! Yet the new emperor chose not to seize this opportunity. The history of the Ch'in dynasty would have taken a course different from the one it later took had he done what a good, conscientious ruler would normally do, such as the delegation of authority to able and virtuous ministers, the concentration of efforts on the cure of domestic ills, the reversal of some of his predecessor's policies that had been proved harmful and self-defeating, the granting of fiefs to the descendants of those who had performed great deeds for the regime, the establishment of a feudal system in conformity with the best of China's tradition, the humanization of the penal code to minimize the necessity of massive imprisonment, the elimination of such statutes as those authorizing the enslavement of a convicted criminal's wife and children so that his relatives, despite his crime, could continue to live in peace, the opening of the granary for the hungry and the distribution of money for the poor, the reduction of taxes and corvée assignments, the simplification of the legal code to curtail punishment which should be imposed only as a last resort, and many other measures that can be cited. The purpose of these measures was to turn a new page for all the people in China who, in this case, would be so grateful to their government for its goodwill that they would be most careful about their own conduct. Meanwhile the government would reap the reward of having not only satisfied people's aspirations but also won their loyalty and support. When people were happy and contented and were most afraid of any disruption of a good life, they would not harbor the thought of withdrawing support for their government, even though one may find among them knavish elements who manufactured turmoil for its own sake. As long as the government enjoyed popular support, disloyal subjects could easily be exposed for what they were, and any conspiracy against the government could be crushed quickly and with ease.

Unfortunately Erh-shih did not do any of the things described above. On the contrary, he heightened the evil of his predecessor. He continued the construction of the Afang Palace,[4] rewrote the penal code to make it even more complex and draconian, employed harsh, heartless men as law enforcement officials, rewarded and punished according to his whims, and taxed as if there were no limit. The nation was then plagued with turmoil which officials could not control; people were destitute, but they could not expect any relief from the government. It was under these circumstances that illegal and conspiratorial acts multiplied, that deception and self-deception were practiced at all levels of the government, and that numerous people were convicted of crimes for which they paid dearly with their lives. Who would not suffer, living in a time like this! Everyone, regardless of his social position, was seized with fear and personally experienced one facet or another of this miserable state of affairs. Everyone was unhappy with the way things were and became susceptible to illicit ideas. Ch'en Sheng, the first man to raise the standard of revolt, possessed neither great virtue nor high position; yet, when he raised up his arm in Tatse [modern Anhwei province] and called for rebellion, the whole nation responded to him. Why? The people could no longer endure the Ch'in tyranny, not even for a single day!

Having examined closely the relationship between cause and effect and thoroughly familiarized themselves with each turning point in the march of events, from survival to extinction and vice versa, the sage kings of ancient times stated time and again that the first principle in government is the attainment of peace and security for all the people in the nation. Once this objective is attained, the government will become secure itself, since no one enjoying peace and security will respond to a call of rebellion. "It is as easy to induce contented people to do good as it is to agitate unhappy people to do evil"; there is indeed a great deal of truth in this statement. Honorable though he was as the Son of Heaven and wealthy though he was as the owner of all of China, Erh-shih, in the end, died at the hands of an assassin.[5] Who, indeed, was responsible for his death? It was none other than Erh-shih himself who, instead of facing the challenge in a time of extreme danger, had chosen to pursue a policy of national suicide.

Notes

1. The Five Autocrats *(wu pa)* were Duke Huan of Ch'i, Duke Wen of Tsin, Duke Mu of Ch'in, Duke Hsiang of Sung, and King Chuang of Ch'u, all of whom lived during the Spring and Autumn period (722–481 B.C.). Each had attempted, at one time or another, to restore some order in the relationships among the various states in China.

2. The founders of the Three Dynasties, namely, Yü of the Hsia dynasty, T'ang of the Shang dynasty, and King Wen and King Wu of the Chou dynasty.

3. Erh-shih, or "Second Emperor," ascended the throne in 210 B.C.

4. The construction of the Afang Palace was begun during Shih Huang-ti's reign and was not yet completed at the time of his death. After his death the working force, said to have consisted of seven hundred thousand men, was transferred to Mount Li to build the dead emperor's mausoleum. Upon the completion of the mausoleum the working force was reemployed for the palace's construction.

5. In 207 B.C. Erh-shih was murdered by Chao Kao, his chief minister.

(12)

Chu-fu Yen / *The Advisability of Dividing Large Feudatories into Small Ones*

The average size of a feudatory in ancient times did not exceed ten thousand square *li;*[1] consequently it was easy for the imperial government, being infinitely stronger, to control all of its feudatories. Today the situation is different. Some of the feudatories have a territory measuring one million square *li,*[2] comprising dozens of cities. They tend to be arrogant and contemptuous if the imperial government is generous and lenient and become openly rebellious, even to the extent of making military alliances among themselves to attack the nation's capital, if the imperial government chooses to be strict with them. This open rebellion occurred once before when the imperial government, following the recommendation of Ch'ao Ts'o [d. 154 B.C.], attempted to reduce the territorial size of some of the largest feudatories.[3]

It seems that a violation of the principle of love and filial piety has occurred when a feudal prince, having a dozen or more sons and younger brothers, designates only one of them to inherit all of his domain when he dies, while the rest of them, who are as close to him in blood as his heir apparent, receive little or nothing. I therefore recommend this measure for Your Majesty to consider: that a decree be issued ordering all the feudal princes to grant territories and titles to their sons and younger brothers as a special favor. When acted upon, this measure will bring gratitude from all the parties concerned, each of whom will receive what his heart desires. Meanwhile the large feudatories will be broken into smaller ones and will become much weakened as a result.

Notes

1. Approximately eleven hundred square miles.
2. Approximately one hundred eleven thousand square miles.
3. This refers to the Seven States' Rebellion (154 B.C.). Though the rebellion was crushed, Ch'ao Ts'o, who recommended the reduction of the largest feudal domains, was executed by the imperial government to appease the princes in rebellion.

(13)

Tung Chung-shu / *The Harmony between Heaven and Man*

In a most enlightened decree couched in the words of the wise, Your Majesty inquires of your humble servant the meaning of Heavenly mandate and the nature of man. How can your humble servant, benighted as he certainly is, possibly provide a satisfactory reply? However, he has studied the events as recorded in the

Spring and Autumn Annals; he has also observed the interactions between Heaven and man. From these studies and observations has emerged a lesson of vital importance which, with Your Majesty's permission, he wishes to discuss.

Whenever a nation is in the process of losing her virtue, Heaven will signal its disapproval by sending out natural disasters. If the nation does not examine herself and change her evil ways despite this signal of disapproval, it will warn and frighten her with the occurrence of strange, unexplainable phenomena or events. If she still refuses to mend her ways, she will inevitably suffer catastrophic defeat. This shows that Heaven loves the person whom it has installed as the king of all men and will try to stop the development of events that could be disastrous to him. Unless the king, living in an age when moral values have totally disappeared, insists on injuring himself and committing political suicide, chances are that Heaven will continually support him. In short, the security of a king lies in his own relentless effort to do good for the nation.

First, there should be a relentless effort to learn. Learning broadens the horizon of knowledge and sharpens the edge of intellect. Second, there should be a relentless effort to perform virtuous deeds, the attainment of which will, slowly but increasingly, refine the character of those who are making the effort. Both efforts are easy to begin and quick to yield concrete results. The *Book of Odes* says, "How dare I relax, day or night!" The *Book of History* says, "How exuberant the king is! How exuberant the king is!" The authors of both books emphasize for us the importance of relentless effort.

Ethical and moral values are the very foundation of a good government, since no government can be regarded as good without being loving in intention and righteous in deeds. There are also, of course, rites and music that form the center of its educational program. The reason that the regimes established by our ancient sage kings could each last several hundred years is because these sage kings, during their lifetimes, had used rites and music to teach and refine their subjects. Before introducing music of his own, the founder of a new dynasty usually adopts that part of the music of his predecessors that is judged most appropriate for his own time, so no interruption will occur in the continuous refinement of all the people in the nation. For the cultural refinement of the people is impossible without them being instilled with psalms and songs. Therefore, once a king has successfully established himself as the ruler of all men, he introduces music of his own, which is meant not merely as a medium whereby his own achievement can be eulogized, but most importantly, as a means of directing the people and their customs, habits, and folkways toward the good. It is easy to change the people, but it is much more difficult to refine them.

The harmonization of sounds constitutes music, but music would not be music if it were not an expression of human sentiments and emotions. Music comes from without, penetrates through our skin and flesh, and is then buried in the marrow of our bones. It outlasts government and politics. After a political regime has long declined as a moral force, music originally composed to eulogize it nevertheless persists. That is why Confucius, when traveling in the state of Ch'i, heard the Songs of Shun, even though the regime founded by Shun had long disappeared from the face of the earth.

All kings in the world wish to preserve their crown and deplore any development of events that may pose a threat to it. Yet there were numerous kings in the past who had lost what they cherished most. Why? They either employed bad men or pursued incorrect policies. They, consequently, witnessed the continuous deterioration of their respective regimes until these regimes ceased to exist. While it is true that the sound policies as formulated by the founders of the Chou dynasty lost their momentum at the time of King Li [r. 878–828 B.C.] and King Yu [r. 781–771 B.C.] this does not mean that the policies themselves had been outdated at this time. The deterioration of the dynasty had nothing to do with the policies which remained sound; it deteriorated because these two kings had failed to carry them out. King Hsüan [r. 827–782 B.C.], on the other hand, did exactly the opposite. Reminding himself of the great virtues of the dynasty's founding fathers, he opened up what had been hitherto clogged and provided remedies for what had gone wrong for a long time. Because of his effort, the glorious deeds of King Wen and King Wu appeared once again, and the royal house of Chou shone brightly throughout the empire. This was the time the poets sang. "May Heaven protect him and bless him with virtuous aides!" they pleaded in their song. People continued to sing this song long after the Chou dynasty had disappeared; even today we can still hear it. How was King Hsüan able to achieve such great fame? The answer is that he worked diligently for the people's welfare and did not dare to relax, day or night.

Confucius says, "Man enlarges virtue, but virtue cannot enlarge man." This means that it is man who determines the course of events, peace or war, good or bad government. It is absurd to assume that the course of events, once determined by Heaven, is irreversible by man. If a king, by virtue of his own conduct, deserves Heaven's approval, the approval, in the form of propitious omens, will come by itself. In other words, the mandate for continuous rule has nothing to do with prayer or pleading; it remains valid and viable if the people love and support their king in the same way they love and support their parents. The *Book of History* says, "White fish jump into the king's boat; fire transforms itself into black crows the moment it enters the king's house."[1] These two auspicious omens, originated in Heaven and bestowed upon King Wu of Chou, were credentials of approval. Being fully aware of their significance, Duke Chou exclaimed: "Heaven has signified its approval! Heaven has signified its approval!"

Confucius says, "A virtuous man does not stand alone; he induces others to become virtuous." This shows that goodness, when practiced consistently, will generate further goodness. It was only during the later periods of our history that excessive misdeeds brought about a moral decline and the government, consequently, could no longer govern well and successfully. Feudal princes revolted against the central government and attempted to annex one another's territories, causing enormous suffering to the people in the process. They replaced moral exhortations with the penal code as a means of persuasion, and the punishments provided in the penal code were so severe that they generated universal complaints among the people they ruled. While complaints were accumulated below, evil deeds multiplied above—in short, a discord of dreadful proportions had thus been created between the rulers on one hand and the ruled on the other. This discord caused the imbalance between the *yin* and the *yang*, which in turn brought about the occurrence of inauspicious omens. All the abnormal, harmful events, including natural disasters, could be traced to this origin.

Your humble servant has heard that fate is the order of Heaven, nature constitutes the essence of life, and emotions are derived from the will of man. Some of us live longer, while others die earlier; some of us are kindhearted, while others are bent on mischief. No potter can make all of his vases perfect; nor can all men have the same awareness of moral values. How much a person is morally oriented depends very much upon the time in which he lives. Confucius says: "A gentleman can be compared to wind, and all other people can be compared to grass. The grass bends toward whichever direction the wind blows." Thus, when Yao and Shun ruled China by virtue of their good examples, their subjects not only were more benevolent but also lived longer. When Chieh and Cheo[2] ruled China through the use of violence, their subjects not only were less humane but also died earlier. The enormous influence of the rulers over the ruled and the invariable imitation of the rulers by the ruled can be compared to the molding of a vessel by a potter or the casting of an iron piece by a metalworker: the potter or the metalworker can shape his product in the way he wishes. This is what Tzu-kung meant when he said: "Comfort them; they will come. Elevate them; they will be elevated."[3]

Your humble servant, having examined carefully the text of the *Spring and Autumn Annals,* believes that he has found the entry that explains the essence of all good governments. The entry is: "Spring; King; Upright Month."[4] "Spring" precedes "King," and "King" precedes "Upright." Spring is a product of Heaven, just as uprightness should be the characteristic of a king. What this entry really means is that a king, imitating Heaven above, should govern his own conduct by the principle of uprightness which is in fact the principle of all governments. It also means that whatever the king intends to do, he should seek guidance from Heaven above.

The wishes of Heaven are expressed in the interaction between the *yin* and the *yang,* and this interaction is the principle that governs everything on earth. The *yang* is virtue positive; the *yin,* on the other hand, is punishment negative. The former generates life; the latter resembles death. Summer is represented by the *yang,* as everything grows most luxuriantly during this season. Winter, on the other hand, is dominated by the *yin,* since it is inactivity or void that characterizes this time of the year. It is clear from the above observation that Heaven relies on virtue positive, rather than punishment negative, for all of its activities. It is Heaven's utilization of the *yang* that makes a year's work, while the *yin*, having been kept dormant, only emerges at the end of the year as a complement to the *yang* in order to make the year complete. The wish of Heaven, in this case, is that a year should begin and end with the *yang*.[5]

In observance of the wishes of Heaven, a sage king governs his country via the positive institution of teaching rather than the negative method of punishment. It is as impossible for a king to govern his country successfully through the use of punishment as it is for Heaven to employ the *yin* to do a year's work. The reliance on the penal code as a means of governing cannot but be interpreted as a violation of the wishes of Heaven, a violation in which none of our ancient sage kings dared indulge. Would we not commit the same violation if we abolish all the governmental posts responsible for people's moral education and rely solely on law enforcement officials for governing, as some have suggested that we should do? Confucius says, "Sentencing a person to death without having ever taught him the difference between right and wrong is an act of tyranny." No government can inspire respect abroad if it practices tyranny at home.

The *Spring and Autumn Annals* has in it the concepts of "oneness" and "uprightness." "One" marks the numerical beginning of all creatures under Heaven, and "uprightness," according to the *Appendix to the Book of Changes*,[6] means the "enlargement of goodness." When the author of the *Annals* used the word "upright" instead of "one" to indicate the first month of the year, he had in mind the continuous enlargement of goodness once a beginning was made and the adherence to essentials in the management of governmental affairs.[7] He dug deep to see where the essentials were and then worked backward to trace their beginning. The beginning was what he regarded as most important.

A king, therefore, must rectify his own heart before he can rectify his family. He must rectify his own family before he can rectify his officials. He must rectify his own officials before he can rectify his subjects. He must rectify his own subjects before he can rectify foreigners abroad. Once foreigners are rectified, all people on earth, wherever they happen to be, will be united as one. Once they are united as one, no evil deeds will ever appear to alienate them from one another. By then the *yin* and the *yang* will be in equilibrium with each other; wind and rain will arrive timely; and all the creatures on earth will live in perfect harmony with one another. Crops will ripen according to schedule; trees and grass will grow most luxuriantly. As natural abundance permeates Heaven and Earth, all the people within the Four Seas, inspired by the king's virtuous conduct, will pledge themselves as his most loyal subjects. Auspicious omens of all kinds will make their appearance, since the ultimate of what a good government should be will finally have been realized. Confucius says: "The phoenix has not arrived; nor has the dragon-horse emerged from the River.[8] Alas! There is no more I can do." What saddened Confucius is that being a commoner without authority, he could not induce the appearance of these auspicious animals.

Now that Your Majesty has acquired the most honorable position as the Son of Heaven and has become the wealthiest man as the owner of all of China, he is better equipped than anyone else to bring about the appearance of these auspicious animals. Furthermore, Your Majesty is most upright in conduct and most generous in the performance of good deeds. He is enlightened in judgment and selfless in intention. He loves his subjects and honors his scholars. He, indeed, is a most righteous sovereign! Yet Heaven has not responded with the ordering of propitious omens. The reason, if your humble servant may say so, is Your Majesty's failure to introduce an educational system that could be used successfully to rectify the conduct of all of his subjects. People follow their self-interest in the same way as water seeks its own level. As water can be stopped from moving downward by the construction of dams, people can be prevented from the pursuit of self-interest by education. Only through education can wrongdoing be avoided in advance; without it one has to invoke the law to punish the wrongdoers. The necessity of invoking the law for punitive purposes spells failure, namely, failure to teach people in advance.

The sage kings of ancient times knew this well and regarded education as a most effective means of successfully governing the empire. They established a central university in the capital and schools in each of the local communities. Through these educational institutions people were slowly but steadily induced to goodness without consciously realizing this fact themselves. Since they had been conditioned by education to conduct themselves properly, they would not violate any law, even though the penalty for violating the law was light. When education works, good custom results.

Having risen at the end of a chaotic age and established a new dynasty, a sage king would most naturally wish to sweep away the traces of the old and restore and invigorate education as a means to cultivate healthful customs and ideas. This is what King Wu did at the beginning of the Chou dynasty. His descendants carefully preserved this beautiful heritage and prospered for the next five or six hundred years. It was not until the latter part of the Chou dynasty that this beautiful heritage slowly dissipated; when it disappeared, the Chou dynasty died too. The Ch'in regime, which succeeded the Chou, could not reverse the trend; in fact, it made what was bad, worse. It banned books and punished book owners. It downgraded the virtue of propriety and righteousness which it detested and would have liked to destroy all the saintly ways of ancient times if it could. The result was a self-serving, most arrogant dictatorship that placed power and profit above love and righteousness. It is no wonder that it lasted only fourteen years. Since history began, there has never been a regime as brutal as the Ch'in that attempted to cure violence with violence and subjected all of its citizens to a reign of terror. Even today the traces of its poison can still be seen. Our customs remain bad; our people continue to be untruthful in words and outrageous in conduct. Most regrettably, they are so stubborn in adhering to the old ways that they refuse to make changes for the better. Confucius says, "You cannot sculpture a piece of rotten wood; nor can you paint a wall made of manure." This is the unhappy situation we are facing today.

What should we do, now that the Han dynasty has inherited from the Ch'in pieces of rotten wood and rows of manure walls? The law is noted more in its violation than its compliance; an order, once issued, is quickly followed by sabotage and obstruction. Under the circumstances the invocation of the law as a means of governing can be likened to the use of hot water to stop boiling or the use of charcoal to fight fire—it merely makes a bad situation worse. Like the strings of a lute which have to be tuned before they can yield harmonious sounds, a policy that has not worked must be readjusted before it can successfully be carried out. Even an expert lutist cannot make music with an untuned lute; likewise, even a most able statesman cannot carry out a policy that is inherently faulty. Ever since its establishment, the Han dynasty has always wanted to bring about the best kind of government; yet it has not succeeded. Why? This is because it has not introduced basic changes when changes are needed.

Now that the Han dynasty has ruled the country for more than seventy years, it is time to introduce basic changes, by means of education, to bring about the best kind of government. Once the country is well governed, natural disasters will disappear and in their wake will arrive good fortunes. The *Book of Odes* says, "He who brings benefit to the people will be richly rewarded by Heaven." There is no question whatsoever that a ruler who has worked diligently for the welfare of his people will receive reward from Heaven. Love, righteousness, propriety, wisdom, and faith: they are the five constant virtues that must be cultivated by all conscientious rulers. He who cultivates these virtues will be protected by Heaven above and blessed by all the gods and spirits. Thus blessed and protected, he will be able to extend his goodness to the four corners of the earth. He and his good deeds will be enshrined in the heart of every one of his subjects.

Notes

1. This quotation appears in the "Oath of Ch'in" *(Ch'in shih)*. These two auspicious omens allegedly appeared to King Wu of Chou during his military campaign against Cheo, last ruler of the Shang dynasty.

2. Last rulers of the Hsia and Shang dynasties, respectively.

3. Tzu-kung was a disciple of Confucius. This quotation appears in the *Analects,* roll 10.

4. The Chinese original reads *"Ch'un Wang Cheng-yüeh,"* which is the first entry in the *Spring and Autumn Annals. Cheng-yüeh* actually means the "first month." Since *cheng* can also mean "upright" or "truthful" and since it is this meaning that Tung Chung-shu intended to play with, *cheng-yüeh* is hereby translated as "upright month." The terseness of the entry provides ample room for all kinds of interpretations or, more frequently, misinterpretations. Tung Chung-shu was determined to read into it moral and political connotations when actually, as most historians today would agree, there are no such connotations in it. A rational interpretation of this entry would be "the First Month of Spring in the King's Calendar."

5. A year begins and ends with spring when life *(yang)* emerges.

6. *Yi hsi-tz'u;* see note 1, p. 7.

7. See note 4 for clarification of some of the ambiguous points that may be encountered in this paragraph.

8. According to the *Great Commentary on the Book of Changes (Yi ta-chuan),* a dragon-horse emerged from the Yellow River during the time of Pao-hsi, also known as Fu-hsi. The stripes on the dragon-horse's body were supposed to have

inspired Pao-hsi to draw the Eight Diagrams. The appearance of the phoenix or the dragon-horse was regarded as an auspicious omen.

(14)
Tung Chung-shu / *The Plight of the Peasantry*

In ancient times the tax rate did not exceed 10 percent of the produce, and the length of time required for corvée assignment amounted to only three days a year. Peasants, consequently, did not find their obligations toward the government too burdensome, since they had enough to support their families after having met these obligations. Being happy with their government, they had no objection to following its leadership.

The situation was different during the time of the Ch'in regime, which undermined this ancient system with Shang Yang's laws.[1] The well-field system[2] was abolished, and land could be bought and sold legally. Consequently, while the wealthy had land that extended from one tract to another, the very poor did not have a spot of earth where they could plant their two feet. Besides, the wealthy monopolized all that our lakes and rivers could produce and owned outright many of our mountains and forests. They lived a life so extravagant that it exceeded the limit imposed by law and they competed with one another in conspicuous consumption, the increase of which meant to them the enhancement of prestige. They were honored like members of the nobility in their respective communities, since they owned wealth unmatched even by dukes and counts.

Not surprisingly, peasants became poorer and poorer as the wealthy became richer and richer. Each peasant had to serve one month per year as a member of the local militia, in addition to his obligations toward the imperial government that called for one month of duty for labor services and another month of duty as a soldier, serving in areas outside his own community. In short, labor obligations alone were thirty times heavier than those of ancient times. There were other forms of imposition, too, such as the poll tax, taxes on harvested crops, and indirect taxes resulting from the government's monopoly of the salt and iron industries.

All these impositions were twenty times heavier compared to those practiced in ancient times. If the peasant, unfortunately, happened to be a tenant farmer and tilled the land of others, he would have to pay half of the harvested crops to his landlord as rent. It is not surprising that he and other poor people ate the kind of food too coarse even for dogs and pigs and wore the kind of clothes that even horses and cattle would be ashamed to wear. As if their lives were not miserable enough, cruel and corrupt officials constantly looked for excuses to punish them for imaginary crimes. In desperation many of them left their homes and repaired to mountains and forests where overnight they degenerated into thieves and bandits. Any day one could see captured bandits being marched on the nation's highways; thousands of them were convicted and sentenced to death each year.

The situation described above did not change with the establishment of the Han dynasty.[3] While it is doubtless difficult to reintroduce the well-field system of ancient times in toto, we should nevertheless adopt its spirit by imposing a limit on land ownership, so that land aggrandizement will be effectively stopped and the very poor will have a better opportunity to earn a livelihood. Moreover, the monopoly by the government of the salt and iron industries should be abolished forthwith, so that profits from these industries will be returned to the people. The right of owners to punish their slaves by death should be revoked; taxes and corvée obligations should be substantially reduced so that people will have more resources to take care of their own needs. Only in this way can the people be successfully governed.

Notes

1. Shang Yang (d. 338 B.C.), a Legalist, served as Ch'in's chief minister during the fourth century B.C.

2. A land distribution system prevalent during the early period of the Chou dynasty.

3. This is Tung Chung-shu's subtle way of describing the deplorable situation as he saw it in his own time. He used this indirect approach in order, hopefully, not to offend the emperor. Speaking of the Ch'in, he was actually talking about the Han. For instance, governmental monopoly of the salt and iron industries, which he deplored, was actually introduced in 118 B.C. by the very emperor to whom he was addressing this memorial.

(15)

Pan Ku / *The Market Stabilization Program*

As an impetuous person, Wang Mang had to be active all the time. Yet, he would not introduce a new program unless someone could prove to his satisfaction that its introduction was justified in accordance with the contents of some ancient classics. Responding to this need, Liu Hsin, the Grand Tutor, reported to him as follows: "It is recorded in the *Chou Institutions (Chou kuan)*[1] that one of the duties of the imperial treasurer is to purchase one kind of goods that has glutted the market and to sell another kind which the market has evidenced strong demand. This duty of the imperial treasurer is in total agreement with a statement contained in the *Book of Changes*, which says, 'The conformity of financial management to the principle of equity is a most effective means to prevent people from committing crimes.' " Thus convinced, Wang Mang issued the following decree:

"The *Chou Institutions* speaks of loans and credits; the *Record of Music*[2] mentions market stabilization. The concept of governmental intervention in economic matters can be found in many ancient books. I am, therefore, ordering the establishment of banks for the granting of credit, the introduction of market control to stabilize prices, and the installation of various governmental agencies to manage the private section of the economy. The purpose of this measure is to prevent financial aggrandizement on the part of the strong so that everyone in the nation will have a satisfactory livelihood."

In observance of this decree the offices of market stabilization were opened in Ch'angan[3] and five other major cities, namely, Loyang, Hantan, Lintzu, Yüan, and Chengtu.[4] Two offices were opened in Ch'angan: the one in charge of the East Market was called "Capital *(ching)* Office," while the other in charge of the West Market was called "Royal *(chi)* Office." The office in Loyang was called "Central," while the offices in the remainder cities were named "Eastern," "Western," "Southern," and

"Northern," respectively. In each of these offices were five exchange officials and one treasurer. A producer of goods or a merchant could present to any of these offices gold, silver, copper, lead, tin, tortoise shells, cowries, and other valuables and exchange them for other goods or cash. The office, having assessed the market's demand or the lack of it, would decide whether to entertain this exchange or, having decided to entertain this exchange, would inform the producer or merchant concerned of the kind of goods or the amount of cash he could expect to receive.

Wang Mang also followed the *Chou Institutions* in the enactment of a new tax law. The farmer who chose not to cultivate his land would have to pay three times the amount of taxes that he would normally pay if he cultivated it. The city dweller who chose not to plant trees, bushes, or vegetables when there were spaces available for that purpose would have to deliver to the government three times the amount of cloth that he would normally deliver if he planted them. A man who chose not to work when work was available would have to pay one bolt of cloth in addition to his regular tax assessment. If he were too poor to pay, the local government would put him on relief at the public's expense. In return he would have to work on whatever project the government assigned him to do.

According to the new law, people of different occupations—hunters; fishermen; ranchmen; housewives engaged in making or weaving silk, or making or mending clothes for pay; artisans; medical doctors; magicians, mediums, and necromancers; merchants and peddlers; hotel owners and innkeepers, including those who let part of their residences for rent—were required to report to the local government their earnings (namely, gross income minus expenses); and the local government, having been satisfied with the accuracy of the reports, would take 10 percent of the reported earnings as taxes. If a person chose not to make a report or chose to make an inaccurate report, all his earnings would be confiscated by the government, and the confiscated earnings would become part of a general fund for administrative expenses.

In the second month of each quarter an office of market stabilization would determine the maximum, minimum, and normal prices for each item of merchandise under its jurisdiction and, by means of buying or selling this merchandise, maintained its price at a normal level. The prices determined at one office did not have to be the same as those determined at any of the other offices.[5] At the time of abundant supply when a producer or merchant could not dispose of the goods he owned without suffering financial losses, he could offer these goods, whether they be grain, cloth, silk, or floss, to the office of market stabilization for sale. The exchange officials in the office would examine the quantity and quality of the goods offered and would then determine, in consultation with the seller, the cost involved in the production of these goods. The goods would be purchased at cost, to make sure that the seller did not lose any money in the process. If, on the other hand, the price of a particular product had risen by 10 percent above the normal price as determined by the office of market stabilization, the office would sell this product in the open market at the normal price. It would not intervene, however, if people chose to buy or sell this particular product at prices below what it had predetermined as a normal price. The purpose of this abstention from intervention was to prevent hoarding by ruthless merchants to force prices up.

A person who needed money for religious worship or funeral expenses could apply to the office of market stabilization for a loan. The treasurer in the office, with capital drawn from the profits that had been realized in the office's commercial transactions, would grant the loan without charging any interest. In order to be qualified for this loan, the borrower had to promise in advance that the length of religious worship and mourning observation would not exceed ten days and three months, respectively. A person who needed capital to start a business of his own could also borrow money from the market stabilization office. The interest charged on this kind of loan was limited to 10 percent of the net profit (gross income minus expenses) the borrower realized in his business, to be computed on a yearly basis.

Notes

1. The *Chou kuan* (or *Chou li*) was attributed by tradition to Duke Chou of the Chou dynasty (twelfth century B.C.). Actually it was an anonymous creation of a much later period.

2. The *Record of Music*, or *Yüeh yü*, formed part of a massive collection owned by King Hsien of Ho-chien (Ho-chien Wang Hsien) who, during his

lifetime in the second century B.C., had made a continuous and sustained search for all the books that survived Ch'in Shih Huang-ti's book-burning campaign. Though available at the time Wang Mang issued this decree, it has since been lost.

3. Capital of the Former Han regime.

4. Located in modern Honan, Shansi, Shantung, Honan, and Szechuan provinces, respectively.

5. This means that prices could vary from one city to another. For instance, the prices determined at Loyang did not have to be the same as those in Ch'angan.

(16)
Pan Chao / *The Seven Feminine Virtues*

I do not worry about the boys of our family who will manage somehow when they grow up. I am deeply concerned, however, about the girls who, on the threshold of marriage, may not have been educated sufficiently to know what a woman should or should not do. They may, after their marriage, speak or act improperly and thus bring shame and dishonor to the family that gave them birth and was therefore responsible for their education. I have been ill for a long time; my life may end soon. As long as I live, I cannot but be continually concerned about the way you girls are. I have therefore written this little essay entitled "The Seven Feminine Virtues" and asked each of you to copy it at least once. Hopefully it will be helpful to you when you become a young woman in your new household. Be gone, girls; best luck to all of you!

The first feminine virtue consists of meekness and humility. In ancient times a female infant, on the third day after her birth, was placed underneath her parents' bed and given a spindle to play with. Meanwhile her father would fast and do penance and report to the familial ancestors on the arrival of a female child. The placement of a female infant underneath the bed indicates her inferior position, and the provision of a spindle as her first toy is to familiarize her, at the earliest possible moment, with the importance of diligence and hard work. The fact that her arrival is reported to the ancestors shows that she, when she grows up, will have the honor as well as the obligation to host ancestor worship. In the acknowledgment of her own inferior position, in the lifelong devotion to work, and finally in the obligation to host the ritual of ancestor worship lies the essence of womanhood, enshrined in customs and tradition and regulated by law. As a woman, she should always be modest and respectful; should keep herself constantly in the background, whatever she does; should never speak of her own goodness or flinch from the performance of her assigned duties, however unpleasant; and finally, should be able to endure all the humiliations and insults, from wherever they come. This is what I mean by the acknowledgment of her own inferiority—her inability to live up to it should be her constant worry and fear. More concretely, she should be the first to get up in the morning and the last to go to bed in the evening and should work every minute in her waking hours. She undertakes every task inside the house regardless of its difficulties, proceeds with it in an orderly and efficient manner, and completes it in time. This is what I mean by diligence. She waits upon her husband with seriousness and integrity and conducts herself in a most refined and unsullied manner. She of course never indulges in any form of frolic, including laughter. At the time of ancestor worship, she sees to it that all religious offerings, such as food and wine, have been prepared most carefully for this occasion.

A woman who has met successfully the three demands described above (i.e., acknowledgment of her own inferiority, diligence in work, and reverence in ancestor worship) will earn a good reputation which is her due and will certainly not bring any dishonor to her family or herself. Conversely, if she has failed to meet these three demands, there is no way she can keep away humiliation and insult, let alone earn a good reputation for herself.

The second feminine virtue has to do with a woman's relationship with her husband. The principle that governs a husband and his wife corresponds to the eternal law underlying the relationship between the *yin* and the *yang*. It is an extension of the principle of Heaven and Earth, sacrosanct and inviolable, since the sexual relationship forms the basis of all other relationships, such as that between parents and children. That is why the *Book of Rites* speaks of sexual propriety and the *Book of Odes* begins with a poem of love. A wife who lacks feminine virtues cannot serve her husband well, just as a husband who fails to inspire respect cannot govern his wife. A husband who cannot govern his wife has lost his manhood; a wife who refuses to serve her husband has condemned herself as a social outcast. When either of these two situations occurs, marriage itself fails, since a harmonious relationship between husband and wife, which is essential to a successful marriage, can no longer be maintained.

The gentlemen of our time, realizing that the ability to govern one's wife and the necessity of inspiring respect are prerequisites to the cultivation of manhood, have been most careful in the education of their male offspring, including education of a bookish kind. They fail to recognize that the purpose of cultivating masculinity for their sons cannot be achieved if in the meantime the daughters of other families have not been taught the importance of feminine virtues. In short, one cannot succeed in teaching a boy how to become a man without in the meantime teaching a girl how to become a woman. According to the *Book of Rites,* a child should be taught to read at the age of seven and should be able, under normal circumstances, to pursue his own independent studies by the time he reaches fourteen. It does not say that this education is precluded as far as female children are concerned.

The third feminine virtue has to do with reverence and obedience. A man and a woman should conduct themselves differently for the simple reason that the *yang* and the *yin* are totally different. Since hardness characterizes the *yang,* a man should be resolute and strong. Since softness characterizes the *yin,* a woman should be weak and pliant. As a popular saying goes: "Even if your son is as aggressive as a tiger, you should be concerned that he might turn out to be a mouse. Even if your daughter is as meek as a mouse, you should be concerned that she might turn out to be a tigress." As far as a woman is concerned, there is no better way to fight the strong than compliance and no better way to cultivate herself as an ethical being than reverence. "Reverence and obedience," as another saying goes, "are the most important in womanhood." Reverence has no meaning unless it is constantly pursued, and obedience, to be true, has to originate from the obedient of their own accord. Constancy in reverence can be achieved only when the parties involved know how to stop airing their differences when it is time to stop. Voluntariness in obedience, on the other hand, requires a conscientious effort to inspire respect from the other side and to maintain respect for oneself. The marital relationship is that of a lifetime; unavoidably there are occasions when the married couple disagree with each other. In a quarrel that ensues, excess in words tends to be followed by excess in emotions. This is the time when a woman often becomes contemptuous of her husband, even though she is supposed to honor and obey him at all times. The problem can be avoided if she knows how to stop airing her own opinions when it is time to stop. A husband can be right but can also be wrong. It is natural for his wife to support him when he is right and argue against him when he is wrong. But under no circumstances should she allow anger to precede the soundness of judgment, since anger, in its final analysis, reflects the absence of self-respect. A wife invites scolding when she shows contempt for her husband and serious beatings when she becomes angry over an argument. Marital harmony rests on the dual pillars of reciprocal respect and mutual affection, both of which are instantly undermined when scoldings or beatings take place. Once the two pillars are destroyed, marriage itself has ceased to exist.

The fourth feminine virtue is related to a woman's conduct as a woman. There are four standards whereby a woman is judged: her ethics, her words, her appearance, and finally, her domestic work. These four standards, when expressed in a popular form, mean, really, that she does not have to be unusually talented, particularly articulate, strikingly beautiful, or remarkably proficient. Thus by personal ethics is meant that she is quiet and docile, orderly and clean, self-contained and unemotional. She adheres to the principle of honor, whatever she does, and will not make a move unless she is convinced that it is consistent with custom and convention. When she speaks, she chooses her words carefully, none of which should even remotely resemble vulgarity. She does not speak unless the occasion calls for her speech and will immediately stop when she has apparently become a bore to others. This is what people mean when they say that she should mind her words. As far as her appearance is concerned, society dictates that she should wash and keep herself clean, bathe regularly, and wear fresh but not necessarily new clothes. Finally, in the matter of domestic work, she is supposed to devote herself to spinning and weaving, abstain from any form of frolic, including laughter, and prepare food and wine in a most satisfactory manner when her husband entertains. These four standards are the most important that a woman should attempt to reach and are by no means difficult if she is determined to reach them. Confucius says, "How can *jen* [love, benevolence, etc.] be too far away? If I wish to have it, it will be there." The same thing can be said about these four standards.

The fifth feminine virtue has to do with devotion. The ancient classics command a man to remarry after he has lost his wife; there is no mention whatsoever that a woman can do likewise after she has lost her husband. "The husband is Heaven," say the classics. As Heaven cannot be defied, a wife cannot desert her husband. Heaven punishes a man if he chooses to violate its rule; likewise, a husband is entitled to downgrade his wife if she commits transgressions against convention. The *Code for Women*[1] says that winning a man's affection marks the beginning of a lifelong relationship, while losing it precedes an immediate and permanent departure. Therefore, a woman has to dedicate herself to winning her husband's affection if she wishes to be successful as a wife. But this does not mean that she has to be clever in words, charming in appearance, or liberal in attitude toward sex. It means instead that she never loses her serious countenance and never for a single moment violates the principle of propriety and righteousness. She refuses to listen to vulgarity and never looks at anyone sideways. She does not dress up seductively when she goes out; nor does she degenerate into an unkempt mop after she returns home. She does not gather with other women for a party of fun; needless to say, she never stands in the front door or peeps through a window to see what is going on outside. If she follows these rules religiously, she has indeed attained the goal of devotion.

The sixth feminine virtue comes about when a woman bends her own will in order to accommodate herself to the wishes of others. It has been stated earlier that winning or losing a husband's affection marks the dividing line between eternal joy and permanent departure, a statement that is meant to strengthen a woman's devotion to her husband. Since such devotion is of obvious importance to her welfare, how can she in the meantime afford not to win the affection of her parents-in-law? A marriage can fail for two reasons, subjective and objective. In the former case the couple involved have lost affection for each other; in the latter case the husband or wife has created so many difficulties with a third party that the continuation of the marriage becomes impossible. I have in mind particularly a woman who, despite her husband's great love for her, has in the end to leave his household for no other reason than the fact that she has been unable to get along well with his parents. The only way to solve a problem of this nature is for her to bend her will to the wishes of her parents-in-law—there cannot be any other choice. She should obey every order of her mother-in-law and carry it out faithfully, whatever her private feelings. Needless to say, there should never be an argument as to who is right or who is wrong. That is what the *Code for Women* means when it says that a woman's obedience will yield its own reward.

The seventh and last feminine virtue has to do with the maintenance of cordial relations with the brothers and sisters of one's husband. A woman should keep in mind that the success she has achieved as a wife is primarily because her husband's parents are fond of her as a daughter-in-law and that the success she has achieved as a daughter-in-law is primarily because her husband's brothers and sisters have found in her a good friend. In short, whether she can succeed as a member of her adopted family depends very much upon the relations she has developed with her husband's brothers and sisters who, in fact, can praise or condemn her as they please. How can she afford not to win their friendship? Many women, unfortunately, are either unable or unwilling to maintain a most cordial relationship with their husbands' brothers and sisters, even though they know the importance of this relationship to their own welfare.

Since no one except a sage can be faultless all the time, a woman, however intelligent or virtuous, is bound to make errors at one time or another. (Confucius spoke highly of Yen Hui [a disciple of Confucius], not because Yen Hui was always faultless but because he never committed the same error twice.) Whenever an error occurs, the knowledge of it will stay inside the house, if the woman involved has had a most cordial relationship with all members of her husband's family; otherwise the error, in a most exaggerated form, will be broadcast, causing enormous damage to her reputation as a woman. The *Book of Changes* says,

"Two persons sharing the same will are as strong as a sharpened sword; their words are as persuasive as the fragrance of an epidendrum." Given the natural rivalry between a woman and her husband's younger sisters,[2] it is mandatory for the former to win the latter's friendship, so that they, as allies, will continue to speak of her goodness and gloss over her weakness. Her parents-in-law will be greatly pleased; so will her husband. Her reputation as a good wife and obedient daughter-in-law will spread far and wide; she, in that case, will bring honor and pride to her own parents. If, on the other hand, she is stupid enough to think or act as if she were superior to her husband's younger sisters, or, relying on her husband's affection for her, becomes prideful or careless toward them, they will inevitably become resentful, exaggerating her shortcomings and hiding her goodness. Her parents-in-law will become angry; so will her husband. Her failure as a wife and a daughter-in-law will spread far and wide; she, in that case, will bring shame and dishonor not only to herself but to her parents as well. Moreover, she places her husband in a most difficult situation, no matter how great his love for her is.

The choice to win the friendship of her husband's younger sisters or to alienate them is indeed the choice between honor and shame, fame and notoriety. How can she win their friendship? The answer can be summarized in two words: modesty and pliancy. The *Book of Odes* says, "I see no evil in him; nor does he see any in me." This should be a guideline for all of us, women as well as men.

Notes

1. The nature and authorship of *Nü hsien*, or *Code for Women*, cannot be easily identified.
2. Her husband's elder sisters, if any, must have been married by then.

CHAPTER

4

Disintegration and Amalgamation

HE was criticized for being stubborn after repeated efforts had failed to abort him while he still remained in his mother's womb; in retaliation his mother was murdered soon after his birth. He was eight years old when his father died, and his father's death was followed, several months later, by the murder of his foster mother as well as his elder brother. At the age of fourteen he was married; twelve years later he was forced to witness the murder of his wife. As if this were not enough, at the age of thirty-nine he lost the job that he had inherited from his father and was never to have another job again. How did he react to this series of misfortunes? A few sighs and tears—that is all historians managed to record. In the end, however, he was able to achieve what most of his relatives had failed to achieve, namely, a natural death at the comparatively advanced age of fifty-three. This may not mean much to an average person, but it was a truly remarkable achievement for a man of his profession.

The man in question was Han Hsien-ti (181–234), the last emperor of the Han dynasty. In many ways his own life epitomizes a much larger tragedy then in existence: the disintegration of the empire and deaths and sufferings across the length and breadth of the nation. In the capital one strong man emerged to replace another, only to be replaced later by a stronger person. Whoever he happened to be, he had nothing but contempt for the emperor. As far as Han Hsien-ti was concerned, the worst of his tormentors was a man named Ts'ao Ts'ao (d. 220) who, by 200, had emerged as the strongest man in North China. Ts'ao could easily have deposed the royal puppet but, for his own reasons, chose not to do so (selection 17). In 220 he died; Ts'ao Pi (187–226), his eldest son and successor to the post of prime minister, lost no time in doing what his father had promised never to do. Properly "inspired," Han Hsien-ti issued a series of decrees condemning his own "unworthiness" and praising the "great virtue" of the Ts'ao family which, according to these decrees, had been mandated by Heaven to found a new dynasty. Ts'ao Pi repeatedly declined the honor, as custom dictated, and accepted it after false modesty had properly run its course. "Haha!" he exclaimed. "Now I know what the sages meant when they said that Yao and Shun had voluntarily abdicated the throne on behalf of the country's most virtuous" (selection 2). Once a precedent was established, the farce was repeated throughout this period (220–589). In each case the so-called most virtuous man on whose behalf the reigning emperor had "voluntarily" abdicated was none other than his strongest and worst enemy whom he would have liked to banish for life but could not. Not surprisingly, this period ended in the same fashion as it had begun. In 589 a strong man named Yang Chien (541–604), having forced a boy emperor (aged seven) to abdicate on his behalf, established a dynasty called Sui and ushered in a new period.

Between the Wei dynasty which Ts'ao Pi founded and the Sui regime that eventually unified China, numerous kingdoms came and went, with life-spans that ranged from a score of years to more than a century. While claims to royal prerogatives were anything but uncommon in Chinese history, the proliferation of pretenders during this period was most unique in the sense that most of these self-styled Sons of Heaven were actually non-Chinese aliens. Beginning in the first decade of the fourth century, wave after wave of northern nomads descended upon a divided and weakened China, burning and killing as they went. Once settled in North China, some of these nomadic chieftains continued to act in a most barbaric fashion, while others, having been thoroughly assimilated, outshone even their Chinese counterparts in promoting everything Chinese (selection 18). None of them was able to conquer all of China, however, thus enabling a succession of Chinese regimes to maintain their independent status in the south. It was in South China, away from the center of political struggle and war, that some stability remained.

It would be wrong to say that all the miseries during this period were caused by barbarian invasions, since we know that long before the invasions China as a cohesive society had declined.

Philosophically, Taoist skepticism had replaced Confucian optimism as the doctrine for the educated elite, and such orthodox virtues as filial piety and fealty to the king were as much noted in their violation as in their observance. Even on the institutional level one notices the same decline. For instance, the selection system of recruiting bureaucratic personnel according to talent, which the Han dynasty had introduced during its more glorious years, gave way to the nine-rank system which made its first appearance in 220. Though hailed by its supporters as a logical extension of the selection system, the nine-rank system, in practice, strengthened social stratification and stifled social mobility and defeated the very purpose that the selection system had attempted to achieve. Political power and social prestige gravitated into the hands of an oligarchy of elite families, thus denying the government a popular basis for support (selection 19). Living in a hostile and oppressive environment with which they were unable to cope, many of the best products of this period either played out their worst instincts or dropped out from society altogether (selection 20). With misery abounding, more and more people sought solace in Buddhism, which promised a better life in the next existence (selection 21). In this age of war and chaos, it was the preservation of life, rather than its improvement, that concerned most people in China.

As if in sympathy with the tempo of the time, cultural activities in general and prose writing in particular also declined. Not a single Tung Chung-shu or Ssu-ma Ch'ien emerged, and the quality of history writing, which inevitably varies along with the quality of other prose writing, was no longer the same. Nevertheless, by then a tradition had been established that every political regime, however insignificant, had to have a dynastic history as the final word on its achievement or the lack of it, and there was no lack of writers willing to undertake this project. A number of dynastic histories emerged, and jointly they form the basic material covering this period. Their quality is uneven, of course, as they range from the carefully thought out *History of the Three Kingdoms (San-kuo chih)* to the hastily composed *Book of the Sung (Sung shu)*. A list of these books, with brief comments, follows:

History of the Three Kingdoms by Ch'en Shou (233–97). A native of Szechuan and a precocious scholar, Ch'en Shou devoted practically all of his adult life to writing and rewriting this book, even though, consisting of only sixty-five rolls, it is comparatively short. One century and a half later, a scholar-official named P'ei Tzu-sung (372–451), who served with distinction as a provincial arbitrator under the nine-rank system, added to Ch'en Shou's book extensive comments drawn from materials then still in existence. Ts'ao Ts'ao's short essay about himself, appearing here as selection 17, can be found in one of P'ei Tzu-sung's comments.

History of the Tsin (Tsin shu) by a committee headed by Fang Hsüan-ling (seventh century). The committee met for the first time in 644 and completed its work twenty years later. Consisting of 130 rolls, the book is rich in material; but, like most works written by a committee, its quality is extremely uneven. It has often been criticized for treating supernatural phenomena and hearsay as if they were proved facts.

Book of the Sung (Sung shu) by Shen Yo (441–512). An expert in phonetics credited with the first identification of the four tones in Chinese characters, Shen Yo was more famous for his poetry than for his prose. Nevertheless, considered the most learned man of his time, he was commissioned by Emperor Liang Wu-ti (r. 483–93) to write a history of the Liu Sung period (420–78) in 487. The whole project, consisting of one hundred rolls, was completed in less than one year. None but Shen Yo has been able to write a dynastic history in such a short period.

History of the South Ch'i (Nan-Ch'i shu) by Hsiao Tzu-hsien (494–537). Though praised for his poetic talent during his younger years, Hsiao Tzu-hsien devoted most of his adult life to writing history. He was reported to have authored five books, including a collection of essays and poetry, but his best-known work has always been the *Nan-Ch'i shu.*

History of the Liang (Liang shu) by Yao Ch'a (533–606) and his son Yao Ssu-lien (d. 637). According to his son, Yao Ch'a read ten thousand words per day beginning at the age of five, composed expertly at the age of eleven, and debated with the country's learned scholars at the age of twelve. Though a son tends to exaggerate when writing about his father, there is no question about the erudition of a man who had served three successive dynasties (Liang, Ch'en, and Sui) as an adviser on academic affairs. The first draft of the *Liang shu* was completed sometime before 606, though the present version of fifty rolls, revised and edited by Yao Ssu-lien, was not made public until the 630s.

History of the Ch'en (Ch'en shu) by Yao Ssu-lien. The *Ch'en shu* bears Yao Ssu-lien's name alone; but, like its predecessor *Liang shu*, it is mostly Yao Ch'a's work. Having only thirty rolls, it is the shortest of the dynastic histories.

History of the Wei (Wei shu) by Wei Shou (d. 572). Talented but unprincipled, Wei Shou openly admitted that he would use his book to reward his friends and punish his enemies. "You have been very good to me," said he to his friend Yang Hsiu-chih. "Since I have nothing to offer in return, I shall write favorably about your father." Thanks to the fact that he did not have too many friends to reward or too many enemies to punish, his book of 130 rolls is not only rich in material but also basically accurate. Completed in 554, all historians have relied on it for an understanding of this period.

History of the North Ch'i (Pei-Ch'i shu) by Li Pai-yüeh (565–648). The author, who served as a decree writer *(she-jen)* in the First Secretariat *(Chung-shu sheng)* during most of his adult life, was commissioned by Emperor T'ang T'ai-tsung (r. 627–49) to write the *Pei-Ch'i shu* in 627 and he completed his work in 636. The book has fifty rolls.

History of the Chou (Chou shu) by a committee headed by Ling-hu Teh-fen (583–666). The writing of this book was commissioned by Emperor T'ang Kao-tsu (r. 618–26) in 622 and completed in 636. It has fifty rolls.

History of the Southern Dynasties (Nan shih) by Li Yen-shou (d. ca. 649). This book of eighty rolls covers four dynasties (Liu Sung, Ch'i, Liang, and Ch'en) and 169 years (420–589). It is a revision of the *Sung shu, Nan-Ch'i shu, Liang shu,* and *Ch'en shu* previously described.

History of the Northern Dynasties (Pei shih) by Li Yen-shou. Consisting of one hundred rolls, this book covers the period from 386 to 618 that witnessed the rise and fall of four separate regimes (North Wei, North Ch'i, North Chou, and Sui). The author had as his basic sources the *Wei shu, Pei-Ch'i shu,* and *Chou shu,* all of which have previously been described, and also the *Sui shu,* about which more will be said in the next chapter.

(17)

Ts'ao Ts'ao / *I Have No Ambition for Myself* [1]

When, as a young man, I was chosen as a member of the most virtuous,[2] I knew that I could not, for the rest of my life, pursue the career of a learned hermit. Lest I be mistaken as a man of mediocrity, I began to entertain the ambition of becoming a district magistrate and, in that capacity, of bringing about an honest and efficient administration. In this way, I thought, I should be able to make a name for myself throughout the nation. Later, when this ambition was fulfilled, I, as the magistrate of Tsinan,[3] dedicated myself to the elimination of corruption and incompetence and to a fair and honest administration of the selection system. My effort in this regard made me an enemy of the eunuchs in the capital as well as of many of the local leaders. Fearful for the safety of my family, I resigned from the magistracy by invoking the excuse of a nonexistent illness.

I was still a young man at the time I lost this official post. Looking around, I noticed that many of those who had been elected members of the most virtuous in the same year as I was did not consider themselves old, even though they were fifty years old or older. I thus said to myself that I would be no older than these gentlemen twenty years from then and I should devote these twenty years to bringing about peace throughout the country. When peace was finally achieved, I would retire to my birthplace, Ch'iao [modern Anhwei province], in the eastern suburb of which I should build a fine cottage, approximately sixteen miles away from the city. There I would devote myself to reading from summer to autumn and amuse myself with archery and hunting from winter to spring. I would shut myself off from outside contact and bury myself in anonymity. Unfortunately I have not been able to fulfill this wish.

While still in retirement, I was called upon by my government to serve as a district commander. Soon I was promoted to the post of provincial commander. In the latter capacity my ambition was to eliminate the rampaging bandits [known as the Yellow Turbans] and perform a great deed for my government. I would then

be invested with an earldom and titled a marshal. After my death
my tombstone would bear this inscription: "Here Lies Ts'ao
Ts'ao, an Earl and Marshal of the Han Dynasty." This was my
ambition at that time.

At the time of the Tung Cho disaster,[4] I, like many others,
recruited an army to combat the imposter. While others tried to
make their armies as large as possible, I imposed a limit on the
size of my own, knowing only too well that the larger the size of
an army, the more it tended to be arrogant and complacent, and
that arrogance and complacence were a sure cause of disaster. In
the Battle of River Pien the army under my command numbered
only several thousand.[5] Later, upon my return to Yangchow
[modern Kiangsu province], the total number of troops I recruited there did not exceed three thousand. All this indicates
that whatever ambition I had, it was very limited in scope.

Still later, as governor of Yen,[6] I defeated and captured three
hundred thousand Yellow Turbans. Meanwhile at Chiuchiang
[modern Kiangsi province], Yüan Shu was prepared to assume
the imperial title—his attire was patterned after that of an emperor; all his subordinates referred to themselves as "His Majesty's humble servants"; and his two wives were competing with
each other for the designation as empress. Yet, when urged to
ascend the throne and proclaim himself the Son of Heaven, he
replied, "As long as Mr. Ts'ao is still around, I cannot do it."
Shortly afterward, I captured alive four of his generals and took
as prisoners all of their soldiers. Driven to despair, he died of
sudden illness. After the death of Yüan Shu, his cousin Yüan Shao
continued to occupy the area north of the Yellow River. His army
was strong; my own assessment was that I could in no way defeat
him. Yet, mindful of the fact that in case of defeat my death for
the country would enable me to become a model for posterity to
follow, I risked all I had for the confrontation. Fortunately I was
able to defeat him and capture his two sons, who were subsequently beheaded as a warning to others. To the south there was
one Liu Piao who, priding himself as a member of the royal clan,
was most treacherous as a person. He vacillated from one side to
the other and, by virtue of occupying the province of Ching
[modern Hupeh province], wished to fish in muddy waters. By
defeating him, I was able to bring peace to the nation as a whole.[7]
Now that I have become the prime minister, the highest post any

subject can ever hope to obtain, I have no further ambition for myself.

When saying all this, I am trying to be as candid as I can, not because I wish to be boastful in any way, but because I want to put a stop, once and for all, to the idle speculation on any further ambition of my own. It is true that had it not been for my effort many people would have called themselves emperors or kings; this does not mean, however, that I myself wish to make such a claim. This speculation on what I intend to do, though totally unwarranted, results from the appreciation of the great power I presently hold and the fact that I have never believed in such a thing as the mandate of Heaven. Understandable though it may seem, this speculation has troubled me a great deal.

The reason that Duke Huan of Ch'i and Duke Wen of Tsin have been able to enjoy a fine reputation throughout history is that despite their great power, they continued to serve faithfully the house of Chou.[8] Confucius says: "King Wen was a most virtuous man indeed! Having won fealty from two-thirds of the nation, he continued to pay obeisance to the house of Yin."[9] In both cases, virtue came about when the strong were willing to serve the weak. Having escaped to Chao, Yüeh Yi declined the request that he should collaborate with the king of Chao to plot against his own state, Yen, saying tearfully that he could no more fight against Yen than he could fight against Chao if, in some future time, he was forced to live in another state after having offended the king of Chao. "I am as loyal to Your Majesty today as I have been loyal to King Chao of Yen," he continued. "Since I cannot visualize the possibility of harming even a commoner in Chao if I were forced to leave here and found myself living in another state, how can I, at this time, permit myself to participate in a plot against the rightful heir of Yen?"[10] Before committing suicide by drinking poison, General Meng T'ien said to Hu Hai's envoy as follows: "From my grandfather to me, the Meng family has served the royal house of Ch'in for three generations. Now, at the head of three hundred thousand troops, I have the power to stage a rebellion if I wish to do so. The reason I prefer death to rebellion is my unwillingness to bring disgrace to my forebears and my reluctance to forget the honor that the late emperor [Ch'in Shih Huang-ti] has generously bestowed upon me."[11] Every time I read the statements by these two men [Yüeh Yi and Meng T'ien], I was moved to tears.

From my grandfather to me, the Ts'ao family has been entrusted with great responsibility of the state and has certainly won confidence from the royal house of Han. If you count my children who at present also serve the state, the Ts'ao family has been most favorably regarded by the royal house for more than three generations. I shall always be loyal; how can I possibly be otherwise? Today I am saying this to you, but you do not realize that I have been saying this to my wife and concubines for a long time. "After my death," I said, "all of you should remarry. You should tell others how I felt, so no one will have the slightest doubt in this matter." Duke Chou placed his prayer in a sealed cabinet, precisely because of his fear that others might choose not to believe him.[12]

Some people have suggested that I should hand over my military command to other responsible officials and that I myself should return to my fief as Earl of Wup'ing. But this is an impractical suggestion. Why? Once I leave the army, very likely it will be used by others to advance their own ambitions, causing great sufferings to the people as a result. My departure from the army would indeed place the nation in a most precarious position, not to speak of the fate of my own children. By remaining in the army, on the other hand, I am placing myself in a most precarious position, besides earning the undeserved reputation of being vain. But I do not have any other choice. Formerly I resolutely declined the honor of investing my three sons with the title of earl; now I am accepting it on their behalf, not because I have suddenly become vainglorious, but because I need outside support in order to assure my own safety.

Whenever I read about Chieh Chih-t'ui's self-imposed exile to avoid reward[13] and Shen Pao-hsü's flight from the capital to decline honor,[14] I push the book aside and sigh with admiration. Both of these men have always been an inspiration to me. Thanks to the nation's gods and spirits, I have been able to win against the strong and the numerous, weak and small though my own army was. So far I have been able to fulfill every wish of mine. Now that the country is being pacified, I can honestly say that I have not failed my lord [Han Hsien-ti]. All these achievements have nothing to do with my talent or ability; they come about because Heaven has decided not to desert the Han dynasty.

At present I enjoy a fief of four districts that have in them thirty thousand households. Do I really deserve this generous reward?

Since the nation has not been entirely pacified,[15] I cannot very well resign from my present post. On the other hand, I can return some of the fiduciary rewards that have been bestowed upon me. I am now returning to the government the districts of Yanghsia, Che, and K'u that have in them twenty thousand households; shall retain, however, the district of Wup'ing that consists of ten thousand households.[16] I am doing this to refute the slander that has been unjustifiably directed against me, so I shall enjoy peace with myself.

Notes

1. This essay was written in 210 after Ts'ao Ts'ao, as the prime minister, had succeeded in defeating many of his enemies and bringing North China under his control. As the new strong man, he was suspected of harboring the ambition of overthrowing the Han government and replacing it with a dynasty of his own. He wrote this essay and circulated it widely to show that he had no such ambition. Source: *San-kuo chih*, roll 1.

2. The election of the most virtuous *(hsiao-lien)* in local communities was part of the selection system first introduced by Han Wu-ti in the second century B.C. During the Later Han dynasty when Ts'ao Ts'ao lived, each year one member of the most virtuous was elected for every two hundred thousand people in each district or province. The election qualified him as a governmental appointee at the lowest rank. Ts'ao Ts'ao was elected at the age of nineteen (twenty according to the Chinese way of calculation).

3. Capital of modern Shantung province. Ts'ao Ts'ao was appointed magistrate of Tsinan in 184.

4. Tung Cho, a military governor, marched into the capital of Loyang in 189. He deposed the reigning monarch and placed on the throne a boy emperor later known as Han Hsien-ti.

5. The Battle of River Pien was fought in Yingyang, modern Honan province, in 190. Ts'ao Ts'ao was defeated by Tung Cho's troops in this battle.

6. Modern Shantung province. Ts'ao Ts'ao was appointed governor of Yen in 192.

7. This statement is an exaggeration. Szechuan, the Lower Yangtze, and the areas farther to the south were not brought under his control.

8. ,Duke Huan of Ch'i (Ch'i Huan-kung) was the strong man in North China between 686 and 643 B.C. Duke Wen of Tsin (Tsin Wen-kung) occupied the same position before his death in 629 B.C. Both, however, acknowledged the house of Chou as their common sovereign.

9. King Wen was a founder of the Chou dynasty. The house of Yin was the royal house of the Shang dynasty. This quotation comes from the *Analects of Confucius*, roll 4.

10. This event occurred in 284 or 283 B.C. The "rightful heir" referred to here was King Hui of Yen who, listening to slander, had intended to bring Yüeh Yi

to trial for alleged treason. Yüeh Yi, consequently, escaped to Chao to save his life.

11. Hu Hai is better known as Ch'in Erh-shih ("Second Emperor") who, fearful of the military power Meng T'ien then commanded, had fabricated a charge and imposed a death sentence on the general. The duty of the envoy was to carry out the death sentence. This event occurred in 210 B.C., the year Ch'in Shih Huang-ti died and Hu Hai ascended the throne as the Second Emperor.

12. When King Wu (r. 1122–1115 B.C.) was ill, Duke Chou, his younger brother and close adviser, wrote a prayer which he subsequently placed in a sealed cabinet. In the prayer the duke requested gods to take his life, instead of that of the king, though rumor had it that he intended to usurp the throne the moment the king died. The king died shortly afterward despite his prayer, and Duke Chou, to kill the rumor once and for all, exiled himself to Loyang, far away from the capital. After King Ch'eng, King Wu's son, ascended the throne, he opened the sealed cabinet, found the prayer, and was more than convinced of the duke's loyalty to his father and himself. The duke was called back to serve the new king, and under his guidance the Chou dynasty entered its most glorious era.

13. Chieh Chih-t'ui was one of the retainers who accompanied Prince Ch'ung-erh in an odyssey that lasted nineteen years. Upon Ch'ung-erh's return to Tsin as Duke Wen in 636 B.C., all the retainers sought rewards and received them, with the exception of Chieh Chih-t'ui who retired to Mount Mien with his mother and intended to live as a hermit. Duke Wen repeatedly requested him to come out from the mountain to receive the reward that was his due, but Chieh declined in each instance. As a last resort, the duke ordered the mountain to be burned on all sides with the exception of one, through which, hopefully, Chieh would be forced by the ravaging fire to emerge. Chieh, however, chose death by fire rather than worldly rewards. As for Prince Ch'ung-erh's odyssey, see selection 4.

14. When the state of Wu launched an all-out attack against Ch'u in 506 B.C., the king of Ch'u sent Shen Pao-hsü to the state of Ch'in to seek help. Arriving at Ch'in, Shen "cried for seven days and seven nights" in the palace until the king of Ch'in was moved to come to Ch'u's rescue. The arrival of Ch'in troops forced the Wu invaders to withdraw. Knowing that he would be richly rewarded for his successful effort in saving the Ch'u state, Shen fled from the capital and lived in anonymity, so the king could in no way reward him. Ts'ao Ts'ao cited the example of Chieh Chih-t'ui and Shen Pao-hsü in order to show the importance of modesty.

15. See above, note 7.

16. All four districts mentioned here were located in modern Honan province.

(18)

Fang Hsüan-ling and Wei Shou / *Barbarian Chieftain and Sinicized Monarch*[1]

Shih Hu (r. 335–50)

Later in his years Shih Hu was plagued with obesity and could no longer mount a horse. Yet he continued to love the game of chase. To enable himself to hunt, he ordered the construction of one thousand game chariots, each of which was to be thirty feet in width and eighteen feet in height. Above each chariot was a superstructure that measured seventeen feet in height. He also ordered the construction of forty slaughterhouses mounted on wheels. Each of the slaughterhouses was two-storied, with three staircases connecting one floor to another. After a date was set for the chase, he would order his censors to provide special protection for the animals in the hunting area; any person who had harmed or captured these animals was punishable by death. Having thus been armed with enormous power, the censors quickly abused it to advance their own interests. Whenever a peasant had a daughter, horse, or ox that a censor wished to appropriate for himself but had failed in his attempt to acquire it, he would falsely accuse the peasant of having violated the game protection law and arbitrarily convicted him. From Haitai to Hochi[2] no one had a moment of peace whenever Shih Hu decided to enjoy a game of chase.

At one time Shih Hu conscripted 260,000 peasants to construct his Loyang Palace. At another time he requisitioned without pay twenty thousand head of cattle to be shipped to the province of Shuo [modern Shansi province] so that the forester in that province would have more cattle in his jurisdiction.

While in power, Shih Hu introduced a system of twenty-four ranks for female officials, and those of the first twelve ranks were assigned to serve in his Eastern Palace. In addition, there was a nine-rank system, also for female officials, applicable in the more than seventy feudatories that comprised the empire. To staff the newly created posts, he launched a vigorous campaign of collecting beautiful women between the ages of thirteen and twenty and successfully recruited thirty thousand of them. The women were then graded according to their beauty and talent and, in accordance with the rank they received, were assigned to live in one of the three kinds of houses he built for them. Provincial and district officials, in order to please Shih Hu, would forcibly conscript any woman whom they regarded as unusually attractive, regardless of her marital status. In fact, more than nine thousand married women were recruited in this manner. Many married women, unwilling to leave their families, committed suicide.

Following the example set by their king, other men in power, including the king's younger brother Hsüan, set out to collect beautiful women for their own individual harems. The number of women they collected totaled approximately ten thousand. When all these beautiful women, including the king's own collection, were gathered in the capital, Shih Hu conducted an inspection tour among the houses where the women lived, and he was greatly pleased with what he saw. After the tour, twelve recruiters were titled dukes in recognition of their outstanding service. Few mentioned to him, however, that more than three thousand women had committed suicide by hanging when it became evident to the recruiters that only by killing their husbands could they successfully take their wives away from them. . . .

Sometime later, Shih Hu found it necessary to kill even his own younger brother. Having been presented with irrefutable evidence that it was his younger brother, Hsüan, rather than somebody else, who had killed General Liang T'ao, his anger was as great as his grief. He ordered Hsüan arrested and thrown into the dungeon. In the dungeon the prisoner was tied to a post with a chain that was tight enough to cut deep into his chin. A wooden trough was placed before him so he would be fed in the same way as dogs and swine. Day and night the prisoner was tapped with the same sword that he himself had used in killing General Liang. The tap was strong enough to draw blood but not strong enough to kill him. Suffering from intense pain, the prisoner cried incessantly, and his cry could be heard all over the palace grounds. On the day he was scheduled to be executed, Shih Hu ordered the construction of a pyre north of the capital. A long pole was set up on top of the pyre, and a ladder was then placed against it. Through the use of pulleys, workmen were able to transport additional firewood up the ladder until it could be placed on top of the pyre.

After the prisoner had been brought to the pyre, Shih Hu gave the privilege of escorting the doomed man up the ladder to General Liang's two best friends, namely, Ho Chih and Liu Pa. The two men, having been so privileged, led the prisoner by his hair and tongue while climbing the ladder. Once on top of the pyre, Ho Chih tied the pulley rope to the chain that cut deep into the prisoner's chin and then, by operating the pulleys, raised the prisoner higher and higher toward the top of the pole. Meanwhile, as the body slowly ascended, Liu Pa, brandishing a sword, cut off the prisoner's limbs one by one, besides poking his stomach and eyes repeatedly. This was the way Hsüan had killed General Liang; this was the way that Shih Hu wanted the killer to be killed.

After Hsüan had been raised to the top of the pole, Shih Hu ordered the lighting of the pyre. In a minute flame and smoke shot up toward the sky. Several thousand people, including Shih Hu and his First Concubine, watched the fire from a central platform. After the fire died out, Shih Hu ordered Hsüan's ashes to be scattered at all the gates and all the main streets in and around the capital.[3]

Subsequently Shih Hu also ordered the execution of all of Hsüan's wives and children, with one exception. The exception was Hsüan's youngest son, then only four or five years old, whom the king loved dearly. At the time of the execution Shih Hu was holding the boy in his arms and trying his best to comfort him. "My son," said he tearfully, "it was not your fault, and no one in the world will dare to harm you." But his ministers, insisting that the boy had to be killed to forestall any future difficulties, tried to take the boy away from his arm. The boy clung to Shih Hu as tightly as he could and cried loudly for help. Seeing the boy's struggle for life, all the retainers found tears in their eyes. Nevertheless the boy was taken away and was soon killed.

Wei Hsiao-wen-ti (r. 471–99)

Even as a child, Wei Hsiao-wen-ti had a most natural disposition to love and respect his parents. At the age of three, when his father suffered from a boil, he volunteered to suck the pus out in order to ease the pain. He sobbed beyond control when, at the age of four, his father abdicated on his behalf.[4] Questioned by his father why he was overcome with grief on a most happy occasion, he replied, "The saddest moment in life is the time when one has to assume the responsibilities of one's parents." His father sighed upon hearing this remark and knew that his son, when grown up, would be an extraordinary person.

Dowager Empress Wen-ming, fearful that the young emperor, when grown up, might initiate measures against the interests of the Feng clan from which she came, secretly plotted his deposition.[5] For three days she locked the emperor inside a small room without supplying him with food and clothing, even though the weather was bitter cold. She summoned Hsi, a younger brother of the emperor, to the palace and intended to install him as the new ruler. Only through the vigorous protest of such elder statesmen as Yüan P'i, Mu T'ai, and Li Ch'ung did she change her mind and was the emperor able to preserve his throne. Yet the emperor did not hold any grudge against the dowager empress, though he was deeply grateful to Yüan P'i and others who supported him at a most crucial moment. Nor did he show any semblance of resentment against his younger brothers, including Hsi, toward whom he remained affectionate. In fact, he maintained a most cordial relationship, based upon mutual respect, with all of his relatives throughout his life.

Generous and compassionate, the emperor simply dismissed as insignificant some of the offenses committed against him as a person. At one time a servant spilled hot soup and burned his hand; at another time he found dead insects in his food. In both cases he merely laughed and did not choose to blame the servants involved. One eunuch slandered the emperor in front of the dowager empress and the latter, furious, ordered the emperor to be punished by flogging. The emperor received the punishment without complaint; he did not even try to refute the charges that were patently false. After the death of the dowager empress, he could have punished the eunuch who had caused this miscarriage of justice; but, true to his generous nature, he did not even bother to mention it.

He listened to sound advice and adopted policies that he believed would be most beneficial to his subjects. He cared particularly for the poor and the destitute. Not a day passed without him searching for new ways to improve their lot. He personally attended all the religious services, such as the worship of Heaven, Earth, and imperial ancestors, regardless of the weather conditions. He read all the important petitions submitted to him by the Imperial Secretariat and often asked himself whether any measure he had initiated was indeed beneficial. He paid close attention to the work of all officials and made sure that their actions were just and proper. "The worst thing that can happen to a king is his inability or unwillingness to be fair and honest," he said at one time. "If he is truly honest, he can convert savages into civilized men." "Record the events as you see them and do not hide," he said to the royal historian. "If the country detests the king for the use of power only to his own advantage and yet you do not record this deplorable situation as you should, the king will have no fear of condemnation by posterity and will indeed continue his misdeeds." Responding to recommendations that roads should be rebuilt before each of his inspection tours, he said that only bridges should be repaired to accommodate horses and sedan chairs of the royal entourage and that there was no need to level roads in order to make travel more comfortable. In short, he would not impose additional corvée unless it was absolutely necessary. In his tour of Huainan [modern Kiangsu province, south of the Huai River], he ordered the military to pay silk to the local people if for any reason their trees had to be felled. There was no destruction of crops whatsoever.

Hsiao-wen-ti had no use for taboos, prayers, offerings of sacrifices, and similar practices unless they had been clearly authorized in the Confucian classics. He loved to read; it was a rare moment when he did not have a book in his hand. He could speak meaningfully on any subject contained in the *Five Classics* after reading it only once; and he interpreted it according to his own insight instead of following any particular school. Besides the classics, he also read history and different schools of philosophy extensively. He conversed knowledgeably on Taoism, but it was in Buddhism that he really excelled. As an intelligent and learned man, he wrote in a variety of forms: poetry in the *shih* or *fu* style,[6] prose in the form of remembrance or eulogy—the form varied in accordance with the occasion. He personally dictated to his secretary whenever an important document was to be drafted, and the end product was usually so good that no polishing was regarded as necessary. After the tenth year of the T'ai-ho period [486] all the decrees were the emperor's own writing. He also wrote more than one hundred essays for his own amusement.

Most inquisitive in nature, Hsiao-wen-ti loved to meet with the country's learned men. Whenever one was found, he would employ him in accordance with his specialization or ability. Though occupying the highest position in the nation, he often wished that he had been a commoner. Looking beyond the ordinary concept of power and wealth, he would not let petty matters blind him to the real meaning of kingship. Physically strong, he loved to hunt in his early teens. He could break a ram's bone with one shot and fell any animal in sight. Beginning at the age of fourteen, however, he decided that it was wrong to kill an animal without cause, and for the rest of his life he never hunted again. He lived simply and wore old clothes. The saddle and bridle for each of his horses were made of ordinary wood and metal.

This, in summary, is the unpretentious and yet most elegant kind of life Emperor Wei Hsiao-wen-ti lived.

Notes

1. The sections on Shih Hu and Wei Hsiao-wen-ti are translated from *Tsin shu*, rolls 106–7, and *Wei shu*, roll 7b, respectively.

2. From Shantung to Honan province.

3. So the spirits of the dead could not gather to seek revenge.

4. Hsien-wen-ti (also known as Hsien-tsu), Hsiao-wen-ti's father and predecessor, abdicated in 471 and died in 476. Rumor had it that he was murdered by Dowager Empress Wen-ming. As for Wen-ming, see below, note 5.

5. Dowager Empress Wen-ming was a wife to Hsiao-wen-ti's grandfather but was not related to the emperor by blood. The emperor's own mother came from a Li family and died in 469. During the time the emperor was a minor, the dowager empress acted as the regent.

6. Generally speaking, a poem written in the *shih* style contains lines of equal length, namely, equal numbers (four, five, or seven) of Chinese characters (syllables). A poem written in the *fu* style contains lines of uneven length. Compared with *shih*, it is more ornate and generally longer.

(19)
Liu Yi / *The Nine-Rank System*[1]

Your humble servant has heard that the efficient operation of a good government depends upon the talent and ability of the officials it employs, and the successful recruitment of talented and able officials lies in the mastery of three difficulties that the government inevitably faces. The three difficulties, put in the form of questions, are: First, how does the government know that a person is able and talented? Second, how does the government know that prejudice, in the form of love or hate, has not played an important role in the recruitment process? And finally, how does the government know that a candidate to a governmental position has told the truth about himself? The mastery of these three questions is most essential to the successful running of a good government.

Under the nine-rank system which is in force today, the evaluation of prospective officials, or the mastery of the three difficulties described above, is administered by provincial and district arbitrators, rather than by the imperial government where it properly belongs. These arbitrators elevate or downgrade people as they please and have in their hands the power of honoring or humiliating anyone they choose, thus usurping the authority that belongs to the imperial government. With enormous power in their hands, they judge people according to their own likes and dislikes and evaluate each person's claim according to their own intuition or whims. Once a judgment is made, they tolerate no appeals. Under the circumstances it is not surprising that the evaluated persons will use every means they can find to ingratiate themselves with the arbitrator in whose hands their fate is. The custom of modesty deteriorates as a result and the shameless habit of resorting to expediency comes to replace it. The good reputation of our dynasty inevitably suffers when all the people, regardless of their true worth, strive for no nobler goal in life than to be ranked higher and higher.

The purpose of ranking can be achieved only when fame corresponds to the talent that a man actually possesses and when ranking reflects the degree of ability that is demonstrable in him.

The importance of this point cannot be overemphasized since fairness in the evaluation of personnel marks the beginning of a good government, while its absence inevitably brings about anarchy and chaos. In evaluating personnel a major factor to be kept in mind is that different people possess different talents and that rarely can one person be so versatile as to be an expert in every field. Furthermore, some people bloom early, while others mature late. In the opinion of your humble servant, those who have made honest efforts to correct past mistakes should receive special recognition for having the courage to redeem themselves and those who, by their words or deeds, defy the popular norm when the popular norm is wrong should obtain extra credit as men of principle and integrity. Those who are so occupied with the essential as to neglect the frivolous should be recognized for their sense of priority, and those who are too honest and straightforward to be orderly or polished in their daily conduct should be regarded as men of sound character. Even those whose conduct may not meet with public approval and yet whose talent is too useful to be wasted should be entrusted with the kind of responsibility corresponding to his talent. Since there are different roads leading toward one destination, different people with different styles of life can be regarded as equally righteous as long as their goal in life remains substantially the same, namely, serving society rather than themselves. . . .

Unfortunately today's arbitrators have violated all the standards of fair play in the evaluation of personnel. They emphasize the superficial at the expense of the substantial; they make judgments in terms of sectional or clannish interest rather than the true merit of the persons involved. They pay no attention to the principle of equity and rely instead on their own likes and dislikes as a basis for decisions. They invent good deeds to elevate those whom they like and magnify trifles to downgrade those whom they dislike. They rate a person according to the amount of power or influence he has and judge his conduct in accordance with their own preconceived ideas. Their standard varies as the mood of society changes, devoid of any objective measurement that transcends the change of times. If a man is on his way up on the ladder of worldly fortunes, he inevitably finds himself to have been ranked higher. If on the other hand he is moving down on the same ladder, somehow he has become less worthy in the eyes of the arbitrators. His rank could be changed in a matter of days, even though the man remains exactly the same. Aspiring to be ranked higher, some offer bribes to the arbitrators, while others invoke the assistance of a third powerful party. Through these efforts these men are duly recognized and become instantly "famous." Meanwhile those who persevere in the maintenance of their integrity remain anonymous and unrecognized throughout their lives. Since the arbitrators reward or punish according to what the evaluated person can do for them and since only the wealthy and the influential can offer the kind of favor they have demanded, it is not surprising that under the nine-rank system we are practicing today, there are no poor families among the higher ranks; nor can the old elite be found among the lower rated. There may be a few exceptions to this statement, but these exceptions arise from unusual circumstances. In short, the nine-rank system has not only outlived its usefulness but also posed a direct affront to the dignity of the emperor. It creates anarchy and is most detrimental to the cause of good government. It is for this reason that I request Your Majesty to abolish it.

Second, the duty of a provincial arbitrator is supposedly to canvass public opinion and reach a consensus on the talented persons within his jurisdiction and to arbitrate differences whenever differences occur in connection with any particular person or persons under evaluation. Yet how can one man know all the talented persons in as large an area as a province and rate them in a way that reflects their true worth? Is it fair to punish him for making errors involving as few as one person as the present law stipulates? None of our ancient sages, from Pao-hsi[2] to Confucius, would be able to serve successfully as a provincial arbitrator if they were alive today. It is true that an arbitrator's decision may be reviewed in case of a miscarriage of justice, real or imagined (a fact that in itself is indicative of the insignificance of his person as compared to the importance of the post he holds), but the review, more often than not, becomes even more controversial than the original decision. The reviewer, dispatched from the capital, does not enjoy much respect in the province where he conducts his reviews; nor are the reviews the proper function of his regular post. How can the people in the province be satisfied with his judgment? Not surprisingly, whatever decision he makes would generate another round of accusations and counter-accusations, which results in bitter resentment among the parties involved. This, your humble servant submits, was not the intention of the initiators of the nine-rank system; nor is it compatible with the maintenance of good customs. In the case of Tiao Yu,[3] for instance, the dispute involved not only local leaders but also, eventually, ministers of state who lined up on either one side or the other. Factions were formed for combat, and litigations were carried on from one end of the country to another. The seeds of discord were sown, and the evil consequences arising from this dispute have yet to be erased. It is for this reason that I request Your Majesty to abolish the nine-rank system.

Third, the rationale of ranking is that an orderly difference exists among men, in terms of natural endowment and acquired ability, and by making the minimum but required achievement the norm for the lowest ranked we can proceed to grade the rest in ascending order. The nine-rank system, implemented in this manner, will be well proportioned in shape, having a head as well as a tail. Unfortunately this is not the way in which today's arbitrators interpret the system. Some of them deliberately maintain an unusually high but impractical standard, so much so that no one, in their opinion, deserves top ranking. Meanwhile they elevate or downgrade the low-rated at will, following no discernible standard whatsoever. Seemingly impartial and objective, each of their decisions is actually aimed at the furtherance of their own selfish interests. Since a gentleman will never complain, whatever the injustice to him is, and since no devices exist to prevent these arbitrators from making arbitrary decisions, they are able not only to deceive the government but also to make a farce of the nine-rank system. The worthy occupy positions in lesser ranks, while the undeserving are among the highest rated. A head has become a tail, and vice versa. It is for this reason that I request Your Majesty to abolish the nine-rank system.

Upon ascending the throne, Your Majesty, in a most generous manner, spoke of the necessity of opening up lines of communication so that all the ministers could speak candidly on matters of national concern, thus enabling Your Majesty to keep abreast of the change of events throughout the empire. Your Majesty, by making this noble wish of his known, has laid a firm foundation for peace and stability and established an admirable precedent for future generations to follow.

Today all the people in the nation, with one exception, are indeed subject to governance by law and are rewarded or punished in accordance with their performance. The exception is an arbitrator who shoulders great responsibility and yet is accountable to no one. It is true that all men harbor selfish motives whenever they decide upon a certain course to follow, but an arbitrator, without prior restraint, is more likely than others to abuse the power entrusted to him. Litigation often results whenever an evaluated person feels that he has been unjustifiably discriminated against. What should the government do under the circumstances? If it entertains the litigation, there will be endless litigations to follow. If it does not, people who have been wronged will have no avenue for redress, and the injustice that has persisted in the past will doubtless continue. Now that the government has decided that the injustice resulting from the lack of avenue for redress is more than offset in importance by the inconveniences and the expenses caused by the multitude of litigation that is bound to follow if the avenue for redress is made easily available, a policy of silencing the entire nation in order to advance the power of one group of persons, namely the arbitrators, has been adopted *ipso facto*. Now the arbitrators can do whatever they wish without any fear whatsoever. Their victims, who have hitherto believed the idea that truth and justice will prevail in the long run, will have to bury their grievances in silence, since the door to retribution has been permanently closed. The lines of communication, which Your Majesty has intended to open up, are now cut off for good. It is for this reason that I request Your Majesty to abolish the nine-rank system.

Fifth, let it be recalled that during the time of our ancient sages it was comparatively easy to identify evildoers among the citizenry in view of the good customs that prevailed, the harmonious relationships among men, the respect of the young for the elderly, and a school system that educated people on the importance of good behavior. Even then the elders in each community were specifically allowed to petition the emperor on the merits of a person or persons about whom they had most intimate knowledge. Meanwhile the local magistrate was mandated by law to report on the performance of all the officials within his jurisdiction, and the imperial government, based upon this report, would then decide whom to promote or dismiss. Each person in the community, consequently, devoted himself to the cultivation of his virtue, instead of openly promoting his own name and prestige. When local communities stress personal integrity and fair play and when, in the meantime, the imperial government is impartial in the evaluation of a person's worth, as was the case in ancient times, the selection of governmental personnel will indeed be just and equitable, since the vain and the hypocritical, however ingenious, will be exposed for all to see.

Nowadays there are a thousand or more scholars in each of the provinces who have to be evaluated under the nine-rank system. Some may have moved to areas other than their places of birth; others may have changed their means of livelihood. The arbitrator may not recognize them even if he saw them face to face; how much can he possibly know about their talent or ability? Not knowing them personally, he promotes them if they have been highly recommended by powerful families and demotes them if rumor and hearsay have been circulated to their detriment. If he bases his judgment solely upon his own insight, obviously he has no use for all the information available to him. If, on the other hand, he chooses to use this information, obviously he has to decide how much faith he should place in it: whether to believe or not to believe this or that part of the information. If he knows the person under evaluation, his personal likes and dislikes will doubtless play a most important role in his decision. If he does not know the evaluated person, his judgment will most likely be based upon "politics," including bribery, which makes a mockery of justice. Without either a local consensus or an imperial directive to guide him, he, because of the reasons enunciated above, is wittingly or unwittingly encouraging the evaluated persons to adopt improper and immoral methods to influence his judgment. When personal ethics and public opinion have no role to play in a person's advance to a higher rank or admission to officialdom, a situation has been created that is most detrimental to good government. It is for this reason that I request Your Majesty to abolish the nine-rank system.

Sixth, the purpose of ranking is to find men of talent and ability to serve the government, but the nine-rank system we are practicing today defeats this very purpose. No matter how well he has performed as an official, a person will immediately be demoted to a lower rank once he leaves his office. On the other hand, a person who has done nothing particular to distinguish himself will be promoted to a higher and still higher rank as long as he stays in office. In short, we punish one man with solid achievement while continuously rewarding another man for no other reason than the prestige that is attached to his office. This kind of reward and punishment not only denies the government the right to promote or demote according to merit but also encourages mediocrity among officials. It is for this reason that I request Your Majesty to abolish the nine-rank system.

Seventh, different people have different talents, and different officials have different tasks to perform. Only when the talent fits the task can the task be satisfactorily performed and can the official in charge be regarded as successful. If the performance of a certain task calls for the possession of a particular talent, the official in charge must have that talent or he will see the task unperformed or poorly performed; in the latter case he himself will be in serious difficulties. Under the nine-rank system each rank, theoretically, reflects the degree of approval, in the eyes of the public, concerning the rank holder; it does not indicate the kind of talent he has. If the government insists on assigning the holder of a particular rank to a certain post, the person so assigned may not have the kind of talent appropriate for that post. If, on the other hand, the selection is based upon past performance regardless of rank consideration, the rank system itself will lose much of its validity. By saying all this we imply, of course, that rank corresponds roughly to ability, which unfortunately is not the case. The reality is that a scholar, being so obsessed with promotion to a higher rank, neglects to cultivate further whatever talent he already has, influenced primarily by the fact that the arbitrator pays no attention to such things as talent and makes his decision on the degree of closeness he feels to the evaluated person. The accomplishments of those to whom the arbitrator does not feel close can be deemphasized, just as easily as the shortcomings of those to whom he does feel close can be covered up. In short, name does not correspond to reality, and vice versa. How can a man selected in this manner be entrusted with the great responsibilities of the state? It is for this reason that I request Your Majesty to abolish the nine-rank system.

Last, Your Majesty at one time issued a decree ordering all the arbitrators to write down, in explicit terms, the reasons why a particular person should be promoted or demoted. Because of this decree, the arbitrators, for a time, were more cautious and less arbitrary in handing out promotions and demotions. Now the situation is once again reversed. An arbitrator who promotes a man does not have to list the man's merits; nor does he have to mention the man's offenses if he decides to demote him. As usual, he promotes or demotes according to his likes and dislikes, makes no distinction between the good and the bad, and acts in this way or that way only to advance his own interest. It seems that he will not be satisfied until all the scholars within his jurisdiction become his personal followers. Clearly he has violated the decree referred to above. As the deserving are not rewarded and the unworthy are not punished, reward and punishment have lost their meanings, and the result is as harmful to individuals as it is to society. It is for this reason that I request Your Majesty to abolish the nine-rank system.

In summary, the lack of a sound system for the selection of arbitrators and the investment in them of great responsibilities without holding them accountable for the decisions they make underlie this deplorable state of affairs we are in. They are arbitrators in name but conspirators in fact. The system has nine ranks but contains in itself eight elements, as described above, that are harmful to our political system. It generates suspicion and resentment among even the closest relatives, so much so that a son sometimes fails to come to his father's rescue when the latter is publicly attacked. The damage it has done will be felt for generations to come. An enlightened monarch makes laws in conformity with current demand and will change them if they have been proved inadequate to forestall conspiracy and deceit. It is for this reason that the Chou dynasty changed many of the laws that it had inherited from its predecessor the Shang dynasty. The absence of the nine-rank system in ancient China does not mean that the sage rulers of those days failed to make their governmental apparatus complete; it merely means that these rulers clearly recognized that this system was not necessary to running a good government. Since its introduction during the Wei dynasty, the nine-rank system has not produced any man of note, while in the meantime it has generated much ill will and served as a great divider among our own people. It has brought more damage to good government and sound custom than anything else. Ignorant though your humble servant is, he respectfully requests Your Majesty to abolish it, so we can introduce a new, better system as a replacement.

Notes

1. Liu Yi (d. 285), an incorruptible and outspoken official who served in a variety of capacities during the Wei and Tsin dynasties, wrote this memorial in 280 or thereabouts. Though his recommendation was rejected, his criticism of the nine-rank system was often quoted by other scholars or officials who shared his opinion. Source of this selection: *Tsin shu*, roll 45.

2. See selection 1.

3. Tiao Yu, who served in the censorate of the imperial government, was dispatched from the capital to conduct a review of some of the decisions made by a provincial arbitrator but challenged by his critics.

(20)
Fang Hsüan-ling et al. / *T'ao Ch'ien*[1]

Even as a young man T'ao Ch'ien had lofty ideas of what life was about. He read extensively and wrote well. Unconventional in his conduct and behavior, he prided himself as a man true to himself while honest with others. His friends and neighbors appreciated him greatly for what he was. At one time he wrote a short article, entitled "Gentleman of the Five Willows," as a way to express himself. Part of this article reads as follows:

We know neither his name nor the place wherefrom he came. Because there are five willows beside his house, we refer to him as "Gentleman of the Five Willows."

The "Gentleman of the Five Willows" loves solitude and speaks little. He aspires to neither fame nor wealth, though he reads a great deal. When reading, he cares little how much he comprehends. When he does comprehend, however, he is so happy with himself that he even forgets his own meals.

The "Gentleman of the Five Willows" loves to drink. But, being poor, he cannot have all the wine he wants. His relatives and friends, knowing this situation, often invite him to indulge himself. Once he arrives, it is a foregone conclusion that he will intoxicate himself. Once intoxicated, he will excuse himself and leave, not minding what other people might think of his conduct.

As for his house, it consists of four barren walls and a leaking roof that cannot protect him from the elements. His jacket, having been mended often, has patches all over. His drinking and eating wares are more often empty than not. He takes all this in stride, however. As far as he is concerned, there has never been a happier person.

He writes often to amuse as well as to express himself. He cares little for gains or losses and intends to live this way for the rest of his life.

To T'ao Ch'ien's contemporaries this description was a true record of the author's own life. Since his parents were old and his family was poor, T'ao Ch'ien had at one time served as a provincial academician. But, unable to endure the bureaucratic life, he resigned shortly after his appointment. Later, informed by his relatives and friends that occupying an official post would enable him to sing and to drink as much as he liked, he accepted a post as magistrate of P'engtse [modern Kiangsi province]. Upon his arrival at the new post, he decreed that all the public land within his jurisdiction be planted with glutinous millet, the kind of grain that was used exclusively for wine making. "From now on I can get drunk all the time," he remarked happily. His wife and children pleaded with him to change his mind, since they would have liked to have something to eat. Finally he agreed that only one-half of the public land should be planted with glutinous millet, while the other half would be cultivated with nonglutinous rice.

Even as an official, T'ao Ch'ien lived a simple and unpretentious life. He did not attempt in any way to ingratiate himself with his superiors. One day upon hearing that a high official from the provincial capital was about to make an inspection tour through his district and that he, as magistrate of the district, was required by custom and law to receive him in his official attire, T'ao Ch'ien left the district seal in his office and departed from his post without a word. "I cannot humiliate myself before a boor for five bushels of rice," he explained. This event occurred in the second year of Yi-hsi [406], less than three months after he had acquired the post.

Returning home, he wrote a song which reads as follows:

It Is Time To Return Home

It is time to return home when wild growth has taken over my garden and field. Having subjected the mind to the service of the body, I once lost myself and grieved alone over the sad state. As the past cannot be recalled, fortunately the future is still ahead. The sheep have strayed; they must and shall return to the road.

As the boat moves forward, a breeze plays gently with my clothes. A woodsman informs me of the road ahead; how impatiently I wait for daybreak. Soon there is home to which I run joyfully like a child. My infant son smiles from the doorstop, and all others join in. "Welcome home," they say. The paths around the house have been abandoned to wild growth; but the chrysanthemums and the pines—how much they have grown in my absence! I carry my son inside the house, where I see goblets and cups, all full of wine. I sip the wine slowly, while looking at the trees outside. Beyond the south window soars my fantasy; beneath it is the little world that contains all of my joy and pride.

A cane in hand, I wander daily in the garden. The gate is there, but who bothers to open it since there are no visitors in sight? Upward I look at the sky: the clouds, rolling on aimlessly, leave no traces when they pass by. Even the birds, when tired of flying, have to return to their nests. The sun is setting, and shadows slowly descend as the day darkens into the night. As I caress the lone pine and walk around, I smile at the day ahead.

It is time to return home as I bid farewell to the world. The world and I have nothing in common—why should we even attempt to accommodate? Here at home I rejoice at the chat of my dear ones and rely on my lute to dispel melancholy. Farmers rush in to announce the coming of spring: that soon they will have to sow the western field. With a boat I explore coves along the meandering river; riding a wagon I move on the winding road to reach the top of a mountain. Trees stretch out their joyful arms; streams murmur inviting music. How much they are alive! How much they love me as one of them!

Stop your sermon, as life is ephemeral and transient. How can you afford not to do as you please? Why should you scurry hither and thither to seek trifles? Fame or wealth is not what I want; nor am I certain that I shall ascend to heaven. Here I am: taking a lone walk when the weather is good and raking and weeding when I feel so inclined. I mount the eastern hill to sing aloud and stand by a clear stream to compose a new poem. Life comes and goes; but I shall enjoy this moment.

Soon after his return, T'ao Ch'ien was offered, but declined to accept, a position as a governmental scribe. Having cut off all of his official contact, he had as his friends such men as Chang Yeh, Chou Hsüan-jen, Yang Sung-ling, and Ch'ung Tsun, all of whom shared his ideas about life. When they invited him for a drink, he never refused. When a stranger invited him for a drink, he usually brought his friends along with him. As soon as he felt intoxicated, he excused himself and returned home, never bothering even to inquire about his host's name. Needless to say, he would not make another call of his own accord. He spent most of his time either in the field or wandering about between mountains and rivers.

In the year of Yüan-hsi [419] Governor Wang Hung, one of his admirers, invited the poet to meet him. T'ao Ch'ien declined. The governor, undaunted, traveled all the way to the village to make the same request. T'ao Ch'ien again declined on the ground of a nonexistent illness. "I am not a man of the world," he later explained to his friends. "I live the way I do not because I want to create the impression that I am better or nobler than anybody else but because it is best for me. I should feel very guilty indeed if a man of such high position as the governor presently enjoys should find something exemplary in me."

But the governor did not give up easily. Having heard that T'ao Ch'ien was about to visit Mount Lu, the governor dispatched an old friend of his, a man named Ch'ung T'ung-tzu, to set up a wine stand in a pavilion that the road traversed. Upon his arrival at the pavilion, T'ao Ch'ien was invited for a drink. How could he refuse? In fact, he was so happy with the occasion that he forgot that he still had some distance to travel. "The right moment has arrived," said the governor who subsequently emerged from a corner of the pavilion to introduce himself. The governor and the poet liked each other instantly; they toasted and dined together like old friends. Noticing that the poet was barefoot, the governor ordered a pair of new shoes to be brought in. The poet nonchalantly raised his feet to receive the shoes, while continuing drinking.

"I would like to welcome you as my guest in the capital," said the governor. Hearing no objection, the governor ordered his two sons and a retainer to take turns carrying the poet in a bamboo basket, since the poet, suffering from a foot disease, could not walk far by himself. Upon arriving at the governor's mansion, T'ao Ch'ien acted as if he were in his own house: he drank and laughed without the slightest inhibition. He was neither impressed nor unimpressed by all the luxuries around him.

From then on the governor usually waited in a mountain or near a lake whenever he wished to see his poet. Knowing that he was very poor, the governor sent him rice and wine from time to time.

Showing no interest in the management of family finance, T'ao Ch'ien entrusted his sons and servants with all mundane affairs. When friends and relatives brought wine to his house, rarely would he refuse to drink with them. He never showed irritation or anger with anyone. He inevitably became intoxicated whenever wine was available but sang even when there was no wine. He once stated that the best moment in life was to lie down beneath a northern window in summer months and let the gentle breeze caress one's body and face. Though knowing little about music, he played the lute and sang whenever friends came to see him. "In music it is not the sound that matters," said he. "The most important thing is how one feels."

T'ao Ch'ien, the poet, died in the fourth year of Yüan-chia [427] at the age of sixty-one.

Notes

1. Source: *Tsin shu*, roll 94.

(21)

Wei Shou / *Buddhism during the North Wei*[1]

During his numerous military campaigns Emperor Wei T'ai-tsu [also known as Toba Kuei or Tao-wu Huang-ti, r. 386–409], founder of the North Wei, issued strict orders that none of his soldiers be allowed to molest Buddhist monks and nuns or disturb their temples, having always been impressed with the Buddhists' devotion to their religion and their respect for lay officials. Though a Taoist devotee himself, he had from time to time read

Buddhist scriptures. As the dynasty was only newly established and the country remained to be pacified, no institution had yet been set up to promote the Buddhist cause. There was no question, however, as to where his sympathies lay. For instance, he issued the following decree in the first year of T'ien-hsing [409]:

> During the long time of its existence Buddhism has brought benefit to the dead as well as the living. The Buddhist claim to knowledge of the supernatural is unquestionably valid since it has been proved by irrefutable evidence. The responsible officials are hereby authorized to build new temples in the capital or to renovate old ones, so that all the faithful will have a proper place to live.

Wei T'ai-tsung [also known as Ming-yüan Huang-ti, r. 409–23], T'ai-tsu's eldest son and successor to the throne, followed in his father's footsteps by patronizing Buddhism as well as Taoism and promoted the Buddhist cause by encouraging the erection of Buddhist statues and the painting of Buddhist images. He specifically instructed all the monks and nuns to serve as a catalyst in the refinement of the nation's custom.

Meanwhile in Ch'angan the Indian missionary Kumarajiva had already arrived and was accorded great respect by Yao Hsing.[2] A deep thinker who was proficient in both Chinese and Sanskrit, he gathered at the Ts'aot'ang Temple more than eight hundred scholars to help him translate many of the Buddhist scriptures, including such learned monks as Tao-t'ung, Sen-lüeh, Tao-heng, Tao-p'iao, Sen-ch'ao, and T'an-ying. Jointly they rendered into Chinese more than ten sutras of Mahayana Buddhism. In the translation each sentence or passage was carefully annotated and explained, so a reader would have no doubt about its true meaning. Ever since their rendering into Chinese, these sutras have been studied by all the Buddhist monastics in China. Among Kumarajiva's learned colleagues Tao-t'ung was unquestionably the most outstanding. It was he who helped Kumarajiva in the choice of words in all the translations and, working alone, provided the comments for the *Vimalakirtinirdesa (Sutra Spoken by Vimalakirti)*. He also wrote several treatises on Buddhism, each of which, noted for its insight, was highly praised by other Buddhist scholars.

While Kumarajiva was translating Buddhist scriptures into

Chinese in Ch'angan, a monk named Fa-hsien set out for India to search for other sacred texts hitherto unavailable in China. He traveled in more than thirty kingdoms; in each of the kingdoms he visited, he learned the native language before embarking upon the translation task. He stayed in India for ten years and finally, at Ceylon, boarded a merchant ship to sail eastward toward China. After two hundred days on the high seas during which he was barely conscious, he finally arrived at the Ch'ang-kuang district in the province of Ch'ing [modern Shantung province], south of the Lao Mountains in the second year of Shen-shui [415]. During his sojourn in India, he kept a detailed record of the kingdoms he visited, which is still read today. After his return, he used the texts he had obtained to correct their Chinese equivalents in which he found many inaccuracies. Later, seeking additional assistance, he journeyed to the Lower Yangtze where he consulted with the Indian master Bhadra Lo. One result of this consultation was the latest edition of the *Rules of Discipline (Vinaya)*, more complete than any in existence.

Previously a monk named Fa-lin had sailed from Yangchow to India where he acquired an original copy of the *Garland Sutra (Avatainsaka)*. Several years later, with the assistance of Bhadra Lo and a monk named Fa-yeh, he translated it into Chinese and circulated it among the Buddhists.

Wei Shih-tsu [also known as T'ai-wu Huang-ti, r. 424–52] inherited the throne in his prime and placed the pacification of China, through the use of military force, above any other matter of national concern. Although he had been converted to the Buddhist faith and pledged himself to honor its clergy, he did not feel strongly enough about it to read any Buddhist scriptures. Nor did he place much credence in the Buddhist theory of reincarnation. By the time he was introduced to the teachings of K'ou Ch'ien-chih, he was more than convinced of the superiority of Taoism over Buddhism. At that time the imperial counselor was a man named Ts'ui Hao who, because of his erudition, was consulted often by the emperor on important matters. Ts'ui Hao himself was a follower of K'ou Ch'ien-chih and often criticized, in front of the emperor, the Buddhists and their beliefs which he dismissed as absurd. Being an articulate man, he was able to persuade the emperor to follow his line of beliefs.

When Kai Wu raised the standard of rebellion at Hsingch'eng

and caused enormous disturbances among the populace in Kuanchung [modern Shensi province], Emperor Wei Shih-tsu decided
to lead an army to suppress the rebellion himself. In due course
he arrived at the city of Ch'angan. The Buddhists in Ch'angan
had a long tradition of growing wheat inside their temple compounds; after the emperor's arrival, the government designated
these wheat fields as grazing ground for the royal stable. One day
while the emperor was watching his horses grazing inside one of
these temple compounds, he was informed by some of his retainers, who had been invited inside the temple to drink with the
monks, that they had seen with their own eyes a large store of
military weapons. "What do the monks need military weapons
for?" the emperor responded angrily. "They must be in secret
collusion with the rebel Kai Wu and waiting only for the right
moment to use these weapons against the people." He ordered
a thorough search of the temple and found not only sophisticated
wine-making equipment but also thousands of valuable items
that had been stored for safe keeping by rich people throughout
the empire. Inside the temple were also found secret chambers
which the monks used to carry on illicit affairs with the wealthy
women of the city.

Taking advantage of the emperor's anger, Ts'ui Hao recommended the execution of all the monks in Ch'angan and the
destruction of all of their statues and images. Similar measures
should also be taken in the provinces, he added. Having been
thus persuaded, the emperor issued the following decree:

> The Buddhist monastics, advocating absurdities that originated from
> an alien land and speaking falsely of supernatural appearances, can by
> no means be relied on to bring about good customs. Members of nobility
> who have patronized Buddhist monastics are hereby ordered to sur-
> render them to the appropriate authorites. Under no circumstances will
> evasion be tolerated! The deadline for surrendering these monastics is
> the fifteenth day of the second month [28 March 446], beyond which
> the monastics concerned, together with the person or persons who
> refuse to surrender them, and also all members of their families, will be
> punished by death.

Crown Prince Kung-tsung, who had been a Buddhist devotee
himself, repeatedly petitioned the emperor on the inadvisability

of killing Buddhist monastics and destroying Buddhist statues and images and recommended instead that all the Buddhist temples be left alone and be allowed to deteriorate by themselves, since their renovation would not be permitted under the new law, so that, in due course, the Buddhist faith would die of its own accord. The emperor turned down this request and issued another decree that read as follows:

Formerly there was a degenerate monarch of the Later Han dynasty who, bewitched by a false, heretical idea, made the unsubstantiated claim that he had had an unusual dream and then used this dream as a pretext to serve the evil spirits that originated in an alien land.[3] By honoring these evil spirits, he violated the eternal law of Heaven and Earth, thus causing an unprecedented event of the greatest tragedy. The boastful words spoken by the Buddhists, though patently absurd, were nevertheless convincing enough to the degenerate monarchs of a degenerate age. The Buddhist impact has proved to be disastrous to government and people alike, since the way of the sage kings inevitably declined as the way of the evil spirits rose steadily to replace it. It is not surprising that chaos and wars have become a normal state of affairs since the introduction of Buddhism to China, as Heaven invariably punishes those who have chosen to defy its rules. Cities have been reduced to ashes; countless people have lost their lives; much of the countryside has been so devastated that one can walk miles without seeing a single soul. This tragedy would not have come about had there been no Buddhism in China.

Having received from Heaven the mandate to rule at the end of a degenerate age, I, most naturally, would like to eliminate falsehood and reestablish truthfulness, so that the kind of peace and prosperity that prevailed in ancient times will be with us again. It is therefore my intention to banish all alien deities from this beautiful land and root out their presence forever. If we succeed in doing this, we shall have no apology to make to future historians. . . .

From now on anyone who willfully worships these alien deities or causes statues to be made for the same purpose is to be punished by death. . . . All Buddhist statues, images, and books are to be burned or destroyed, and all Buddhist monastics, regardless of their age, are to be put to death.

The above decree was issued in the third month of the second year of Chen-chün [446].[4]

Though his proposal was rejected, Kung-tsung was nevertheless able to delay the enforcement of this decree so that all the

Buddhists, laymen as well as the clergy, would have enough time to make the necessary arrangements to assure their own safety. As one might expect, all the Buddhist monastics went into hiding and few, if any, were actually sentenced to death. Even in the capital all the Buddhist monks and nuns were safe from persecution, thanks to the efforts of the crown prince. Most of the gold and silver statues, together with the invaluable collection of Buddhist scriptures, had been carefully hidden before the enforcement of the emperor's decree and were consequently spared from destruction. But Buddhist temples and pagodas, which could not be hidden, had been all but totally destroyed.

Before and during the persecution, both K'ou Ch'ien-chih and Ts'ui Hao served as members of the emperor's advisory council, and the former repeatedly requested the latter to use his influence to reduce the harshness of the emperor's edict. When Ts'ui Hao refused, K'ou Ch'ien-chih remarked, "I do not see how you and your family can escape death either." Four years later, Ts'ui Hao was indeed sentenced to death and died at the age of sixty-nine. After Ts'ui's death, the emperor began to regret the persecution he had ordered but, facing a *fait accompli,* could not completely reverse himself. Even Kung-tsung did not dare to advocate openly the reconstruction of Buddhist temples. Yet, during the last seven or eight years of Wei Shih-tsu's reign, the persecution of Buddhism had been greatly relaxed, and the most devoted could indeed study Buddhist scriptures or worship in private without causing the government to intervene. The only thing they could not do was exhibit their Buddhist enthusiasm in public, at least not in the capital.

Not until the ascension to the throne by Wei Kao-tsung [also known as Wen-ch'eng Huang-ti, r. 452–66] did a complete reversal of policy take place. The new policy was contained in a decree which read as follows:

Honoring deities above and promoting good deeds below, the sovereign of all men will most naturally lend his support to all the activities judged beneficial to his subjects, no matter how ancient these activities were in terms of their origin. That is why the *Spring and Autumn Annals* speaks highly of the rites in honor of the virtuous and the books of worship record the names of all those who have contributed generously to a worthy cause.

Lord Buddha brought benefit to thousands while living and left behind a beautiful heritage when he died. Those interested in the question of life and death admire his stoic outlook and those given to literature are most impressed with his insight. His teachings prohibit what a government has banned by law and help to strengthen the innate goodness that is universal in all men. They cast away all the heretical ideas and pave the way for true enlightenment. It is not surprising that dynasties in the past have honored Buddha sincerely and praised his teachings highly. Our own dynasty has done likewise.

The late emperor, the Most Venerated Shih-tsu, extended his benevolence to the farthest corner of the earth in the wake of his successful military campaigns. Numerous monks and nuns, generally of the most impeccable character, had been induced by his benevolence to come here to live, including many who journeyed from distant kingdoms. Like high mountains and deep seas that invariably hide monstrosities of the weirdest kind, the monastics of his time, being so numerous, had also among them the most unprincipled elements who used temples as a shield for their own illegal and immoral activities. It is these unprincipled elements whom the late emperor intended to punish. But the officials in charge, not knowing the emperor's true intention, went ahead to persecute all the Buddhists. Though saddened by this miscarriage of justice, the late emperor, in the midst of military campaigns, did not find time to revive Buddhist learning and restore Buddhist establishments.

Having been mandated by Heaven to be the sovereign of all men and being mindful of the true intention of my forebears, I hereby decree that any community in the empire, if it so desires, can build a Buddhist temple of its own, that no restrictions should be imposed on its expenditures, and that all persons, regardless of their age, be allowed to join the monastic ranks, at an annual rate of fifty persons for each large province, forty persons for each small province, and ten persons for each border province, provided that the initiated come from a good family and are of impeccable moral character. When each monastic conducts his life in accordance with his religious teachings, not only will a true faith spread far and wide, but also will evil itself be replaced by goodness.

This decree achieved more than its intended purpose. People all over the country lost no time in renovating their temples. Buddhist images and scriptures reappeared in the capital and received the kind of attention that had been absent only a short time before.

In the sixteenth year of T'ai-ho [482] during the reign of Wei

Kao-tsu [also known as Wei Hsiao-wen-ti, r. 471–99] a decree authorizing a semiannual initiation of Buddhist monastics was issued. On the eighth day of the fourth month and again on the fifteenth day of the seventh month of each year, one hundred persons were allowed to join the monastic ranks for each of the large provinces. The numbers of persons entitled to this privilege for each medium and small provinces were fixed at fifty and twenty, respectively. This rule, said the imperial decree, was meant to be permanent.

In the seventeenth year of T'ai-ho [483] the *Rule Relating to the Governance of Buddhist Monastics*, which consisted of forty-seven articles, was promulgated.

In the winter of the second year of Yung-p'ing [509] during the reign of Wei Shih-tsung [also known as Hsüan-wu Huang-ti, r. 500–516] Hui-shen, Superintendent of Buddhist Monastics, memorialized the emperor as follows:

Inevitably there are the dishonest among the Buddhist monastics; sadly it is extremely difficult to differentiate them. Having in mind the necessity of making improvements, I have spoken with many Buddhist masters who voice the same concern. We agree on the need for some general principles that would govern the monastics throughout the empire as well as specific regulations that an abbot of each temple or monastery, with the assistance of his first and second deacons, may choose to devise to meet individual circumstances. All monastics are expected to follow these principles and regulations, the violation of which will constitute a legitimate reason for defrocking and for returning them to civilian status.

As a general principle, monastics are not allowed to own worldly possessions; nor are they exempt from prosecution by law. However, circumstances may occur when it is judged more equitable to enforce a principle or law with some flexibility. For instance, a monk, as a matter of principle, cannot own such things as carriages and oxen and cannot consort with a woman, but it is not right to deny a carriage to a monastic who, being sixty years old or older, cannot walk far without suffering extreme fatigue. By the same token, a man, once joining the monastic ranks, is not supposed to follow the custom of the lay by observing the ritual of mourning, but the principle of equity would be better served if he is allowed a three-day mourning period after his father, mother, or any of his three mentors[5] has passed away in an area other than where he is, or a seven-day mourning period if the deceased has lived, until his death, in the same place as he does.[6]

In addition to the above suggestions, I would also like to recommend the following:

1. If a monk chooses to wander among the civilian population instead of living in the temple to which he belongs and in the process commits violations of a serious nature, he should be defrocked and returned to civilian status.

2. A congregation of fifty monks or more should be allowed to petition the government to build its own temple. In the case of a temple that has been built without this authorization, all the monks in it will be banished from the province where the temple is.

3. Monastic laws are not applicable to laymen who, when found to have impersonated monastics, will be banished to the district wherefrom they came.

4. Monks and nuns from foreign countries are allowed to stay in this country if their conduct is judged in conformity with the high standard as recorded in the Buddhist scriptures. If not, they should be ordered to return to their own country. A foreign monk or nun who has been ordered to leave but refuses to do so will be prosecuted in accordance with the monastic law.

The emperor ordered that the recommendations in this memorial be carried out.

In summary, the following may be said about Buddhism during the North Wei:

During this period altogether 415 different sutras were circulated totaling 1,919 rolls. Beginning with the Cheng-kuang period [519–24], as the empire experienced more and more difficulties and the amount of taxes kept increasing, especially in the form of labor services, many registered taxpayers, unable to meet the increased burden, were more than eager to join the monastic ranks. Nominally Buddhist devotees, they were actually tax evaders. The popularity of Buddhism, unfortunately, was accompanied by an exercise in hypocrisy on an unprecedented scale. At its prime Buddhism could count among its monastic ranks two million monks and nuns, housed in more than thirty thousand temples and monasteries. Knowledgeable persons concluded even then that the spread of this alien faith had gone too far for the public good.

Notes

1. Source of this selection: *Wei shu*, roll 114.

2. Kumarajiva arrived at Ch'angan in 401. Yao Hsing, a monarch of the Later Ch'in regime, then ruled part of North China, including Ch'angan.

3. The so-called degenerate monarch was Han Hsiao-ming-ti (r. 58–76) who claimed to have seen a golden statue of Buddha in one of his dreams. Later he sent envoys to India to search for Buddhist scriptures and constructed the first Buddhist temple in Loyang.

4. This was the first of the "Three Persecutions of Buddhism" in China. The other two occurred in 574–77 during the North Chou and again in 845 during the T'ang dynasty.

5. At the time of a novice's official initiation into the monastic ranks, he needed the presence of three mentors and seven witnesses to make the ceremony valid. The mentors were responsible for his religious training as well as his general welfare.

6. The period of mourning for a deceased parent was normally three years.

CHAPTER

5

Sui and T'ang

IN terms of political development the Sui-T'ang period (590–906) has often been compared to the Ch'in-Han era (221 B.C.–A.D. 220) of several centuries earlier. The Ch'in unified China in 221 B.C. and thus ended a long period of political division that dated from the eighth century B.C. The Sui regime did likewise when it conquered Ch'en, the last of the Southern Dynasties, in the spring of 589. The Ch'in dynasty lasted a short period: two emperors and fourteen years (221–207 B.C.). The Sui dynasty did only a little better: two emperors and twenty-eight years (590–618). Both died of the same causes—heavy taxation and unscrupulous use of manpower. Yet from their ruins emerged two of the longest and greatest eras in Chinese history, the Han and the T'ang periods, respectively. The achievements of the Han and the T'ang dynasties are among the most outstanding in Chinese history, so much so that even today the Chinese still refer to themselves as either *Han jen* (men of Han) or *T'ang jen* (men of T'ang)—a living testimony to the pride they take in these two regimes.

When Yang Chien (also known as Sui Wen-ti, r. 589–604), founder of the Sui dynasty, assumed the imperial title in 589, many hoped, with ample justification, that the foundation of a more durable peace had finally been laid. Yet, like many other empire builders who did not know how to stop when they must and should, he set out to bring some of China's peripheral states to submission after he had unified China. He had some success in a war against the T'u-chüeh (Turks) on the western frontier but unexpectedly encountered strong resistance in the east from the Koreans, who by then had enjoyed independence too long to entertain the thought of being a vassal state to China again (selection 22). Yang Chien's defeat at the hands of the Koreans did not prevent his son Sui Yang-ti (r. 605–18) from attempting the same, as he vowed to "avenge the national honor" by "bringing the Koreans to their senses." In 611 and again in 613 he personally led his troops against Korea but failed miserably in both of his attempts. By then a chauvinistic exercise started by his father had become for him a neurotic obsession and could only end if he or his regime perished in the process. In 614 when he attempted to conquer Korea for the third time, revolts against him had already mushroomed all over the country. With no better future to look forward to, he lived a life of debauchery until, finally, he was assassinated by some of his most trusted lieutenants (selection 23).

The lesson of Sui Yang-ti was not lost on the early rulers of the T'ang dynasty who kept reminding themselves and their ministers that the disastrous series of events that had happened to the short-lived Sui dynasty could happen again if they did not use power with restraint or if they were so self-righteous as to neglect the true interests of the people they ruled. "If anything goes wrong anywhere in the empire," said T'ang T'ai-tsung (r. 627–49), a founder of the T'ang dynasty, to his ministers, "you should let me know immediately" (selection 24). The golden era of the T'ang dynasty lasted approximately 137 years (618–755); it was an era of such poets as Li Po (701–62) and Tu Fu (712–70), of such painters as Li Ssu-hsün (651–720) and Wang Wei (699–759), of full granaries and empty jails, and of such generosity and hospitality that "one could travel across the length and breadth of the empire without having to carry any cash with him." Unfortunately good times, like bad times, had to leave the historical stage at one time or another. When China was again plunged into chaos and war beginning in 755, one could reminisce about the past as if it had existed in a cherished dream. One reason for the economic abundance of an earlier period was a land distribution system introduced in 624 that guaranteed an adequate income for each peasant household. Now that all systems, including the land distribution system, had been either undermined or destroyed altogether in a long period of civil disturbances, new devices had to be found to replace the old ones when the T'ang regime was finally able to achieve some degree of social stability. One of the new devices was the semiannual tax system *(liang-shui fa)* which, with modifications, has been the primary way of raising governmental revenue throughout the rest of Chinese history until modern times (selection 25).

As the general state of affairs worsened after 755, the exuberance that had characterized everything T'ang China did before that date also disappeared. This was especially true in literature where fetishism and resignation had become the dominant moods. Even in the newly developed literary form, known to the T'ang Chinese as *ch'uan-chi* but actually similar to what we today might call short stories, one finds a pervasive atmosphere of Taoist fatalism. One of the best known *ch'uan-chi* is *The Story of the Curly Beard (Ch'iu-jan ke chuan)* by Tu Kuang-t'ing (850–933), appearing here as selection 26.

In history the three major works that cover this particular period are *History of the Sui (Sui shu)*, *History of the T'ang (T'ang shu)*, and *New History of the T'ang (Hsin T'ang shu)*. The *Sui shu*, though bearing the name of Ch'ang-sun Wu-chi (d. ca. 570) alone, was actually written by a committee composed of such eminent scholars as Yen Shih-ku (581–645) and Kung Ying-ta (d. 648). The preparation of this work was authorized by an imperial decree in 627, but the work itself was not completed until 656. Written shortly after the overthrow of the Sui dynasty, it tends to be highly critical of the policies pursued by the two Sui emperors, especially Sui Yang-ti. The *T'ang shu*, the single most important work covering the T'ang period, was written by Liu Hsü (ca. 885–944), a scholar-official noted for his literary talent. The book, consisting of two hundred rolls, was completed shortly before the author's death, in 944 or thereabouts. Several decades later, Ou-yang Hsiu (1007–72), a Sung historian and statesman, decided to write his own history of the T'ang and called it the *Hsin T'ang shu*, on the grounds that the *T'ang shu* was too bulky in volume and too detailed or superfluous in some of its coverage. However, as far as a modern historian is concerned, the *T'ang shu* is definitely more useful, since it is richer in source material.

Another work that includes extensive coverage of the Sui-T'ang period is *History as a Mirror (Tzu-chih t'ung-chien)*, written by Ssu-ma Kuang (1018–86), Ou-yang Hsiu's friend and colleague. Designed as a successor to the *Spring and Autumn Annals*, it covers a period of 1,362 years, from the beginning of the Warring States in 403 B.C. to the last year of the Five Dynas-

ties in A.D. 959. The author began his work in 1067 and completed it seventeen years later in 1084, two years before his own
death. The book, consisting of 294 rolls, is essentially a chronicle
of political developments and, as its title implies, was meant to
"elevate the virtuous and condemn the wicked" and thus provide a guide for future statesmen, especially Chinese emperors
so they would not make the same mistakes as their predecessors
had in the past. While writing this book, the author spoke of the
enormous amount of materials covering the Sui-T'ang period
that had to be winnowed and sifted before they could be used.
Thanks to their inclusion in *History as a Mirror*, we are better
informed about this period than we would otherwise have been.

(22)

Yang Chien (Sui Wen-ti) / *A Letter of Warning to the King of Korea*[1]

Having received the mandate of Heaven to love and cherish all
the people in the empire, I entrusted you with the responsibility
of governing one corner of the earth next to the sea, in the hope
that you would continue to promote the great civilization of
China and that all the people in your kingdom, whatever their
station in life is, would live a peaceful and enjoyable life. As my
vassal, each year you have sent tribute missions to China and
pledged your fealty to the sovereign of all men. However, doubt
still exists about your sincerity since you, as my vassal, have not
followed policies parallel to my own.

First, since you know that the Tungus and the Khitan Tatars
have pledged their allegiance to the Celestial Empire and have
indeed become our vassal states, why do you use force either to
chase them from their home, as in the case of the Tungus, or to
forbid them to move about, as in the case of the Khitan Tatars?
How can you be so brutal and merciless to them after they, like
other peoples who know where righteousness is, have sworn
their loyalty to us?

Second, why do you use bribes to seduce archery makers from China and ship them to Korea, when you yourself must know that you will be provided with artisans of all kinds if you openly request them, since we have a large number of them ready for service anywhere? Is it not true that you prefer this illicit method of smuggling in order to cover up your true intention, namely, making or repairing weapons for an unlawful war against China?

Third, I have repeatedly sent envoys to your kingdom for the purpose of not only assuring you of my kind regard but also inquiring about the conditions in your country, so that I shall be able to provide you with necessary instructions to govern successfully. In each case you subject my envoy to house arrest, thus preventing him from seeing or hearing anything. You must have some evil design of your own; otherwise you would not have been so afraid of his inspection.

Fourth, time and again you have sent cavalrymen across the border to kill and injure people in China. Your agents are also active in the border regions, engaging in not only false propaganda but also conspiratorial activities to the detriment of China. Their action speaks loudly of the evil of your heart.

Fifth, since I regard all men within the Four Seas in the same way as I regard my own children, I have chosen to grant you territories and titles, and my generosity in this regard is well known to all the people in the world. Yet you continue to entertain doubt about my intentions and have gone as far as sending spies to China to seek information. Can this conduct of yours be regarded as proper and right if you mean to remain a loyal subject of mine?

I have often thought that all your misdeeds may have been my fault, owing to the fact that I may not have taught you as well as I should have. If that is the case, you shall have my forgiveness, on the condition that from now on you correct all the mistakes you have made, carefully observe the duties required for a vassal, and abide by the law of the Celestial Empire. Moreover, you shall do your utmost to govern your kingdom successfully, and under no circumstances are you allowed to attack or invade the territory of any of your neighbors. If you can do all this, not only will you continue to enjoy fame and wealth with no worry whatsoever, but also I myself will be greatly pleased. Your kingdom may be small in territory and population, but you, as its king, are as much cherished by me as other subjects of mine. If I dismiss you, I would have to find someone else to occupy your present post which cannot remain vacant long. It is my hope that you will purify your heart and rectify your conduct so that once again you will become my loyal subject and abide by my law. In that case there will be no need for me to find another man to replace you. The law of our ancient kings stresses the importance of love and faith and the necessity of using reward and punishment as means to promote good deeds and discourage misconduct. I have likewise made this law known to all the people in the empire. What would my other vassals think of me if you are innocent and yet I choose to dispatch armed forces to punish you? You must be open-minded enough to take this advice of mine and dismiss any doubt of yours. Under no circumstances should you harbor the thought of traitorous activities.

For more than ten years I warned Ch'en Shu-pao[2] not to oppress his own people and invade our territories. But he, relying on the natural defense of the Yangtze River and the small number of troops under his command, was impudent enough not to listen to my advice. Under the circumstances I had no choice but to send my men to wage war against him, and in three months these men, who numbered only a few thousand, succeeded in destroying him and his bandit clique that had been in power for several generations. The whole area was pacified overnight, thus bringing joy to gods and men alike. You, as I understand, are the only person who expressed regret, and in fact grieved over, the conquest of the Ch'en kingdom.

To punish or reward people in accordance with their merit, or the lack of it, is the duty of responsible officials, and these officials, under the law, would have to reward you had you supported the campaign against Ch'en and would, under the present circumstances, have no choice but to punish you, since you did not support the campaign in question. I, personally, simply do not understand why you relish anarchy and chaos. If you think that the Liao River is wide enough for your defense, let me remind you that it is not as wide as the Yangtze River. Nor is Korea as populous as the Ch'en kingdom. Were I not an extremely patient and tolerant person, I could easily have sent one general to punish you for your misdeeds, and the matter would long have been settled. The reason for my repeated attempts to enlighten you is that I have not given up hope that you could be reformed. I hope you will understand my wishes and act according to your best interests.

Notes

1. This letter of warning was written in 597; the war itself was conducted one year later. Source of this selection: *Sui shu*, roll 81.
2. Ch'en Shu-pao, last ruler of the Southern Dynasties, surrendered when his capital, Nanking, was captured by Yang Chien in the spring of 589.

(23)
Ssu-ma Kuang / *The Last Days of Sui Yang-ti*[1]

As the empire continued to disintegrate, Sui Yang-ti could not but feel insecure about himself. After each conference with his ministers, he often changed into casual attire and, carrying a cane in his hand, strolled in the palace compound and wandered from one building to another. He would not stop wandering until dusk, as if every tour of his might be his last. He had taught himself the art of divination and loved to speak in the Wu dialect.[2] With a wine cup in his hand while looking up at the stars, he would say to Empress Hsiao: "Many people outside this palace wish to harm me, but I shall have no worry. Even when the worst arrives, I can still be another Duke Ch'angch'eng and you another Queen Shen.[3] Why should I worry? Let us drink and enjoy life to the fullest." Needless to say, he became drunk again after each remark of this kind. Observing himself in the mirror, he once said: "What a beautiful head! I am wondering who will have the privilege of cutting it off." Looking at his wife's shocked expression, he merely burst into laughter. "Happiness and sorrow take turns governing the life of a man," he responded. "What is wrong with my stating the obvious?"

Seeing that North China had plunged into chaos and war, Sui Yang-ti thought seriously of not returning to the north. He had in mind the permanent move of his capital to Tanyang [modern

Kiangsu province], thus enabling him to continue to hold the Lower Yangtze even after the loss of North China to the rebels. He ordered his ministers to stage a debate on this issue but was surprised to see the division it caused. One group, headed by Yü Shih-chi, was in favor, while another group, headed by General Li Ts'ai, was vigorously opposed and recommended instead that the emperor should return to Ch'angan immediately. The debate was so heated that Yü Shih-chi and Li Ts'ai continued to exchange angry words as they left the conference. Li T'ung, an official in the Second Secretariat, stated: "South China is damp and mountainous and does not have the resources to support the court and the army. The people will be taxed beyond endurance and in that case chaos and war will inevitably occur as they have already occurred in the north." Li T'ung was censored, however, after having made these remarks, as his critics accused him of having deliberately undermined an established policy of the government. Other officials, sensing the trend, began to say what the emperor had wanted to hear. "The people of South China have waited for Your Majesty's presence for a long time," they stated. "Your Majesty will be most enthusiastically received, as the Great Yü once was,[4] should he decide to pass across the Yangtze River to rule and comfort them." An order was then issued to build palaces at Tanyang where the new capital was supposed to be.

Meanwhile the food supply in Yangchow was about to be exhausted. Most of the soldiers who had accompanied the emperor on his southern tour were natives of Kuanchung[5] and, having been in the south for a long time, were homesick and anxious to return home. Now that the emperor had decided to stay in the south, they plotted to return by themselves. One contingent of troops, led by Colonel Tou Hsien, deserted their ranks and moved westward. The emperor, furious, ordered his cavalry elite to pursue them. When captured, said the emperor, these deserters were to be killed on the spot. The number of deserters continued to increase, however, despite the government's stringent measures to stop them.

As the number of deserters multiplied, General Ssu-ma Teh-k'an, a longtime favorite of the emperor's who was then commanding a crack contingent stationed in the eastern section of the city, approached his friends Generals Yüan Li and P'ei Ch'ien-t'ung and spoke to them as follows: "What should we do,

now that the soldiers are deserting their ranks one after another?
If we report all these happenings to the emperor, we will certainly be held responsible and severely punished. If we do not,
not only we ourselves but also all members of our families will be
in serious difficulties when the emperor finds out the truth himself. As you recall, after Li Hsiao-chung had switched sides in the
losing battle against the rebels in Kuanchung, the emperor threw
his two younger brothers into jail and proposed to try them for
treason. Do you not think that we should be equally concerned,
since our families are still in the north?"

Generals Yüan Li and P'ei Ch'ien-t'ung were frightened upon
hearing these remarks. "What should we do?" they asked.

"Since our soldiers are deserting us," Ssu-ma Teh-k'an replied,
"we may as well desert with them."

The two men approved this idea and began to contact others
for the same purpose. Among those who were contacted and
agreed to become participants in a coup were Yüan Min, Chao
Hsing-ch'u, Meng Ping, Niu Fang-yü, Hsü Hung-jen, Hsüeh Shih-
liang, T'ang Feng-yi, Chang K'ai, and Yang Shih-lan, all of whom
held important positions with the government. They met day
and night and pledged not to betray one another. They aired
their sentiments of rebellion even in public, as if they had nothing to be afraid of.

One of the court women reported the conspiracy to Empress
Hsiao but was advised to report directly to the emperor, "if you
so desire." Hearing the report, the emperor ordered the poor
woman to be put to death on the grounds that the conspiracy, if
there was one, was none of her business. When other court
women continued to make the same report, Empress Hsiao only
sighed with resignation. "The state of the empire has so deteriorated that nothing you and I can do will make any difference,"
she replied. "Telling him the truth only worries him more, with
no difference in the end whatsoever." From then on no court
woman even mentioned the plot any more. . . .

General Yü-wen Hua-chi, who had never been known for his
daring or audacity, was understandably shocked and perspired
profusely when informed by the plotters that he had been designated as their leader to stage a coup against the emperor. Nevertheless, after some hesitation, he agreed to serve as their leader.
Having thus secured the general's consent, Ssu-ma Teh-k'an sent

Hsü Hung-jen and Chang K'ai to the palace to inform everyone they knew as follows: "His Majesty has heard that the northern soldiers intend to stage a rebellion and has therefore ordered their execution by poison. The poison will be placed in the wine during a banquet which His Majesty is scheduled to give in their honor. Having had all of the northern soldiers killed, His Majesty will then feel safe with the southerners." The rumor spread by these two men yielded its desired result, as the northern soldiers could hardly wait for the coup to begin.

On the day of Yi-mao [10 April 618] Ssu-ma Teh-k'an gathered all of the officers of the northern army and instructed them in what to do. "We will do whatever you say, sir," they responded unanimously.

It was a windy and cloudy day, and darkness shrouded the city even at noon. Shortly after 6 P.M. Ssu-ma Teh-k'an arrived at the royal stable, taking control of the horses and ordering all present to ready themselves for the battle. Meanwhile Yüan Li and P'ei Ch'ien-t'ung led their men to the palace compound on the pretense of providing additional strength to safeguard the life of the emperor. T'ang Feng-yi, whose official duty was to guard all of the city gates, secretly communicated to P'ei Ch'ien-t'ung that all the gates would not be bolted on that particular evening.

By midnight, after he had gathered more than forty thousand men in the eastern section of the city, Ssu-ma Teh-k'an ordered the burning of houses as a signal to the allied troops outside the city wall that they should proceed with their part of the plan. In the palace, meanwhile, the emperor was questioning P'ei Ch'ien-t'ung about the fire he saw and the noise he heard. "It is nothing, sir," P'ei Ch'ien-t'ung replied. "Some of the haylofts have caught fire, and people are fighting it." By this time the communication between the palace and the outside world had been totally cut off; the emperor, consequently, had no way of knowing what was going on outside.

Outside the city wall Yü-wen Chih-chi and Meng Ping, commanding approximately one thousand men, launched a sudden attack upon a contingent headed by Feng P'u-yüeh, captain of the city patrol, and captured him alive. Their mission completed, the men were ordered to guard the nearby side streets.

Having sensed that a coup had already begun, Prince T'an of Yen [a grandson of Sui Yang-ti's] secretly entered the city, in the darkness of the night, through an aqueduct next to the Fang-lin Gate. When he was stopped at the Hsüan-wu Gate that led to the palace compound, he told the guards that he had suddenly suffered a stroke, would die soon, and must see the emperor to bid him farewell. P'ei Ch'ien-t'ung, instead of reporting his presence to the emperor, ordered him to be arrested.

Shortly before dawn on the next morning Ssu-ma Teh-k'an ordered the troops under P'ei Ch'ien-t'ung's command to replace the imperial guards as sentries at all the gates leading to the palace compound. Meanwhile P'ei Ch'ien-t'ung himself, commanding several hundred cavalrymen, headed for the Ch'eng-hsiang Palace. When the imperial guards stationed in the palace discovered the intruders' presence, P'ei Ch'ien-t'ung ordered all the gates to be closed immediately, with the exception of the Eastern Gate, through which the imperial guards were ordered to get out. The guards, surprised and overwhelmed, dropped their weapons and hurried out as ordered. Only their commander, a man named Tu-hu Sheng, decided to put up a fight. "Who do you think you are?" said he to P'ei Ch'ien-t'ung. "What do you think you are doing?"

"We have already made the move," P'ei Ch'ien-t'ung replied. "What we are doing today has nothing to do with you. Please stay where you are and do not do anything foolish."

"You old thief," Tu-hu Sheng scolded as loudly as he could. "What kind of talk is this?" Without even bothering to put on his armor, he ordered his immediate followers, who numbered no more than fifteen, to rush into battle. In the ensuing fight all of them, including Tu-hu Sheng, were killed by the rebel soldiers. . . .

Previously, in anticipation of unusual developments, Sui Yang-ti had selected several hundred public slaves, known officially as servitors-at-large, to be stationed at the Hsüan-wu Gate on an around-the-clock basis. These servitors-at-large were chosen for their physical strength and military skill and were treated so well that the emperor even married many of them to the court women he owned. What the emperor did not realize was that Wei Shih, the royal chamberlain in charge of the palaces, had already joined the conspirators and agreed to do whatever he could to facilitate the coup from the inside. Shortly before the coup, Wei Shih, in a forged decree, ordered the servitors-at-large to leave their posts and go to the city to amuse themselves. Thus, when Ssu-ma Teh-k'an arrived with his men at the Hsüan-wu Gate, there was not a single servitor-at-large on guard.

The emperor, finally convinced that the rebels were indeed storming his palace, quickly changed into civilian clothes and ran toward the Western Pavilion. Meanwhile two of the conspirators, P'ei Ch'ien-t'ung and Yüan Li, were pounding the gate that led to the Left Pavilion. Wei Shih opened the gate from the inside and the conspirators, together with their men, found themselves in a narrow corridor. "Where is His Majesty?" they asked. One of the emperor's concubines, who happened to be in the corridor at this time, pointed out the direction in which the emperor had fled.

Lieutenant Ling-hu Hsing-teh unsheathed his sword and ran straight to the Western Pavilion. The emperor, hiding part of his face behind a window curtain, said to Ling-hu Hsing-teh, "Are you going to kill me?"

"How can your servant dare to do a thing like that?" the conspirator replied. "We only wish to obtain Your Majesty's consent to return to North China." Having said this, he helped the emperor down the steps from the Western Pavilion.

Before the coup P'ei Ch'ien-t'ung had been one of the emperor's most trusted lieutenants, dating to the days when the emperor was still a crown prince. Imagine the emperor's shock when he was brought face to face with the conspirator. "Are you not an old friend of mine?" the emperor asked. "What have I done to you that makes you betray me?"

"It is not your servant's intention to stage a rebellion," P'ei Ch'ien-t'ung replied. "The officers and the men are homesick and want to go home. They would like very much to have the privilege of escorting Your Majesty back to the capital [Ch'ang-an]."

"I would like to return to the north too," said the emperor. "The reason for the delay is that the rice ships from the Upper Yangtze have not yet arrived. If you insist, I am going with you now." Despite his consent to return to the north, the emperor remained a captive, as P'ei Ch'ien-t'ung ordered his men to keep constant watch over him.

As soon as the day broke, Meng Ping dispatched several cavalrymen to escort General Yü-wen Hua-chi to the palace com-

pound. The general, trembling and speechless, had to be assisted
to his mount. Whenever someone came near to pay his respects,
he merely raised his head, crouched forward against the saddle,
and kept murmuring: "What a shame! What a shame!" At the city
gate he was met by Ssu-ma Teh-k'an who subsequently escorted
him to the Hall of Audience. As soon as he was inside the hall, the
general was proclaimed prime minister.

In the palace, meanwhile, P'ei Ch'ien-t'ung was preparing the
emperor to proceed to the Hall of Audience to meet with the
leaders of the coup. "All the ministers are ready," he said. "Your
Majesty must go there to comfort them in person." A mount was
brought in, but the emperor, reluctant to leave, complained
about the shabbiness of the saddle. The saddle was changed, and
the emperor, having no more excuses, had to mount. P'ei Ch'ien-
t'ung led the emperor out of the palace by the horse's reins, while
brandishing a sword. Rebel soldiers on both sides of the road,
watching the emperor pass by, shouted with joy.

Yü-wen Hua-chi, the newly proclaimed prime minister, did not
relish the idea of meeting the emperor face to face. "Why does
he have to be taken out of the palace?" he shouted. "Why can he
not be finished off quickly where he is?" The emperor, consequently, was returned to his palace.

Having returned to the palace, P'ei Ch'ien-t'ung and Ssu-ma
Teh-k'an seated the emperor in a chair, while they themselves,
with swords in their hands, stood behind him.

"What have I done to deserve a fate like this?" the emperor
asked.

"Plenty," Ma Wen-chu, one of the rebel leaders, replied. "Your
Majesty deserted his ancestral temple and conducted endless
tours of pleasure. He indulged in military adventures abroad,
while living an extravagant, licentious life at home. Consequently millions of men died in war and millions of women were
left helpless in the gutter. Millions of others lost their means of
livelihood, while banditry and riots mushroomed all over the
country. He trusted nobody except those who knew how to flat-
ter; he protected the guilty and punished the innocent. How can
he say that he has done nothing to deserve punishment?"

"I may have betrayed the common people," the emperor replied. "But certainly I have not done anything wrong to men like
you who enjoy honor and wealth on account of me. How can you

possibly do this thing to me? Who, may I ask, is in charge of today's events?"

"The whole world has grievances against you," Ssu-ma Teh-k'an replied. "Yet you are talking about only one person."

Yü-wen Hua-chi sent Feng Teh-yi to enumerate the emperor's crimes. "You are a scholar," said the emperor. "Scholars do not degrade themselves by doing things like this." With a reddened face, Feng Teh-yi withdrew without completing his enumeration of crimes.

During the exchange of accusing words, Prince K'ao, a lad of eleven and the emperor's most beloved child, was leaning against his father and crying incessantly. Annoyed by the crying and yet unable to stop him, Ssu-ma Teh-k'an cut the boy's head off with one swipe of his sword, causing blood to spatter over the emperor's clothes. "A Son of Heaven must die with dignity, and beheading is not the proper way to end his life," said the emperor, when Ssu-ma Teh-k'an was about to slay him too. "I would appreciate a cup of poisoned wine."

Ma Wen-chu, supported by others, turned down the emperor's request for poison; instead, he ordered Ling-hu Hsing-teh to push the emperor hard against the chair. The emperor, knowing the end was near, untied his silk belt and handed it over to Ling-hu Hsing-teh. The latter strangled him to death on the chair.

Previously, in anticipation of a situation similar to that described above, Sui Yang-ti had prepared a jar of poisoned wine which accompanied him wherever he went. "If traitors show up," he instructed his favorite concubines, "you ladies drink this wine first before I do it myself." When the anticipated moment arrived, all of his favorite concubines had already fled and he could not even find the poisoned wine.

Notes

1. When the event described in this selection occurred, Sui Yang-ti was touring Yangchow (modern Kiangsu province), a city famous for its wine and women. Source of this selection: *Tzu-chih t'ung-chien*, roll 185.

2. The dialect of the Lower Yangtze.

3. Ch'en Shu-pao, last ruler of the Ch'en kingdom, was titled Duke Ch'ang-ch'eng after he surrendered his territory to Sui Wen-ti in 589. Queen Shen was his wife.

4. As for the Great Yü, also known simply as Yü, see pp. 10–11.

(24)
T'ang T'ai-tsung / *On the Art of Government*

As a young man, I loved archery and prided myself as an expert in the evaluation of bows and arrows. Recently I came into possession of a dozen bows, the quality of which was the best I had ever observed. I showed them to the bow makers and was surprised to hear that they were not as good as they looked. "Why?" I asked.

"The center of the wood is not located at the center of the bow; consequently all the wood grain moves in a bizarre fashion," replied the bow makers. "Though the bow is strong and durable, an arrow released from it cannot travel straight for a long distance."

I used a countless number of bows and arrows in unifying the country; yet I still do not know enough about them. Now that I have the country for only a short time, how can I say that I know enough about it to govern it successfully, taking into consideration the fact that my knowledge of it is certainly inferior to my knowledge of bows which I have used throughout my life?

* * * * *

Lately the draft decrees that originate from the First Secretariat are often contradictory and in some cases correct one another. To clarify this point, let me say that the purpose of having both the First and the Second Secretariats is for them to check and balance each other, so that the error of one will be corrected by the other and that an error, whoever commits it, will not remain undetected for a long time and thus cause irreparable damage.

Different people are bound to have different opinions; the important thing is that differences in opinion should not degenerate into personal antagonism. Sometimes to avoid the possibility of creating personal grievances or causing embarrassment to a colleague, an official might decide to go ahead with the implementation of a policy even though he knows that the policy is wrong. Let us remember that the preservation of a colleague's prestige, or the avoidance of embarrassment to him, cannot be compared with the welfare of the nation in importance, and to

place personal consideration above the well-being of the multitude will lead to defeat for the government as a whole. I want all
of you to understand this point and act accordingly.

During the Sui dynasty all officials, in the central as well as the
local governments, adopted an attitude of conformity to the general trend in order to be amiable and agreeable with one another.
The result was disaster as all of you well know. Most of them did
not understand the importance of dissent and comforted themselves by saying that as long as they did not disagree, they could
forestall harm to themselves that might otherwise cross their
path. When the government, as well as their families, finally
collapsed in a massive upheaval, they were severely but justifi-
ably criticized by their contemporaries for their complacency
and inertia, even if they themselves may have been fortunate
enough to escape death through a combination of circumstances.
This is the reason that I want all of you to place public welfare
above private interest and hold steadfastly the principle of righteousness, so that all problems, whatever they are, will be resolved
in such a way as to bring about a most beneficial result. Under no
circumstances are you allowed to agree with one another for the
sake of agreement.

*   *   *   *   *

As for Sui Wen-ti, I would say that he was politically inquisitive
but mentally closed. Being close-minded, he could not see truth
even if it were spotlighted for him; being overinquisitive, he was
suspicious even when there was no valid reason for his suspicion.
He rose to power by trampling on the rights of orphans and
widows[2] and was consequently not so sure that he had the unanimous support of his own ministers. Being suspicious of his own
ministers, he naturally did not trust them and had to make a
decision on every matter himself. He became a hard worker out
of necessity and, having overworked, could not make the right
decision every time. Knowing the kind of man he was, all his
ministers, including the prime minister, did not speak as candidly
as they should have and unanimously uttered "Yes, sir" when
they should have registered strong dissent.

I want all of you to know that I am different. The empire is
large and its population enormous. There are thousands of matters to be taken care of, each of which has to be closely coor-
dinated with the others in order to bring about maximum ben-

efit. Each matter must be thoroughly investigated and thought out before a recommendation is submitted to the prime minister, who, having consulted all the men knowledgeable in this matter, will then present the recommendation, modified if necessary, to the emperor for approval and implementation. It is impossible for one person, however intelligent and capable, to be able to make wise decisions by himself. Acting alone, he may be able, if he is fortunate, to make five right decisions out of ten each day. While we congratulate him for the five right decisions he has made that bring benefit to the country, we tend to forget the enormous harm that results from the implementation of the other five decisions that prove to be wrong. How many wrong decisions will he accumulate in a period of days, months, and years if he makes five such decisions every day? How, in that case, can he not lose his country or throne? Instead he should delegate authority to the most able and virtuous men he can find and supervise their work from above most diligently. When he makes clear to them that he will not tolerate any violation of the law, it is doubtful that they will abuse the authority with which they have been entrusted.

I want all of you to know that whenever an imperial decree is handed down you should carefully study its content and decide for yourselves whether all or part of it is or is not wise or feasible. If you have any reservations, postpone the enforcement and petition me immediately. You can do no less as my loyal ministers.

*   *   *   *   *

Governing a country is like taking care of a patient. The better the patient feels, the more he should be looked after, lest in a moment of complacency and neglect one irrevocably reverse the recovery process and send him to death. Likewise, when a country has only recently recovered from chaos and war, those responsible for running the country should be extremely diligent in their work, for false pride and self-indulgence will inevitably return the country to where it used to be and perhaps make it worse.

I realize that the safety of this nation relies to a great extent on what I can or may do and consequently I have not relaxed for a moment in doing the best I can. But I cannot do it alone. You gentlemen are my eyes and ears, legs and arms, and should do your best to assist me. If anything goes wrong anywhere in the empire, you should let me know immediately. If there is less than total trust between you and me and consequently you and I cannot do the best we can, the nation will suffer enormous damage.

*   *   *   *   *

As the ancients say, a friend in need is a friend indeed. If mutual assistance governs the relations between two friends, how can it not do so between a king and his ministers? Whenever I read of Chieh's execution of Kuan Lung-feng and Han Ching-ti's execution of Ch'ao Ts'o,[3] I cannot but feel deeply about the mistakes these monarchs made. Contrary to these monarchs, I am asking you gentlemen to speak candidly on matters that you believe are most important to the well-being of the nation, even though the opinion you express may not coincide with my own. Needless to say, there will be no penalty of any kind, let alone execution, for opinions honestly held.

Recently I have made several decisions that are clear violations of the law, even though such violations were not apparent to me at the time when the decisions were made. You gentlemen obviously thought that these violations were inconsequential and therefore abstained from speaking about them. The truth is that the most consequential acts are usually an accumulation of acts of less consequence and in order to prevent the greatest harm, one has to make sure that even the smallest harm does not occur. It will be too late to reverse the course after small disasters have coalesced to become a great one. Keep in mind that a government does not fall because of the occurrence of a major catastrophe; rather, its demise usually results from an accumulation of small misfortunes.

It enlightens one to note that not a single person expressed regret when Sui Yang-ti, a brutal and merciless tyrant, met his death at the hands of a group of assassins.[4] If you gentlemen keep in mind the reason why I have been able to overthrow the Sui regime, I, on my part, will constantly remind myself of the injustice suffered by Kuan Lung-feng and Ch'ao Ts'o. Only in this way can you and I be permanently secure.

Notes

1. This selection is translated from *Chen-kuan cheng-yao (Politics in Brief: The Chen-kuan Period, 627–49),* edited by Wu Ching (669–749). Before his death, Wu Ching served as a royal historian under Emperor T'ang Hsüan-tsung (r. 713–55).

2. In 581 Sui Wen-ti forced Chou Ching-ti, aged seven, to abdicate the throne on his behalf. The boy's father had died only one year earlier; his mother was a young widow at the time of the abdication. Four months after his abdication, the boy died under suspicious circumstances.

3. Kuan Lung-feng was a loyal but outspoken minister under King Chieh (r. 1818–1765 B.C.), last ruler of the Hsia dynasty. He was executed because of his criticism of the king's policies and personal behavior. Han Ching-ti (ca. 156–141 B.C.) ordered the execution of Ch'ao Ts'o (d. 154 B.C.) to appease some of the feudal lords who were then in rebellion. Previously Ch'ao Ts'o had recommended breaking up large feudal domains into smaller ones, a recommendation that angered the lords.

4. See selection 23.

(25)

Liu Hsü / *Taxation during the T'ang Dynasty*[1]

The law governing land distribution and taxation that was promulgated in the seventh year of Wu-teh [A.D. 624] read in part as follows:

Each adult male is to be granted one *ch'ing* [100 *mou* or 15.13 acres] of land. A person incurably ill or disabled will receive forty *mou* of land. A widowed wife or concubine will receive thirty *mou.* The head of a household will receive twenty *mou* in addition to his regular allotment. Of the amount of land each person [an adult male] receives, 20 percent is hereditary and the rest is redistributable. Upon the death of the grantee, the hereditary portion can be inherited by the head of the household next in line, while the redistributable portion is to be returned to the government for redistribution among other people.

The yearly tax obligations of each adult male toward the government are threefold: rent *(tsu)* that amounts to two piculs of grain, requisitions *(t'iao)* that vary in accordance with the products of his native district, and labor services *(yung)*. In fulfilling his requisition obligations, he can deliver to the government two *chang* [approximately twenty feet] of damask silk, plus three [Chinese] ounces of floss. If he chooses to pay in cloth, the assessment will be increased by 20 percent, plus three catties of hemp. As for labor services, he is required to work twenty days each year for the government.

If a taxpayer so desires, he can translate his labor obligations into payment in kind, at the rate of three [Chinese] feet of silk for each day of labor services. He will be exempt from requisition obligations if, when the necessity arises, he is called upon to work twenty-five instead of twenty days. He is to be exempt from both rent and requisition obligations if he is called upon to render labor services for a period of thirty days. Under no circumstances should his labor obligations toward the government last for a period longer than fifty days. . . .

The tripartite tax system, as described above, had functioned well during the early period of the T'ang dynasty. It began to deteriorate by the K'ai-yüan period [713–41] when T'ang Hsüan-tsung, a Taoist-oriented emperor who adopted a policy of benign neglect during a time of peace and prosperity, ordered a cessation of population registration for tax purposes. Population increased at a fast rate during this period; yet there was no provision in the law to tax the increased population. Under the circumstances only a short time had to elapse before the tax registers no longer reflected reality and were in fact totally useless. People long dead were still recorded as bona fide taxpayers, while others who had lost their land still appeared as landowners. Many families had become rich, while others had become poor, thus invalidating the old classification of households according to income. Yet the same tax registers, despite their inaccuracy, were still relied on by the government for tax assessment.

No provision in the tax law was more abused than that applicable to the veterans. According to the law, those who served as soldiers on the frontier were exempt from rent and requisition obligations and were supposed to be discharged and allowed to return home at the end of a six-year period. However, because they were called upon to fight so many battles, most of the frontier soldiers died long before the expiration of their tenure of service. But their commanders, doubtless relying on the emperor's good graces, chose not to report their deaths so they themselves could pocket the salaries of the dead soldiers. Thus, long after they had perished on the frontier, the names of these soldiers continued to appear in the books as bona fide taxpayers.

During the T'ien-pao period [742–55] the commissioner of revenue was a man named Wang Kung who insisted that a person whose name appeared in the tax registers must be a tax evader if he could not be located anywhere and, having determined to collect the largest amount of revenue possible regardless of any other consideration, imposed on the families of the deceased soldiers thirty years of taxation, namely, thirty-six minus the six years when these soldiers were legally exempt from taxation. The families involved had no place to voice their grievances, and the tripartite tax system, which had functioned well at one time, was now greatly abused.

The situation worsened further beginning with the Chih-teh period [756–57]. By then the country had plunged into a major war which was inevitably followed by universal conscription, widespread famine, and epidemic disease. The government ordered the requisition of all kinds of goods, and their transportation necessitated the employment of forced labor, which in turn emptied most households of adult males, leaving few bona fide taxpayers behind. To raise more revenue for the war effort, the commissioner of revenue and the commissioner of transport sent their respective agents all over the empire to collect as much as possible. Meanwhile, on the local level, the military governors-general, as well as the military governors, separately and without coordination, did likewise. Thus a taxpayer, if he could still be found, was supposed to pay taxes to all four authorities, none of whom had jurisdictional powers over the others. The imperial government had no idea of what its commissioners were doing; nor were the commissioners informed of the local authorities' tax-collecting activities. Tribute from the provinces, when it occasionally arrived, went straight to the treasury of the royal household, unaccountable and unapproachable by the imperial government. To make the situation worse, the payment of tribute was often manipulated, with cunning and dexterity, by powerful but unprincipled ministers as a means to enrich themselves. They demanded tribute in the name of the emperor but appropriated the tribute for their own uses once it arrived. In most cases, the amount they managed to steal was valued at millions of standard coins.

On the local level such provinces as Honan, Shantung, Ching-hsiang [modern Hupeh], and Chiennan [modern Szechuan] remitted little or nothing to the imperial government. With a heavy concentration of troops at their command, the authorities of these provinces collected taxes for their own support and decided for themselves whether to increase or decrease their administrative personnel or the amount of salary their employees should receive. They in fact did whatever they pleased, with no reference to the imperial government whatsoever. The various excuses under which taxes were levied numbered several hundred, as new taxes were imposed without in the meantime eliminating the old ones. As different forms of taxation piled upon one another, taxpayers toiled to exhaustion to meet the demands and in numerous cases sold their dear ones to fulfill their tax obligations. Hardly had a ten-day period passed by without them having to repair to the local government to pay some kind of tax. To keep on the pressure, many local governments assigned to each unit of one thousand households a tax collector who lived off his charges like an autocratic parasite.

To enable themselves to be qualified for tax exemption, many rich families volunteered their sons as officials of some sort in the bureaucracy; failing that, they sent their sons to the monasteries. Unfortunately these two avenues of tax exemption were not readily available to people of poor families. This meant, of course, that the poor families would have to shoulder more than their normal share of the tax burden. Without the means to pay, people of poor families deserted their homesteads altogether and wandered in the countryside as "floaters"; those who chose to stay numbered no more than four or five in a hundred. This sad state of affairs lasted almost thirty years.

It was against this background that Yang Yen [727–81], in the fifteenth year of Chen-yüan [799], proposed a new tax law known as the semiannual tax system. According to this law, all levies by the government, whether they be rent, requisitions, or labor services, would be combined to form a single tax, to be paid in cash. Before a budgetary year began, the government would calculate its expenses in advance and then fix tax rates in such a way as to yield enough to cover these expenses. For tax purposes the difference between permanent and temporary residences was to be abolished; a person would be registered as a taxpayer wherever he actually lived. Age made no difference in the amount of taxes a person had to pay; the only criterion was income: the rich would pay more and the poor would pay less. As for traveling merchants who had no residence to speak of, they would be taxed one-thirtieth the value of their merchandise by the district or provincial authorities in whose territorial jurisdiction they bought or sold their merchandise. In any case the amount of taxes they had to pay should be neither more nor less than that paid by other people with the same income. Taxes were to be paid twice a year, once in the summer and again in the fall. If this proved to be inconvenient, local authorities were allowed to make the necessary adjustment. Generally speaking, the summer taxes were due before the end of the sixth month and the autumn taxes before the end of the eleventh month. At the end of each year the tax registers would be revised to reflect the increase or decrease of the taxpaying households. The revision was to be conducted by the commissioner of revenue of the Executive Secretariat.

Emperor T'ang Teh-tsung [r. 780–804] was very pleased with Yang Yen's tax proposal and ordered it to be enforced throughout the empire. The tax officials, however, opposed it, on the grounds that the tripartite tax system, which had been in force for more than four hundred years, could not be changed without causing great harm. The emperor went ahead with its enforcement anyway, and his confidence in it was more than justified when all the taxpayers considered it just and convenient. Besides, soon after the enactment of the new tax law, fewer and fewer people deserted their homesteads and more and more people were interested in settling down permanently. Tax revenues increased substantially, even though tax rates remained the same. Tax registers, for the first time in a long period, reflected reality and became most reliable. Moreover, tax collectors also became more honest, since they were given less chance to be otherwise. The imperial government, finally, succeeded in repossessing the power to tax, which it had lost for a long time.

Notes

1. The first four paragraphs of this selection, which deal with the tripartite tax system, can be found in *T'ang shu*, roll 48. The Chinese original of the rest of this selection appears in *T'ang shu*, roll 118.

(26)

Tu Kuang-t'ing / *The Story of the Curly Beard*[1]

When Emperor Sui Yang-ti [r. 605–16] went to Yangchow[2] to amuse himself, he instructed Yang Su [d. 606], the prime minister, to remain in the capital to be in charge of the central administration. Yang, an old and conceited man, regarded himself as indispensable and his own power as incontestable at a time when the empire was already plunged into chaos and war. He lived a life of pure luxury, so extravagantly conducted that it far exceeded the norm customarily allowed among the king's ministers. When guests or other ministers came to pay their respects, they inevitably found him sitting high on a couch among beautiful women, without ever rising from his seat to greet them. Of beautiful women he had many; moreover, their number continued to increase as he became more and more advanced in age. Living for the purpose of pleasure, he, needless to say, had no concept of his own responsibility to hold the empire together, nor did he know how.

One day a commoner named Li Ching [ca. 571–649] paid him a visit and presented to him a plan that could, said its author, save the empire. While receiving this visitor, Yang Su sat high on his couch as usual; the visitor, having a high regard for himself, was greatly annoyed. "The empire is in chaos and rebels can be found everywhere," said Li Ching. "How can you, sir, sit complacently on that couch when you, as the emperor's most trusted servant, should be most concerned with rallying the nation's talents to save the empire?" Quite taken aback by these blunt remarks, Yang Su suddenly became serious and rose from his seat to greet the visitor. He liked what Li Ching had to say and accepted his plan before dismissing him.

While explaining his plan with great eloquence, Li Ching happened to notice that a young woman of great beauty, who held a red horsewhisk[3] beside the prime minister, stared at him time and again. When Li Ching was about to leave the prime minister's residence, the young woman reappeared behind a railing and asked one of the guards who the visitor was and where he lived. Since the question was loud enough for Li to hear, Li replied directly without using the guard as an intermediary. The young woman repeated the answer after Li, being afraid that she might not be able to remember it.

Early in the morning when Li Ching was still lying on his bed in the hotel room, he heard a continuous knocking at the door, interrupted occasionally by a low voice calling his name. He got up, opened the door, and found himself in front of a stranger. The stranger, wearing a large hat and a blue cloak, was holding a cane on his shoulder, at the end of which hung a traveling bag.

"Who are you?" Li inquired.

"I was the person who held the red horsewhisk," the stranger replied.

Having invited the stranger in, Li Ching helped him with his hat and cloak, only to see, happily, the emergence of a beautiful woman. The woman did not wear any makeup, but she did wear the finest clothes. Once her identity was revealed, she curtsied and was saluted in return.

"I have waited on the prime minister long and have seen many prominent men in the world," the young woman spoke calmly without expressing much emotion. "But I have never seen a man like you. As a vine cannot survive long without climbing a tree for support, I have come here to join you of my own accord."

Though happily surprised at the request, Li Ching was nevertheless fearful of the consequences. "What would happen if the prime minister found out about your escape?"

"There is nothing to fear from that corpse," the young woman replied. "Many of his women have already run away, knowing that the old man could die at any moment. The old man went through the motion of locating them but was never really serious. I have thought about this matter for a long time. You should put any doubts of yours to rest."

"What is your name?"

"Chang."

"Any brothers or sisters?"

"I am the oldest of several."

Having decided to take this young woman as his own, Li Ching began to look her over more closely. She was perhaps eighteen or nineteen and had a smooth, flawless complexion; her manner was charming and yet subdued; her speech was cultured and her

use of words impeccable; and, most importantly, her tempera-
ment seemed to be mild and measured. This was the kind of
woman he had always dreamed about; now she was standing
before him and asked him to take her! What on earth had he done
to deserve this grand prize from Heaven? While he was thus
congratulating himself, a sense of doom suddenly struck him: if
they were caught, that would be the end of both of them.
Throughout the morning he was restless, as joy and fear took
turns dominating his mind. The matter was not helped by the
repeated appearance of many strangers outside the room who,
hearing a female voice that aroused their curiosity, tried vainly
to take a peek through the window.

For several days they stayed inside their hotel, never daring to
venture outside. They heard that a search was being made for the
missing woman, but in a routine, casual manner as Chang had
correctly predicted. Finally, convinced that the danger was over,
Li Ching and his woman made preparation to leave and set out
for Taiyuan, several hundred miles northeast of Ch'angan, the
capital.

In Lingshih, a city between Ch'angan and Taiyuan, Li Ching
and his wife (as Chang should be regarded by this time) took
lodging in a country inn. Early in the morning, after they had
made their bed, fired the furnace, and put a piece of meat in a
cooking pot, Li Ching went outside to groom his horse, leaving
his wife alone in the room to dress herself. Since her hair was
extraordinarily long, she combed it beside the bed, so it would
not touch the floor. Slowly she combed her hair, while reflecting
on the marital bliss of the previous evening, occasionally with a
faint smile.

Outside the inn, as Li Ching continued to groom his horse, a
man riding on a donkey slowly appeared in the distance. As he
came close, Li Ching could not help noticing the man's unusual
appearance. The man was of medium height, which impressed
no one; what really impressed him was the thick growth of his
beard. The beard was red, curly, and long and covered not only
the lower part of his face but also the neck and part of his chest
as well. Having arrived at the inn, the man quickly dismounted
from his donkey and went straight in. On his way he caught sight
of Mrs. Li's profile and decided to walk in. Once in, he unloaded
a traveling bag from his shoulder and placed it at the foot of the
furnace. Then, finding a pillow on the bed, he lay on it and began

to watch the young woman combing her hair. He did all this without uttering a single word.

Li Ching was furious. Yet the man went through this series of actions so naturally that Li was quite taken aback, not knowing whether he should be more amused than angered. But an explosion would sooner or later take place, his wife reasoned, if she did not do anything about it. Holding her hair in one hand, she slowly turned around to face the window and then, with the other hand, signaled her husband that he should keep his anger in check. Having little time to lose, she did her hair quickly. As soon as this was done, she rose from her seat, curtsied before the stranger, and asked him what his name was.

"My surname is Chang," the stranger replied while still lying on the pillow.

"What a wonderful coincidence!" she responded enthusiastically. "My name is Chang too. You must be my brother."

She curtsied again and was finally saluted by the Curly Beard in return.

"How do you rank among your brothers and sisters?" she asked.

"I am the third born among them. How do you rank among yours?"

"I am the oldest," she replied.

The Curly Beard seemed to be overjoyed by the answer. "How lucky I am! I have unexpectedly met my first sister."

"Husband Li," Chang cried aloud through the window. "Come here to meet my third brother."

Li Ching came in and saluted. Then all three seated themselves around the furnace and chatted.

"What kind of meat is there in this pot?" asked the Curly Beard.

"Mutton; it must be about ready now," Li Ching replied.

"I am starved," said the Curly Beard.

Li Ching fetched a loaf of bread and handed a large portion over to the Curly Beard. The Curly Beard took a knife from his pocket and cut the bread and the meat with it. Having finished his meal, he chopped the rest of the meat at random and then went outside to feed his donkey with it. He did all this quickly without pausing to say "by your leave," as if he had known the Lis all his life.

"You look like a poor man to me," the Curly Beard spoke again after he had fed the donkey. "How in the world did you manage to find this extraordinary woman for your wife?"

"I am indeed poor," Li Ching replied, "but that does not mean I do not have any ambition."

"What ambition?"

"I do not talk about it very often."

"You have not answered my question."

"I presume I could talk about it with someone who regards himself as my brother-in-law."

Then Li Ching revealed his ambition in detail.

"Where are you two going from here?" asked the Curly Beard.

"Taiyuan," Li Ching replied.

"In that case, we will have to part company soon."

The Curly Beard asked for wine, but there was no wine anywhere in the room. "West of the inn there is a tavern," Li Ching suggested.

"Splendid!" said the Curly Beard. "You must join me. I do not like to drink alone."

In the tavern the two ordered drinks and toasted each other.

"I have some appetizers to go with the wine," said the Curly Beard. "Would you like to share them with me?"

"If you insist," Li Ching replied.

The Curly Beard opened his traveling bag and took out a human head, a heart, and a liver. He returned the head to the bag and started to cut the heart and the liver with his pocket knife. He ate heartily and handed some of his preparation over to Li Ching who also ate it. "This belonged to a heartless, ungrateful individual whom I had hated for ten years," he explained. "Now that I have caught up with him, I shall have no more regret."

"You do not look like an ordinary man to me," the Curly Beard spoke again between sips. "In your destination of Taiyuan, is there any man whom you would regard as truly outstanding?"

"Yes, there is," Li Ching replied. "He is a leader born great, a true Son of Heaven. As for the rest I have heard about, they may someday become generals and marshals."

"What is his name?"

"His surname is Li, the same as mine."

"How old is he?"

"No more than twenty years old."

"What is he doing at the moment?"

"He is a son of the local commander."

"I have suspected that," said the Curly Beard. "I would like to meet him myself. Will you introduce him to me?"

"Liu Wen-ching [568–619], a friend of mine, knows him well," Li Ching replied. "We shall meet the young man through his effort. By the way, why do you wish to meet him?"

"The diviner says that there is something extraordinary in the air of Taiyuan," the Curly Beard replied. "I wish to find out about this myself. You are leaving tomorrow. When do you think you will be in Taiyuan?" Li Ching told him the day when he would arrive.

"Early in the morning on the day after your arrival," said the Curly Beard, "please wait for me at the Fenyang Bridge."[4] Having said this, he hastily took his leave.

Returning to the inn, Li Ching told his wife about the man's words and conduct in the tavern. They reflected on the day's happenings and were not certain whether they should be pleased or alarmed. After a long silence, Li Ching finally said that a man like the Curly Beard would not deceive and that there was no reason why they should be afraid of him. Having agreed on this point, Li Ching and his wife proceeded to Taiyuan the next day.

Li Ching met the Curly Beard on schedule at the Fenyang Bridge and, as agreed, took him to see Liu Wen-ching. "I have brought a famous physiognomist with me," he went to Liu's house and reported. "He has wanted to meet you for a long time. Will you kindly receive him?"

Having always had a high regard for Li Ching's judgment of men, Liu Wen-ching readily agreed to invite the Curly Beard as his guest. Moreover, he wanted to know what the physiognomist had to say about his friend Li Shih-min, the second son of Li Yüan, the local commander. Therefore, as soon as the Curly Beard was inside the house, he sent for Li Shih-min. He had no idea that the primary purpose of this visit, as far as the Curly Beard was concerned, was to take a good look at the famous young man himself.

Shortly afterward, Li Shih-min arrived. He was casually attired, wearing his fur on only one arm, leaving the other sleeve hanging at his side. He was pleasant and cheerful, much more mature than his age would normally indicate. He was handsome, of course; what seemed to make him so different and important was something inside him that radiated outward, something that was intuitively sensed but could never be adequately described. In him the Curly Beard found the unique quality of combined power and trust, authority and compassion, the kind of combination that great leaders had. There was indeed a world of difference, thought the Curly Beard, between this man and Sui Yang-ti who killed anyone impudent enough to bear him bad tidings.

The Curly Beard, as the physiognomist, sat at the end of the table, scrutinized the young man, and never uttered a word. Having reached a decision, he called Li Ching aside and told him what he thought. "A true Son of Heaven," he whispered. Li Ching in turn conveyed the verdict to Liu Wen-ching who was greatly overjoyed as a result.

"I am more than 80 percent certain about my opinion of that young man," said the Curly Beard as soon as he and Li Ching were outside in the street. "I have to consult a Taoist friend of mine before I can be absolutely certain." He asked Li Ching to return to the capital with his wife and to meet him again in a tavern on a certain day. "The tavern is called Mahsingtung, and the time of the meeting is noon," he continued. "When you see two donkeys at the entrance of the tavern, you will know that my Taoist friend and I are drinking upstairs. Walk right in and proceed immediately to the second floor."

After returning to his hotel room, Li Ching consulted with his wife as to what they should do next. Without hesitation, she urged him to follow the Curly Beard's instructions by returning immediately to the capital.

On the day of the meeting, Li Ching arrived at the Mahsingtung Tavern at noon and, surely enough, there were two donkeys tied to the post in the tavern yard. Entering the inn, he quickly ascended a flight of stairs that led to the second floor. At the end of the staircase he saw the Curly Beard and a man in the Taoist robe. Both seemed to be extremely pleased with his punctual appearance and invited him to drink. They had one drink after another; considerable time elapsed before the Curly Beard spoke of the purpose of their meeting. "In a wooden chest downstairs there are one hundred thousand pieces of silver," said he. "Use part of the money to buy a decent house for your wife in a secluded area; the rest should go to her for living expenses. You have to be away from her for awhile since I need your service." Then he told Li Ching the date when they should meet again at the Fenyang Bridge.

Both the Curly Beard and the Taoist priest appeared on the day of the meeting. Li Ching, guessing correctly the purpose of this meeting, invited both of them to see his friend Liu Wen-ching. Liu was playing chess when the three arrived. After a few pleasantries, he asked the Taoist priest to join him in a friendly game. A message was then sent to Li Shih-min, saying that a good game was in progress and that he should by no means miss the fun. The game turned out to be very good indeed, as each player fought vigorously for every piece on the board.[5] Both Li Ching and the Curly Beard watched it from the side with intense interest.

The game was not yet completed when Li Shih-min arrived. They all rose to greet him, including the Taoist priest whom he met for the first time. Having heard how well the game was being played, he asked the Taoist priest about his strategy in winning a chess game. "Do not let me interrupt the game," said he finally after he had conversed for a few minutes. The Taoist priest returned to the game, but he could no longer concentrate, try as he might. He decided to concede, even though the eventual outcome of the contest was far from clear. "The game is lost." He uttered a long sigh and pushed the board aside. "It is a total loss; what else can I say?" He left with the Curly Beard shortly afterward.

"China will not be yours since she has already found her own leader," the Curly Beard heard the Taoist priest say as soon as they were outside. "But you should by no means feel totally rejected. Outside China there are places where you can invest your talent and energy more profitably and succeed in doing what you cannot accomplish in China." The Taoist priest's remarks canceled whatever reservation the Curly Beard had had about his own judgment of Li Shih-min. They had come to Tai-yuan to make a final assessment of their own prospects vis-à-vis Li Shih-min's. A unanimous verdict had been handed down; there was nothing more they could do.

Before leaving Taiyuan, the Curly Beard had another meeting with Li Ching. "The day after your return to the capital," said the Curly Beard, "come to visit me at my home and make sure to bring your wife with you." This was the first time that the Curly Beard mentioned his home, since they had always met somewhere else. "I have something for your wife which neither you nor she should refuse," the Curly Beard continued. "Since I have adopted her as my own sister, I cannot very well let her live a life of poverty, can I?" Without waiting for an answer, he sighed and left.

On the day after their return to Ch'angan, Li Ching and his wife went to see the Curly Beard as they had been instructed. The residence, at least from the outside, was far from impressive. They knocked at a small wooden door, and a female voice responded. "His lordship has waited for you for a long time," said the voice.

Entering the small door, they found a long corridor which led to another door. Then there were a second corridor and a third door. Each door was larger and more decorative than the preceding one; so was each corridor. When they finally reached the main hall, forty maidens lined up on both sides and curtsied as they approached. "His lordship wishes to receive his honorable guests in the Eastern Hall," announced a man who seemed to be the head butler. Suddenly twenty butlers, ten on each side, appeared from nowhere; together they ushered Li Ching and his wife to the Eastern Hall. The Eastern Hall was richly decorated with luxuries: jewels, mirrors, paintings, and silk, the likes of which Li Ching had never seen before. At one end of the hall were two dressing rooms, one for men and one for women, in which Li and his wife were requested to change their clothes from ordinary street wear to the most luxurious. Finally seated in the hall, they waited for the Curly Beard to appear.

"Here comes his lordship," a voice outside the hall announced. At the entrance of the hall appeared the Curly Beard, but not the Curly Beard they used to know. Here was a man of noble bearing, richly attired in furs and impeccable in his manner. He radiated with happiness the moment he saw them. He asked permission to present his wife who proved to be as beautiful and elegant as the occasion would have called for. A table was then set for four and they dined amid music provided by a troupe of female entertainers in the background. After the dinner, they continued to chat, while wine was poured regularly into their cups.

After all had had enough food and wine, the Curly Beard gave a signal, and suddenly a door on one side of the hall swung wide open. Through the door and into the hall came one chest after another, each carried by two servants. The chests, twenty altogether, were then neatly positioned in front of Li Ching and his wife. The servants opened the chests, revealing brocades of the finest embroidery. After the brocades were lifted up, Li Ching saw in each chest hundreds of keys and dozens of registration books.

"These keys and registration books indicate the properties I own throughout the empire, the properties I have accumulated for the performance of a great deed," the Curly Beard explained. "Since I cannot do the things I wanted to do in China, all these properties are of no use to me and are now yours." Before Li Ching could raise any objection, the Curly Beard continued: "If I insist upon fighting it out, the war will last twenty or thirty years, entailing enormous sufferings for all people in China and yet changing little as far as the final outcome is concerned. China has already found her leader; there is no place here for me. In a few years the young man in Taiyuan will unify China and usher in a new era of peace and prosperity which has been long overdue. As a dragon generates the clouds around it, a great leader will attract worthy followers. You, sir, are fortunate to have lived at a time when a true leader exists and, with your talent and ability, will doubtless serve him well. In return, you, of course, will be richly rewarded."

Turning to Li Ching's wife, the Curly Beard continued: "As for my adopted sister, let me say that it takes an unusual woman to recognize an unusual man. In the long run her happiness will result not so much from what you can do for her personally, important though that is, as from your willingness and ability to serve your chosen leader and, through him, to serve all the people in China. I am now leaving China, but by no means should you feel sorry for me. Ten years from today, if you happen to hear about some unusual event that takes place hundreds of miles away in Southeast Asia, you know that I have succeeded. Then you and my adopted sister can toast me while facing the south."

Before Li Ching had time to respond, the Curly Beard ordered all of his servants to line up in the hall. "Mr. and Mrs. Li are from now on your new masters," he announced. "Serve them well as you have served me." Then he gave the order that two horses be saddled immediately; when this was done, he and his wife, accompanied by a servant, rode away. They were never to be seen again.

Having taken over the Curly Beard's properties, including the house, Li Ching became one of the wealthiest men in China. He contributed generously to Li Shih-min's cause; his financial contributions helped the latter, eventually, to unify the empire.

Exactly ten years after Li Shih-min had ascended the throne as Emperor T'ang T'ai-tsung [A.D. 637], Li Ching, then serving as vice-president of the Executive Secretariat, came across a report submitted by a Chinese tributary state in Southeast Asia. "A fleet of one thousand ships, manned by one hundred thousand warriors, invaded the kingdom of Fu-yü[6] from the sea," stated the report. "The latest news is that the invaders have killed the king, pacified the country, and installed their own leader as the new ruler." The report convinced Li Ching that the Curly Beard had indeed succeeded outside China. He hurried home to tell the good news to his wife, who was greatly overjoyed as a result. Then both husband and wife, changing into their formal attire, stepped outside the house and faced the south. Raising the wine cups above their heads, they shouted simultaneously: "Congratulations!"

Notes

1. Tu Kuang-t'ing (850–933) was a prolific writer of the T'ang dynasty, though the short story translated here has remained for centuries the best-known among his writings. Having failed to pass the metropolitan examination as a young man, he entered a Taoist temple as a priest. In the 880s he was summoned from his mountain retreat to enter governmental service, where he remained for the rest of his life. Perhaps because of his Taoist background, most of his writings, including this one, carry a strong sense of Taoist fatalism. The Chinese original of this short story can be found in *T'ai-p'ing Records* (*T'ai-p'ing kuang-chi*), roll 193.

2. Yangchow, a city located in modern Kiangsu province, was famous for its fine scenery and beautiful women throughout Chinese history. Sui Yang-ti went there to enjoy himself in 605.

3. A horsewhisk is a whisk made of horsehair. It is used as a religious or philosophical symbol rather than as a duster. In the hand of a Taoist, it is supposed to sweep away worldly cares. One may still find it in some of the Taoist temples.

4. The bridge, still standing, is located in the eastern section of Taiyuan.

5. The game is called *wei-ch'i* ("game of encirclement") in China, *go* in Japan.

6. Early during the T'ang dynasty the kingdom of Fu-yü was actually

located in eastern Manchuria, not in Southeast Asia. Since the author obviously knew this fact, a possible explanation for this deliberate error is that he wanted to emphasize the fictional aspect of the story, at least that part of the story dealing with the Curly Beard's invasion of the Fu-yü kingdom. There is also the possibility that he did not wish to embarrass the kingdom allegedly or actually invaded.

CHAPTER

6

The Two Sungs (1)

DURING his advanced years Liang Ch'i-ch'ao (1873–1929), a leading intellectual of China at the turn of the century, regretted deeply that he no longer had the time to fulfill an ambition of his younger days, namely, to read all of China's dynastic histories, from the first to the last page. Objectively speaking, Liang should not have felt too guilty, since thousands of scholars in China must have made the same resolution during their youth, only to see years quickly pass by without ever carrying out that resolution. The few who did carry it out include Chao Yi (1727–1814) who, based upon his careful reading of the dynastic histories (twenty-two at his time and twenty-five now), wrote a masterpiece of his own. The masterpiece, *Random Notes on the Twenty-two Dynastic Histories (Erh-shih-erh shih tsa-chi)*, traces the background of each book, explores its inconsistencies, and sometimes points out its errors. More useful, however, is his grouping of scattered materials into one topic, thus enabling a reader, at one glance, to grasp the essentials relating to that topic. An example appears here as selection 27, entitled "Bureaucratic Affluence." Most students of history must have heard of the pampering of intellectuals by the Sung government, but it takes Chao Yi's documentation to dramatize the point.

The Sung dynasty, founded by a scholarly general, conformed better to the Confucian image of an ideal state than any Chinese dynasty before or since, so much so that one is irresistibly tempted to describe it as having a government of intellectuals, by intellectuals, and most unfortunately, primarily for intellectuals. The prestige associated with a learned scholar was enormous, and the criterion whereby an aspiring student would be recognized as one was passing the metropolitan examination under the civil service examination system. As the examination road was the major avenue to power and wealth as well as prestige, the debate on an objective way to administer the examination appeared time and again among the scholars and statesmen of the Sung times. The debate involved not only the kinds of tests to be given and the kind of literary form (prose or poetry) to be emphasized, but also the merit, or the lack of it, of a quota system. The quota system became a major issue because without it, the southern Chinese, who were economically more affluent and consequently had a larger base of educated men, would inevitably dominate every metropolitan examination and provide a much larger group of the intellectual and power elite than the northern Chinese. The northerners, as one might expect, were in favor of a quota system, on the grounds that all of China, the less as well as the more affluent regions, should be proprotionally represented in the power structure. In their judgment, the quota system was not only intellectually permissible but also politically wise (selection 28).

The generous subsidy of the intellectual elite, plus the payment of annual tribute to the various enemies that had at one time or another defeated China, imposed a heavy drain on the limited financial resources of the Sung regime. Sung China had a territory much smaller than T'ang China, and yet its expenditures were much larger. This means that taxes had to be increased time and again to meet the expenses. It is against this background that one must view Wang An-shih's reforms, the primary purpose of which was to raise governmental revenue (selection 29). The key feature of these reforms was the green sprouts program *(ch'ing miao fa)* that authorized the government to serve as banks to lend money to the people, hopefully making a handsome profit in each of the transactions. Interestingly enough, in the debate that followed the introduction of the green sprouts program, the central issue involved not so much the soundness of the principle behind the program (the government's right, or the lack of it, to compete with the people for profit) as the abuses the program generated shortly after its introduction (selection 30). While governmental expenditures kept rising, neither Wang An-shih (1021–86) who introduced the reforms nor Ssu-ma Kuang (1018–86) who strongly opposed them ever advocated a policy of retrenchment. This shows, sadly, that any vested interest, including the vested interest of the intellectuals, is hard to dislodge once it is created, no matter how harmful it has proved to the nation as a whole.

Under the double pressure of financial crisis and foreign invasions, the North Sung regime eventually collapsed when its capital of Kaifeng, North China, was captured by the Nuchens, a seminomadic group related to modern Manchus (selection 31). Meanwhile a new Sung regime, referred to by historians as the South Sung, was established in Hangchow, South China. The South Sung regime lasted 153 years (1127–1280) until it was conquered by the Mongols.

As for source materials covering the Sung period, the standard reference is the *Sung shih (History of the Sung).* Consisting of 496 rolls, it is the richest of the dynastic histories in terms of raw material. Two other works, also classified as dynastic histories, are *Liao shih (History of the Liao)* and *Chin shih (History of the Chin)* which describe Sung's former and later enemies, respectively. All three works were compiled by a committee headed by T'o-t'o (1238–80), a Mongol scholar who once served under Kublai Khan.

Aside from the dynastic histories, the most important sources include *Source Materials Compiled as a Sequel to History as a Mirror (Hsü Tzu-chih t'ung-chien ch'ang-pien)* by Li T'ao (*chin-shih* degree, ca. 1130) and *Annals of the Chien-yen Period, 1127–62 (Chien-yen yi-lai hsi-nien yao-lu)*, by Li Hsin-ch'uan (1166–1243). In the field of foreign relations a definitive work is *Negotiations and Treaties with Our Northern Neighbors in a Period of Three Emperors (San-ch'ao pei-meng hui-pien)* by Hsü Meng-hsin (1124–1205). It is a history of peace and war between Sung and Chin during the crucial period of 1111–62. Consisting of 250 rolls, it contains a large number of original documents.

One cannot leave the source materials of the Sung period without mentioning a monumental work by Ma Tuan-lin (d. ca. 1317), entitled *A Study of Cultural Heritage (Wen-hsien t'ung-k'ao).* Previously, Tu Yu (735–812) of the T'ang dynasty had written a book entitled *A Study of Institutions (T'ung tien)*, the contents of which were organized according to topics rather than years or persons. This breaking away from both the chronological (such as the *Spring and Autumn Annals*) and biographical (such as the various dynastic histories) traditions was hailed by Ma Tuan-lin as a major development in history writing, and Ma proceeded to write a history of his own using the same method. Consisting of 348 rolls, *A Study of Cultural Heritage* traces the development of Chinese institutions from their early beginnings to the Sung times—it is particularly strong on the Sung institutions. Its author records the pros and cons of the major issues involving institutional changes and often concludes with his own assessments.

Aside from sources that are classified as history, there are numerous collections of this period that are classified as literature. But a piece of literature is as much a historical source as an official document, if one knows its background as well as the time in which it was written. For example, a book entitled *Meng-hsi Sketches (Meng-hsi pi-t'an)*, by Shen Kua (1021–85), is generally classified as "miscellaneous literature" *(chi)*; yet it records in detail the personal lives of some of the Sung dynasty's intellectual elite. It is indispensable to the study of the Sung society. The author's description of the movable type invented by his contemporary Pi Sheng in the 1040s remains one of the few primary sources insofar as the history of Chinese printing is concerned.

(27)

Chao Yi / *Bureaucratic Affluence*[1]

In the treatise on bureaucracy, the author of the *History of the Sung*[2] records the compensations for Sung officials as follows:

Premiers and chancellors: 300,000 standard coins per month in cash, plus 20 bolts of damask silk, 30 bolts of gauzy silk, and 100 ounces of floss, to be distributed on a yearly basis.

Vice-premiers and vice-chancellors: 200,000 standard coins per month in cash, plus 10 bolts of damask silk, 30 bolts of gauzy silk, and 50 ounces of floss, to be distributed on a yearly basis.

Other officials in the central government received their salaries and silk allotments in proportion to their ranks and titles.

As for local officials, governors-general and deputy governors-general received a monthly payment of 400,000 and 300,000 standard coins respectively, plus a proportional amount of silk allotments. Other local officials, being inferior in rank, were paid less.

The payments in cash and silk, as described above, were classified as regular salaries. There were also food stipends that amounted to 100 piculs of grain for premiers and chancellors, 150 piculs of grain for imperial counselors and their deputies, and 70 piculs of grain for heads of commissions and departments, 150 piculs of grain for governors-general, 100 piculs of grain for inspectors-general and garrison commanders, to be paid on a monthly basis.[3] Half of the amount was to be paid in rice and the other half in wheat. During the Hsi-ning period [1068–77] the payment in grain for all the officials on the district level was further increased: those who had hitherto received three piculs were now entitled to receive four; those who had hitherto received two piculs were now entitled to receive three; and so on.

In addition to regular salaries and food stipends, each official in the capital also received a payment in cash known as the positional allowance *(chih ch'ien)*. The amount of positional allowance was 60,000 standard coins for the grand censor and the ministers of the Six Ministries; it was 50,000 standard coins for the academicians in the Hanlin Academy. But only officials serving in the central government were entitled to this additional payment, as local officials had their own allowance, known officially as "compensation for public service" *(kung-yung ch'ien)*.

During the Yüan-feng period [1078–85] a revised schedule was put into practice that increased the amount of compensation each official received. For instance, a man serving simultaneously in two positions could receive two salaries, plus other compensations. The schedule was further revised during the Ch'ung-ning period [1102–6] when Ts'ai Ching [*chin-shih* degree, 1070] was the prime minister. It doubled the amount each official received as compared to what his predecessor had received at the beginning of the dynasty.

In addition, the government was obligated to pay for the food and clothing of the servants *(ch'ien jen)* employed by each official. (These servants were referred to as *sui shen,* or retainers, if they happened to be employed by premiers, chancellors, and governors.) The number of servants each official was entitled to have was as follows: premiers and chancellors, 70; vice-premiers and first and second ministers of each ministry, 50; governors-general, 100; deputy governors and inspectors-general, 50; and so on. Each servant received from the government a payment known as the meal fee *(ts'an ch'ien)*, which varied from 20,000 to 5,000 standard coins in a descending scale of seven steps if he happened to be employed by a court official; and it varied from 15,000 to 3,000 standard coins in a descending scale of eight steps if he happened to be employed by an imperial official. As for lesser officials, the scale of the meal fee for their respective servants had nine instead of seven or eight steps. (The servants for officials on the level of ministers in the central government, or of governors in the local government, were entitled to the meal fee as well as food and clothing allowances. All other servants, however, received only food and clothing allowances, without the meal fee.)

Generous though it was, the largess did not end here. Each official was also entitled to receive from the government, without charge, such items as tea, wine, salt, firewood, noodles, and animal feed. Those who served outside the capital received an additional amount known as "compensation for public service," as mentioned earlier. The amount varied from 20 million to 7 million standard coins, in a descending scale of four steps, for premiers and chancellors who served as acting governors-general on an *ad hoc* basis. It varied from 10 million to 3 million standard coins, in a descending scale of four steps, for governors-general.[4] Inspectors-general, garrison commanders, and other lesser officials received lesser amounts.

Aside from "compensation for public service," to each office was attached a certain amount of land, the income of which could be disposed in whatever way the occupant of that office wished. This land was known as "postal fields" *(chih t'ien)*. The Bureau of Barbarian Affairs, for instance, had 40 *ch'ing* [600 acres] of land attached to it. A garrison command had 35 *ch'ing* [525 acres] of land, while lesser offices had lesser amounts. The occupant of an office whose rank was too low to receive any "postal fields" would nevertheless receive a cash payment, known as the "tea and soup fee" *(ts'ai t'ang ch'ien)*.

During the Chien-yen period [1127–30] and shortly after the central government had settled south of the Yangtze River, the premiers and other high officials requested the reduction of their salaries and other forms of compensation to one-third of their original amounts, at a time of war and enormous expenses. When war was renewed during the K'ai-hsi period [1205–7], the same request was made, but this time the reduction was only one-half of the original amount. These reductions, however, were all done on a temporary basis. Once the war was over, the old schedule of payments was revived.

In summary, the compensation to intellectuals, whenever they were employed by the government, was most generous. On the positive side one may say that this generosity enabled all officials to concentrate on the performance of their duties, without being sidetracked by financial worries for their families; and they were generally incorruptible during their tenure of office. Not surprisingly, outstanding ministers emerged time and again during the reigns of Emperors Sung Chen-tsung [r. 998–1022], Sung Jen-tsung [r. 1023–63], and Sung Ying-tsung [r. 1064–67]. When disaster finally struck, many ministers were willing to sacrifice their lives, without hesitation or regret, for the regime they had served. Even after half of China had been lost to the enemy, the Sung regime remained fairly stable, thanks to the loyalty and devotion of its officials. During the Teh-yu period [1275–76] garrison commanders chose to die while fighting, instead of surrendering to the enemy. In fact, during none of China's many dynasties had there been so many scholar-officials who were happy and willing to die for their respective regimes as there were during the Sung dynasty, even though their deaths did not in any way help save the regime. Nevertheless, their preference of death to surrender indicates clearly their heartfelt gratitude to the government they had served.

On the negative side this generous payment to the nation's officials imposed an enormous drain on the nation's financial resources. The Sung policy seems to have been, "There is no such thing as overgenerosity to its officials; there is no such thing as overtaxation of its taxpayers." In the long run this does not seem to be a good policy for any government to follow.

Notes

1. *Erh-shih-erh shih tsa-chi*, roll 25.

2. See p. 187.

3. To appreciate the generosity of these payments, one must compare them with the income of a well-to-do farmer in the countryside who cultivated 100

mou of land (15 acres) and reaped an annual harvest of approximately 300
piculs of grain, a sizable portion of which had to go to the government as taxes.
  4. The "compensation for public service" was paid on a yearly basis.

(28)
Ssu-ma Kuang and Ou-yang Hsiu / *Two Views on the Civil Service Examinations*[1]

Ssu-ma Kuang:

In each of the metropolitan examinations the examiners who
make up the test are without exception chosen from the scholars
in the Hanlin Academy or one of the Three Institutes.[2] What
these scholars like inevitably becomes the academic fashion of
the time. This gives the examination candidates in the capital an
undisputed advantage over those in more distant areas since
they, being knowledgeable of the change of academic trends,
adjust their writing style accordingly and will, in due course, be
able to write in such a way as to enhance their chance of success
in the examinations. How can the candidates in a remote province, denied this advantage, possibly compete with them?

Confucius says, "In every ten households there must be a man
as virtuous as I am." Even in the most backward area, the master
seems to say, there can be men of true talent. Following the
principle implied in this statement, the governments of ancient
times assigned a quota of successful candidates to each district or
province in proportion to its population—some of these candidates were chosen because of their exemplary conduct while
others were chosen on account of their talent and ability—regardless of whether they were as close as blood relatives or as
remote as distant barbarians. Only in this way were all men of
merit given the opportunity to serve the country and its people.

The situation today is entirely different. Sometimes an entire
province cannot produce a single successful candidate, indicating clearly that something is wrong with the examination system
itself. According to the way we are recruiting governmental personnel today, a man cannot obtain a position of importance with

the government unless he has passed the metropolitan examination and received the "advanced scholarship" *(chin-shih)* degree. But he cannot pass the metropolitan examination and receive the "advanced scholarship" degree unless he knows how to
write prose and poetry in a way that conforms to the academic
trend prevalent in the capital at that time. To keep abreast of the
change of academic trends, scholars all over the country take
leave of their homes, desert their parents, and congregate in the
capital. Among them are many unsavory elements who, having
a bad past to hide, journey to the capital to avoid the close
scrutiny of their relatives and friends at home. Being what they
are, they cannot acquire the necessary permits in their home
districts in order to take the examination in the capital. Once in
the capital, however, any of them can claim to have come from
a district that knows him not and thus be allowed to purchase a
permit to take the examination. In recent years the number of
unsuccessful candidates who choose to stay in the capital instead
of returning to their home districts has increased enormously,
despite the various measures taken by the government to discourage them.

One reason for their continuous stay is their desire to save the
time and the expense involved in a round trip away from and
back to the capital especially if they intend, as most of them do,
to take the next scheduled examination. But there is also another
reason. In each of the metropolitan examinations most of the
successful candidates are those whose permits to take the examination have been issued by either the Department of Cultural
Affairs or the Mayoralty of Kaifeng, indicating clearly that those
who choose to remain in the capital have a better chance of
success than those who do not. Who, under the circumstances,
wishes to return to his native district? It seems that we are doing
two things simultaneously that are basically contradictory. On
one hand, we are using all kinds of inducement—power, fame,
and wealth—to encourage people to take the examinations; on
the other hand, we are enacting strong measures to discourage
them from exploiting every opportunity they have in order to be
successful in these examinations. Not surprisingly, these strong
measures exist only on paper since they cannot be effectively
enforced. This is like diking a flood with a handful of earth—the
result is known before the attempt is made.

Ou-yang Hsiu:

The examination system we are practicing today is more impartial and less subject to foul play than in any of the preceding dynasties. For this we should be most grateful to the emperors of the past who did their utmost to perfect this system. The principle that underlies this system is very simple: that an emperor, being the sovereign of all men, should regard all of his subjects as members of one family and treat them equally, without discrimination. Candidates from all the provinces are encouraged to gather in the capital to compete, and the only criterion for their success or failure is the amount of talent they have. To assure objectivity, not only are the names of the candidates covered up, but also the answers to the questions are copied before the copied answers are presented to the examiners in charge to be evaluated. The examiners in charge, consequently, have no idea whose papers they are reading, let alone where these candidates come from or whose sons they are. In short, in no way can personal bias or prejudice play any role in the evaluation process. The examination system we are practicing today may or may not be as good as some ancient system for the same purpose; but, in terms of fairness and objectivity, we cannot do better with any other system. Since the founding of this dynasty, it has been more than adequate to meet our needs.

The *Commentaries on the Book of Changes* says, "Do not invent clever devices to replace old institutions." It also says, "Do not make new laws unless the old laws have been proved inadequate." Contrary to the spirit of these two statements, many of our opinion makers constantly speak of reforms before they bother to study the issues involved. In the case of the civil service examinations, for instance, they deplore the fact that most of the successful candidates in the category of "advanced scholarship" come from the southeast and suggest that reform should be introduced in order to increase the number of successful candidates from the northwest. They do not seem to realize that in a large empire like China different regions are bound to have different customs with different emphases. The people of the southeast, being more imaginative, are fond of literature; they, consequently, have produced more successful candidates in the category of "advanced scholarship." The people of the northwest, on the other hand, are more practical; they, consequently, have produced more successful candidates in the category of "expertise in classics" *(ming ching)*. Taking into consideration the successful candidates in both categories, one will find that the total number of successful candidates for the northwesterners is approximately the same as that for the southeasterners. Having looked àt only one side of the picture, namely, only one category in the examinations, many critics immediately suggest changes in the examination system itself. These critics, in my judgment, have committed an error of partiality.

Second, at a time when we are deeply concerned with the continuous enlargement of the bureaucracy, the increase of the number of successful candidates from the northwest will of necessity mean the reduction of the number of their counterparts from the southeast, if we intend to maintain the rate of enlargement at an acceptable level, since under the law a successful candidate has to be given a governmental post to hold. In each of the metropolitan examinations conducted in recent years the number of successful candidates, as far as the southeasterners are concerned, is anywhere between twenty and thirty among a total of two or three thousand who have taken the examination in the category of "advanced scholarship." In short, the ratio of success is approximately one in a hundred—a ratio that indicates clearly that strong measures have been taken to reduce the number of successful candidates among the southeasterners. On the other hand, the northwestern candidates who choose to take the metropolitan examination in the category of "advanced scholarship" have rarely exceeded one hundred in each instance; of these one hundred a dozen or so usually succeed. In short, their chance of success is approximately one in ten, or ten times better than their counterparts from the southeast. If we increase the quota of successful candidates for the northwest while reducing the same for the southeast, as many have suggested, we would be placed in a position to punish those who have already been unjustifiably punished and to reward those to whom we have already been overgenerous. This to me is an unsound proposition.

Third, in the preliminary examinations conducted in the provinces to choose candidates for the metropolitan examination in the capital, approximately ten in a thousand are scheduled to pass, as far as the southeasterners are concerned. Their chance of success is one in a hundred, as it is in the metropolitan examination. As far as the northwesterners are concerned, approximately ten in a hundred are scheduled to pass the preliminary examinations, in a ratio of ten to one. In short, most of the southeasterners who have failed the preliminary examinations are actually better prepared, academically speaking, than most of the northwesterners who have succeeded. Even if a universal ratio of ten to one were applied to both groups, it would still mean that most southeasterners who should have passed actually failed and that most northwesterners who should have failed actually passed. This is because, first, an average southeastern candidate is academically better prepared than his northwestern counterpart and, second, the southeasterners who take the preliminary examinations are many times more numerous. A universal ratio of ten to one, applied to all the provinces, would be a clear case of the miscarriage of justice.

Fourth, a quota system for successful candidates, on the provincial as well as the metropolitan level, would mean that we attach more importance to a candidate's geographical background than to his academic preparation which is supposed to be the only qualification that counts in the examinations. If carried out, a quota system would mean that many succeed in the examination not because they have better training but because they come from the right provinces. It would also mean that many fail in the examination not because they lack the necessary academic qualifications but because they were born in the wrong place.

Fifth, a quota system, if carried out, is supposed to benefit the natives of those provinces who without it would have a difficult time passing the examinations. Do those who advocate it realize that once this system is officially enforced, many candidates who are not natives of these "deprived" provinces can nevertheless claim that they have adopted these provinces as their native residence? In fact, numerous candidates have already appeared in the Mayoralty of Kaifeng to be registered as natives of the so-called adopted provinces. Sadly, conspiracy to take advantage of the law has occurred even before the law takes effect.

Sixth, because of their lack of adequate preparation, candidates from Kwangtung and Kwangsi have rarely succeeded in the metropolitan examination. The general practice in these provinces is to send to the capital whatever talents they happen to have, and these candidates, knowing in advance that they cannot possibly succeed, return home as soon as the examination is over. Since the northerners do not wish to serve in these provinces, these candidates, by virtue of having taken the metropolitan examination, are granted the right to serve as acting officials in their respective districts. This practice, though irregular, has been specifically authorized by the imperial government in view of the unusual circumstances.[3] If a quota of ten to one is made applicable to all the provinces, the examination system will be even more abused in the case of such provinces as Kwangtung and Kwangsi than in the case of the northwestern provinces.

The six items discussed above are the most important I can think of at this moment. If the present law governing the examination is abolished and is replaced by some kind of new law that mandates a universal quota system, I am afraid that more abuses will come about than we can now visualize. The present system which recognizes talent as the only criterion and is therefore impartial to people of all the provinces is, in my judgment, most practical. It should and must be maintained.

Notes

1. Ssu-ma Kuang, who has been mentioned earlier in his capacity as a historian, was born in Hsiahsien (modern Shensi province). Here he speaks for the northerners. Ou-yang Hsiu (1007–72), the acknowledged dean of southern scholars in the capital, was born in Luling, modern Kiangsi province. Here he speaks for the southerners. Source of this selection: *Wen-hsien t'ung-k'ao*, roll 31.

2. The Three Institutes were Kuang-wen ("Cultural Enrichment"), T'ai-hsüeh ("Higher Learning"), and Lü-hsüeh ("Jurisprudence").

3. During the eleventh century Kwangtung and Kwangsi were still regarded as culturally underdeveloped areas.

(29)
T'o-t'o / *Wang An-shih*[1]

As a young man, Wang An-shih loved to read and, having an extraordinary memory, would rarely forget what he had read for the rest of his life. When he wrote, he wrote so fast that his pen seemed to have been equipped with two wings. On the surface he seemed to be careless; yet, once the work was completed, it would generate instant admiration from all those who read it. Tseng Kung [1019–83], a friend of his, showed some of his works to Ou-yang Hsiu, and the latter, also impressed, spoke highly of the young man among his influential friends.

Wang An-shih passed the metropolitan examination with distinction and was subsequently appointed a judge at Huainan [modern Kiangsu province]. Customarily, a successful candidate in the metropolitan examination, after his first tenure of office as a local official, was specifically allowed to apply for a position in one of the Three Institutes[2] by a presentation of his written works. But Wang An-shih chose not to take advantage of this custom. Consequently, after his first tenure of office as a local judge, he was transferred to Ningpo [modern Chekiang province] to serve as its magistrate. In his new capacity he constructed dikes, canals, and reservoirs to promote transportation and agriculture. He also introduced a credit program whereby a needy farmer could borrow grain from the government by paying an interest charge, and the borrowed grain, once paid, would be used as capital to be lent to other farmers in need. This credit program proved to be enormously popular in the rural areas.

Upon his installation as the premier, Wen Yen-po [ca. 999–1090] recommended Wang An-shih for a high position in the capital, bypassing the normal procedure of step-by-step promotions on the grounds that a talented man of such modesty as Wang An-shih should be generously rewarded, in order to discourage the kind of fierce competition by methods other than merit for promotion purposes. Wang An-shih was called upon to apply for a position in one of the Three Institutes; Wang, however, declined. Later, Ou-yang Hsiu recommended him as a member of the imperial censorate, an honor Wang again de-

clined, saying that his grandmother was old and ill and needed
him at home. Nevertheless, believing that the young man
needed a salary to support his family, Ou-yang Hsiu spoke to the
emperor again. As a result, Wang was appointed a judge to supervise the conduct of local officials, while serving simultaneously as
magistrate of Ch'angchou [modern Kiangsu province]. Later he
was transferred to Chiangtung [modern Kiangsu province]
where he served as a criminal judge. Finally, in the third year of
Chia-yu [1058], he came to the capital to work for the Ministry
of Finance.

Wang An-shih relished lofty but strange ideas and, thanks to
the enormous amount of learning he had accumulated, could
usually make these ideas sound plausible. There had never been
any doubt in his mind that, given the opportunity, he had both
the ability and the will to change China for the better. Based
upon this belief, he wrote a long memorial to the emperor [Sung
Jen-tsung], in which he attributed the nation's financial difficulties and the deterioration of its customs to the lack of knowledge
about sound institutions and to the inability and unwillingness on
the part of government officials to follow the policies of the sage
kings of ancient times. He cautioned, however, that these policies
should not be followed in a literal manner; it was their intent, he
said, that really mattered. To follow the intent rather than the
letter of these policies would yield one clear advantage: namely,
that they could be implemented without in the meantime shock-
ing the complacent and generating controversies. The general
principle that underlay these policies was the creation of wealth
by utilizing all the resources at the nation's command and by the
use of this wealth, once created, to promote the good of all men.
The inadequacy of revenues which had plagued all governments
since history began, he said, resulted not from the lack of adequate resources as generally assumed; rather, it resulted from the
lack of able men who knew how to utilize the available resources.
"When able men cannot be found either in the government or
outside of it," Wang An-shih continued, "who is there to assist
Your Majesty in shouldering the nation's responsibilities when
and if an emergency arises,[3] even though we have been blessed
with peace for a long time? To arrest this aimless drift, Your
Majesty is hereby requested to introduce new programs as a
means of facing any contingency that might arise. To forestall

opposition, these programs should be introduced gradually, one at a time." Whatever merit this memorial had, it became the ideological foundation of all the programs Wang An-shih later introduced when he was in power.

Before he was widely known, Wang An-shih, as a southern scholar, befriended Lü Kung-chu, Han Chiang, and Chiang's younger brother Wei. The purpose of these friendships, as far as Wang An-shih was concerned, was to promote his own career by association, since the Lü and Han families were among the most influential and prestigious in the nation. These three friends of his spoke of him highly wherever they went, and Wang An-shih, consequently, became widely known. When Sung Shen-tsung was the crown prince, Han Wei, as his secretary, would not claim credit for himself whenever the crown prince praised a particular point of view that impressed him. "This is not my point of view, sir," Han would say. "It originates from my friend Wang An-shih." Later, Han Wei recommended Wang An-shih to be the master tutor to the crown prince when he himself was scheduled to fill that post. One can imagine how much the crown prince would have liked to meet Wang An-shih in person.

As soon as Sung Shen-tsung ascended the throne, he promoted Wang An-shih to the magistracy of Nanking. Several months later, he summoned Wang to the capital to serve as an academician in the Hanlin Academy and simultaneously as an imperial counselor. In the fourth month of the first year of Hsi-ning [1068] the emperor met with Wang An-shih for the first time. "What is most important in the creation of a good government?" the emperor asked.

"The most important thing in the creation of a good government," Wang An-shih replied, "is the choice of the right method to create it."

"Will you not say that T'ang T'ai-tsung was a model monarch?"

"The example Your Majesty should follow is not T'ang T'ai-tsung, but Yao and Shun," said Wang An-shih. "The way of Yao and Shun is simple and uncomplicated and extremely easy to follow. Not knowing this fact, scholars of later ages thought that it was too lofty to be attainable."

"Your remarks have indeed posed the greatest challenge to me," the emperor responded. "As I look at myself, I am afraid that I might not be able to live up to the standard you have assigned to me. In any case, help me in the best way you can and together we may be able to attain what has been regarded as unattainable."

In the second month of the second year of Hsi-ning [1069] Wang An-shih was appointed prime minister. "Not knowing what you are and what you can do," said the emperor, "people say that you are only a bookworm, totally ignorant of practical matters."

"Sound theory is the foundation of sound practice," Wang An-shih replied. "The scholars of later days are so mediocre that they cannot understand the inseparability of theory and practice."

"What, then, is the first priority in launching a successful administration?" asked the emperor.

"The most urgent is a change of atmosphere and the introduction of new programs," Wang An-shih replied.

The emperor agreed to this assessment and ordered the establishment of the Finance Commission. From then on a series of programs was introduced, dealing with a variety of topics such as land utilization, irrigation and flood control, "green sprouts," tribute transport, *pao-chia*, draft exemption, marketing and exchange, horse conservation, and land survey. Together they were called the New Program. More than forty new posts were created to carry out the New Program throughout the empire.

The green sprouts program called upon the government to lend money to all who applied for it at a semiannual interest of 20 percent, with capital drawn from the ever-normal granaries. Normally the applicants received the money in spring [when the sprouts were green], to be paid in full in fall [after harvests had been collected]. In the tribute transport program the officials in charge were authorized to purchase goods for tribute at the lowest price possible and at a place closest to the capital, instead of having them transported from different parts of the empire. In addition, the goods thus purchased would be those actually needed by the government, instead of those produced in each of the tribute-bearing regions. According to the *pao-chia* program, every ten households in the rural areas were organized to form a *pao* ["mutual protection"], and one of every two able-bodied men in each household was required to join the militia.[4] The militiamen were drilled in the use of weaponry and the methods of warfare. In the draft exemption program all households in the empire were required to contribute to the draft assistance fund in proportion to their income, and the government would then use this fund to hire men to serve in the army, instead of having them drafted from the reluctant households. A household that had no able-bodied men or only one able-bodied man and had hitherto been exempted from military obligations was also subject to the assessment of fund contributions under the new program.

As for the marketing and exchange program, it enabled a person to borrow money from a district treasurer by submitting as collateral his land, house or houses, gold and silver, silk or silk products. The interest was 20 percent per annum, but the borrower would be assessed a penalty of 2 percent per month if he failed to pay the principal whenever it was due. The horse conservation program called for lending one horse, or the amount of money necessary to purchase one horse, to a household that chose to participate in this program. A government-appointed veterinarian was to examine the horse once every year; if the horse died of disease or some other cause, the borrower was obligated to compensate the government for the lost horse. According to the land survey program, all agricultural land was divided into sections, each of which was measured 1 million square paces, or 4,166 *mou* and 160 square paces. Land survey was conducted in the ninth month each year and, in accordance with its fertility, each section was graded on a scale of five. The amount of taxes to be paid varied in direct proportion to land fertility, rather than the amount of crops the land actually yielded.

An enormous amount of interest in agriculture was generated throughout the empire as a result of introducing the programs described above. Old dikes were repaired and abandoned reservoirs were renovated—all this indicated a new mood of the nation.

Wang An-shih also wrote commentaries on the *Book of Odes, Book of History,* and *Chou Institutions;* and these commentaries, entitled *New Interpretations (Hsin yi),* were later decreed by the Board of Education as required reading for all students and scholars. During his old age when he retired to live at Nanking, he wrote *On Words (Tzu shoh),* a book full of distortions and tinged with Buddhist and Taoist ideas. At the time when he was in power, the officials in charge of the civil service examinations tested the candidates on their knowledge of the *New Interpretations;* students and scholars, consequently, could not but read this book, even though, by following its content, they had a difficult time being consistent with themselves. The situation became so bad that all other commentaries on the classics, including those written by great scholars of the past, were abolished for examination purposes. Even the *Spring and Autumn Annals* suffered the same fate after it had been dismissed by Wang An-shih, only half in jest, as an incomplete collection of headlines in a court record.[5]

The reputation of Wang An-shih as a learned man of impeccable integrity was the talk of the capital long before his arrival to assume a position of power and influence. He did not like luxuries of any kind and was extremely frugal in the conduct of his personal life. He wore unwashed clothes and seldom took a bath. Yet all the scholars and statesmen praised him highly as a virtuous man. The only exception was Su Hsün [1009–66] who denounced him as a hypocrite and, in an essay entitled "How Can You Tell a Hypocrite" *(Pien chien lun)*, compared him to the worst demagogues of the past. Being stubborn in nature, Wang An-shih had no regard for any opinion except his own and, during the debate on the New Program, insisted on its immediate implementation despite strong opposition from other ministers. Once he made up his mind, he would not change it, whatever the circumstances. He interpreted the classics in such a way as to rationalize his own opinion and, being an unusually talented man, could easily and quickly write a rationale of such eloquence that his political opponents had a difficult time refuting him. He once remarked: "There is nothing to fear from Heaven; nor are the laws of our forebears relevant. Why should I care about what other people think of me?" During his tenure of office, he dismissed practically all the old and conservative ministers and replaced them with young men of high intelligence but of little experience. Eventually he resigned from the premiership when a nationwide drought occurred. Later, he was called upon to assume responsibility again, but his second premiership lasted only one year. From then on and for the last eight years of Sung Shen-tsung's reign, he received no calls from the imperial government.

Notes

1. *Sung shih*, roll 327.
2. See note 2, p. 197.
3. This refers to a possible invasion by Liao and the ensuing warfare.
4. According to other sources, all able-bodied men in each household, with the exception of one, were required to join the militia.
5. *Ch'ao pao*, here translated as "court record," was a daily account of important events in the imperial government, sometimes including complete texts of outgoing decrees and incoming memorials. It was more like the British *Parliamentary Papers* or American *Congressional Record* than a daily newspaper.

(30)
Ssu-ma Kuang and Wang An-shih / *Two Views on the New Program*[1]

Ssu-ma Kuang:

Of all the policies from which the nation suffers most, none is more damaging than the following: First, there is the granting of easy credit under the green sprouts program which increases the people's debt without in the meantime bringing any benefit to the government. Second, the operation of the draft exemption program, whatever its original purpose might be, has only succeeded in exempting the rich from the draft while increasing the tax burden of the poor. All the funds collected under this program have been used for no better purpose than the support of a group of shiftless loafers.[2] Third, the market and exchange program is wrong not only because it places the government in a position to compete with the people for profit but also because it gives official sanction to the waste of government-owned materials. Fourth, to harbor the thought of launching adventures abroad while China itself remains to be pacified cannot but bring us more harm than good. Fifth, the organization of the rural population under the *pao-chia* system[3] and their training in the use of military weapons have brought nothing except unnecessary disturbances to the countryside. Last, the operation of numerous flood control and irrigation projects, run by a group of wild but clever men, has resulted in enormous waste of manpower and material.

In terms of the harm they have brought about, the first two among the six items described above are definitely the worst. Physical strength is born with man and, combined with the natural fertility of the soil, produces such useful objects as grain and silk. But money, in the form of coins, is an artificial product of the government which people themselves are not allowed to produce. Yet, both the green sprouts program and the draft exemption program require, in all transactions, payment in coins, the manufacturing of which is a monopoly of the government.

There was a scarcity of coins long before the introduction of the New Program; they are more scarce today. A wealthy merchant might have them in a moderate amount, but a farmer, certainly, does not have them in abundance. Even a rich farmer thinks of his welfare in terms of enlarging his land ownership so as to harvest more crops, repairing old houses or constructing new ones, or owning his own oxen instead of having to borrow from others. He does not hoard coins. As for a poor farmer, he does not have much to wear or eat; he might even be someone else's tenant, working hard to be able to ward off hunger. He rarely has the opportunity of seeing any coins, let alone owning them. Recognizing this fact, the enlightened governments of ancient times taxed people according to what they actually possessed or produced, namely, the payment of grain and silk and the rendering of labor services. Not until the latter part of the T'ang dynasty, after a major disaster had occurred, was the payment of taxes in cash enforced for the first time.[4] When Po Chü-yi [a poet, 772–846] spoke of the lack of mints among private individuals and the absence of copper mines in the crop fields, he meant to criticize the government for ordering people to pay what they neither owned nor produced.

Today all individuals, wherever they happen to be or whether they are rich or poor, are constantly pressured by government officials for money. After a bumper harvest when the price of grain is low, they have to sell their crops at one-third of their normal price in order to raise enough cash to pay the government. Not infrequently, they have to offer 20 percent of the purchasing price as a fee in order to find a buyer. The situation becomes definitely worse during a bad year when they have no grain to sell and yet the government's demand for money remains the same. Nor is it possible for them to sell their land, houses, or oxen since everyone, in order to raise cash to meet the government's demand, wants to sell them at the same time. Out of desperation, they ax down their date and mulberry trees, or sometimes wreck part of their houses, to be sold as firewood. Oftentimes they slaughter their oxen to sell as meat. By taking drastic steps like this they may be able to raise enough cash to meet their governmental obligations for the current year. The question is, How can they survive in the years ahead? Since the introduction of the New Program the plight of the peasantry has been increasingly worse.

Agriculture is the foundation of the nation's economy. If it fails, where can the nation find food to feed itself? Today all goods, including grain, are cheap in terms of money, even though we have had a bad year. Why? This is because the government, in carrying out the green sprouts and draft exemption programs, has done its utmost to exact money from the people. All over the country—from the frigid north to the warm south, from Szechuan in the west to the coastal provinces in the east—there has not been much rain or snow during last fall and winter. Consequently, streams and wells are drying up. There is little farmers can look forward to, as wheat crops have already failed. Summer is now half-gone; yet, because of the lack of rain, they have not been able to plant autumn crops. Most low- and medium-income families have already suffered from the lack of food: not a few depend on grass roots to sustain their lives. What will happen to them in the months to come?

Despite all this, local officials, in enforcing orders from above, keep on the pressure to exact money under the green sprouts and draft exemption programs. They whip people or even send them to jail if payment is not made when it is due. As a result, women and children, as well as men, live in constant fear. Like a man who has been thrown into a caldron of boiling water, people all over China are crying for help, but help is nowhere in sight.

Even the most peaceful animals will become predatory when they are hungry; men, unfortunately, are not an exception. Driven to desperation, the weak will be condemned to a slow death in the gutter, while the strong will gather as bandits. What will the government do when people begin to organize themselves as bandits and rebels all over the country, ravaging the countryside and attacking the cities, and succeed in defying every effort of the government to suppress them? It will be too late then to speak of the abolition of the New Program.

Wang An-shih:

I had the honor of receiving your letter yesterday.

I feel that the real reason behind our disagreement, despite our longtime friendship, is that you [Ssu-ma Kuang] and I differ on the basic approach to the management of state affairs. In whatever way I try to present my side of the disagreement, I remain doubtful that it will ever be appreciated. That is why I have not chosen to answer your objections to the New Program item by item but have relied instead on a brief presentation of my own stand. Having in mind the kindness and generosity with which you have always regarded me, by no means shall I be rude and inconsiderate. In the following I shall state what I believe, hoping earnestly that you will not take offense at what I have to say.

The argument between responsible men is an argument over truth and falsehood, and all responsible men agree that once truth or falsehood has been clearly demonstrated as such, they will come to agreement by themselves, however strongly they once disagreed. You, sir, regard me as having unnecessarily interfered with the normal functions of the government, needlessly created difficulties when there should have been none, ruthlessly sought after profit for the sake of profit, and stubbornly turned a deaf ear to different suggestions. This is why, you stated, I have become a target of universal criticism and complaint. I, of course, do not agree with you on this assessment of myself. I do not regard myself as having unnecessarily interfered with the normal functions of the government when I, in observance of His Majesty's wishes, recommended new programs to be carried out by responsible officials. Nor do I regard myself as having needlessly created difficulties when I attempt to revive the good laws of our ancient sage kings by promoting what is good for the people and by eliminating that which harms them. Needless to say, my efforts to manage the nation's finances most efficiently are not to seek profit for the sake of profit. Lastly, how can the refutation of heresy, as well as the employment of governmental personnel with care and discrimination, properly be characterized as "turning a deaf ear to different suggestions?" As for criticism and complaint, I have not expected anything else.

I am not surprised that most people prefer the status quo, however unpleasant. What disappoints me is that many of our scholar-officials choose to side with them and air their prejudice, when they should know that only through changes can the fortune of our people be improved. His Majesty wishes to do away with this popular inertia and I, without thinking much about the strong opposition I have to face, agree to assist His Majesty in this endeavor. Knowing how strong the inertia is, I am not surprised at all at the intensity of the popular anger. Yet, P'an-keng [a king of the Shang dynasty, r. ca. 1401–1374 B.C.] did not change his decision to move the nation's capital despite the strong opposition of his subjects, including his own ministers, since he knew, as they knew not, that he had carefully studied the problem before he made his decision publicly known. Nor did he regret the decision after he had made it. If you, sir, blame me for having failed to assist His Majesty in bringing about maximum benefit to the people, I shall plead guilty, since I have occupied a position of influence for a considerable length of time. On the other hand, I cannot but disagree with you if you insist that the key to the nation's welfare is the maintenance of the status quo or doing nothing in particular.

As there is no opportunity for me to meet you in person, I am sending you my best regards via this letter.

Notes

1. The two documents in this selection were written in 1074 shortly before Wang An-shih was forced to resign from his premiership as a result of a nationwide drought. A copy of the Chinese original can be found in *A Collection of Essays (Ching-shih wen-tsung)* (Chungking: Huang-chung Press, 1943), pp. 458–61.

2. Under the draft exemption program both rich and poor families were supposed to contribute funds for hiring mercenaries (referred to as "shiftless loafers" here) so their own sons did not have to be drafted.

3. See p. 201.

4. The "major disaster" was An Lu-shan's revolt of 755 and the widespread chaos and war that followed. The payment of taxes in cash, rather than produce, was mandated under the semiannual tax system introduced by Yang Yen in 799. For details, see selection 25.

(31)

Ting T'eh-ch'i / *Last Days of the North Sung*[1]

On the last day of the eleventh month (leap), in the first year of Ching-k'ang [14 January 1127], the Chin enemy, for the first time, agreed to a truce. On the fourth day of the next month [18 January] he sent men to the capital [Kaifeng] to inspect and examine the treasury and ordered all the books to be handed over to him. His purpose was to find out how much treasure the Sung government still had in order to determine how much he should demand for himself.

On the fifth day of the twelfth month [19 January] the Chin enemy sent the Mayoralty of Kaifeng a letter in which he demanded ten thousand horses of the finest quality. On the next day he demanded all the military weapons.

On the ninth day of the same month [23 January] the Chin enemy demanded silk, money, and other valuables. From the city he took with him more than twenty families that had collaborated with him.

On the twenty-third day [6 February] the Chin enemy demanded all the books housed in the Department of Cultural Affairs. He was particularly interested in the works of Su Hsün, Su Shih [1036–1101], Huang T'ing-chien [1045–1105], and Ssu-ma Kuang, such as *History as a Mirror.* On the next day he sent another letter demanding the immediate payment of all the silk and money he had previously requested. He took 10 million bolts of the 14 million bolts of silk he had found in the imperial storage. In addition, the Sung government also agreed to give him 1 million ingots of gold and 5 million ingots of silver.[2] The bullion and the silk, said the enemy, were to be distributed among his soldiers as a reward.

On the twenty-seventh day of the first month, in the second year of Ching-k'ang [11 March 1127], the Chin enemy demanded astronomical equipment, gabelle registers, religious garments, ceremonial hats, sedan chairs, and many other items. A search was made among various governmental agencies, as well as private houses, for the items demanded; they were subsequently presented to the enemy. The enemy also demanded such items as rhinoceros horns, elephant tusks, precious stones, medicine, inks and paints of different colors, clothes, and books.

On the twenty-ninth day of the same month [13 March], the Mayoralty of Kaifeng, in compliance with the enemy's demand, gathered all the prostitutes and entertainers it could find and presented them to him. It also sought servants and slaves among houses of the nobility to fulfill the quota of women the enemy demanded. When the entire group was escorted northward, it also included twenty-five eunuchs and more than a thousand artisans.

On the next day [14 March] the Chin enemy demanded the Eight Treasures,[3] the Nine Tripods,[4] and different kinds of vehicles. He also demanded the surrender to him of certain officials in the Ministry of Public Works and the Executive Secretariat, plus all the documents and archives of the imperial government. He wanted all the printing plates housed in the Department of Cultural Affairs. He wanted particularly a book entitled *The Invocation of Taoist Gods and Spirits (Yin-yang ch'uan-shen tao-chao)*.[5]

On the second day of the second month [16 March] the Chin enemy demanded all the porcelain and jade utensils owned by the imperial household. He further demanded the surrender to him of more artisans, entertainers, medical doctors, and eunuchs, together with their families.

On the seventeenth day of the same month [31 March] the Chin enemy demanded the surrender to him of fifteen hundred imperial concubines, twenty-five royal princes, and forty-nine members of the nobility who had been married to the royal princesses. On the next day he sent another letter demanding the surrender to him of thirty Confucian scholars of the Central University. He promised that these scholars would be employed in their own institutions, accorded esteem appropriate to their profession, and paid well. Thirty scholars in the Central University volunteered, most of whom were either Fukienese or natives of Liangho [modern Honan and Hopeh provinces]. The Sung government gave each of them three hundred thousand standard coins as traveling expenses, and all of them were more than delighted to leave for their new positions.

On the nineteenth day of the same month [2 April] the Chin enemy sent a letter demanding the surrender to him of forty

Buddhist monks and scholars. He also demanded all the printing plates of Buddhist scriptures.

On the twenty-second day of the same month [5 April] the Chin enemy ordered that all members of the royal family, together with its servants and retainers, be ready to leave on the twenty-fifth. All had to go, said the enemy; under no circumstances was an exception to be made.

On the twenty-second day of the third month [5 May] the Chin enemy sent another letter demanding more gold, silver, and silk, plus many other useful items to be distributed among his soldiers.

At dawn, on the twenty-ninth day of the same month [12 May] the reigning emperor Sung Ch'in-tsung and his father the ex-emperor Sung Hui-tsung journeyed northward.[6]

Notes

1. The author was in the city of Kaifeng during its long siege by the Chin forces early in 1127. This selection was taken from his book, *Observations of Ching-k'ang (Ching-k'ang chi-wen)*. Ching-k'ang was the reigning title of Sung Ch'in-tsung, last emperor of the North Sung.

2. An ingot contains approximately ten taels (Chinese ounces) of gold or silver.

3. Eight different chemicals, such as sulfur and nitrate, that could be used for making gunpowder.

4. Symbols of imperial authority.

5. Presumably a work of divination, the book has been long lost.

6. Both emperors became prisoners of the Chin forces and never returned.

CHAPTER

7

The Two Sungs (2)

WHATEVER financial disadvantage one may find in the generous subsidy of intellectuals by the Sung government, it was compensated, at least to some degree, by the creation of a lively intellectual community that concerned itself with issues larger than those on a personal level. After a man had passed the metropolitan examination and received the *chin-shih* degree, he would be virtually free from financial worries and could expect to live, within the framework of an agrarian economy, a comfortable life for the rest of his earthly term. He could then pursue higher interests that ranged from philosophical discussions to practical matters of common concern—public welfare, social ethics, and so on. An intellectual community devoted to the exchange of ideas was of course not new in Chinese history, but its activities had never been so lively nor had they been given so much attention as they were during the Sung dynasty. This was an extraordinary phenomenon in any event, especially in view of the difficulty of transportation and communication during those medieval times.

The elite of this intellectual community were cultural as well as political leaders. Ssu-ma Kuang, a political conservative, was a famous historian. Wang An-shih, a political radical, was an outstanding poet. Su Shih (1036–1101), a political moderate, was an essayist, a poet, a painter, and a connoisseur of beautiful women and vintage wine. In the long run, however, it was in the field of philosophy that the Sung scholars truly distinguished themselves. In terms of achievement, they surpassed the scholars of any of the preceding periods in this field of learning, with the exception, of course, of the pre-Ch'in period when men like Confucius and Lao-tzu predominated. Their impact on the subsequent periods cannot be overemphasized, since it extended beyond the narrow confines of philosophy and profoundly affected people's attitudes toward family and society. Not until the 1920s did the influence of the Sung philosophers begin to recede, largely because of the increasing popularity of Western values.

This outburst of philosophical interest during the Sung period did not spring from the void, of course. The enormous popularity of Buddhism, which dated from the Wei-Tsin period, not only posed a challenge to the defenders of the Confucian faith but also caused the raising of a number of issues in which Confucian scholars of the earlier periods had shown only marginal interest. These issues were primarily cosmological and metaphysical, contrary to the worldly and the human that had been the Confucian's major concern. To the critics Confucian ethics seemed to be shallow without a cosmological or metaphysical foundation, and defenders of the Confucian faith, to answer these critics, had to build, with whatever material they could find in the Confucian classics, a new cosmological system. The man who pioneered this effort was Chou Tun-yi (1012–73) whose short essay "The Absolute" (selection 32) became the nucleus around which all subsequent debates evolved. Once the cosmological issue was resolved, more or less, to every Confucian scholar's satisfaction, the Confucian elite turned their attention to the examination of the mind and the self and the relationship between the self and the universe. The Ch'eng brothers (Ch'eng Hao, 1031–85; and Ch'eng Yi, 1032–1107) of the North Sung period pioneered in this effort, but one hundred years had to elapse before it blossomed into a major academic issue, centered on the ideological differences between Chu Hsi (1130–1200) and Lu Chiu-yüan (1139–92).

Typically Confucian, the issue was concerned with the origin of moral knowledge (sense of compassion and guilt, intuitive knowledge of right and wrong, etc.) which, according to Mencius, was unique to man. Those scholars who had been more influenced by Buddhist ideology, such as Lu Chiu-yüan, tended to emphasize the inner mind as the source of moral knowledge and the rectification of the mind (which was denounced by their opponents as Buddhist meditation in disguise) as the means of acquiring it (selection 33). Those scholars who had been less influenced by the Buddhist ideology, such as Chu Hsi, while not denying the importance of the inner mind and the necessity of its rectification (both of which, after all, had been recorded in one of the Confucian classics), stressed the interplay between the mind and the physical world as a means of acquiring moral knowledge (selection 34). Though the difference was primarily a difference in emphasis (selection 35), the ideological battle went on for the next seven hundred years.

It would be wrong, of course, to regard all of the Sung scholars as ideological doctrinaires. As a government official or a self-appointed defender of orthodoxy, a Sung scholar of necessity had to defend Confucianism and condemn Buddhism or Taoism whenever the opportunity presented itself. But his private life was a totally different matter. Su Shih, for instance, considered himself as much a Confucian as anyone else; yet some of his best friends were Buddhists and Taoists. His official works, such as his memorials to the emperor, are without exception Confucian in outlook; but his less official writings, including his poems, are more often than not Taoist (selection 36). Such a free soul could not have been happy in any kind of ideological confinement.

While the intellectual elite were debating such abstractions as the self and the mind about which the overwhelming majority of the Chinese people, namely the peasants, understood little and cared about even less, a new form of entertainment, called vernacular tales *(p'ing hua)*, had emerged in the countryside and enjoyed enormous popularity. Technically, calling this form of entertainment "new" is incorrect since tales had been *told* by professional storytellers in country fairs and similar gatherings for centuries before the establishment of the Sung dynasty. It is "new," however, to the historians since vernacular tales of the pre-Sung periods, even if they were written, have not survived. The major difference between a vernacular tale of the Sung dynasty and a *ch'uan-ch'i* of an earlier period is that a vernacular tale, written in spoken Chinese, can be *told* and understood by its audience, whereas a *ch'uan-ch'i*, written in literary or classical Chinese, can only be read and understood by a well-educated person. After both have been translated into modern English, it is of course difficult to tell one from the other (selections 26 and 37).

As for sources on the Sung philosophy, each major philosopher has his own complete works bearing his name—*The Complete*

Works of Lu Hsiang-shan (Lu Chiu-yüan), for instance—which
was compiled by either the author or some of his followers or
admirers. Secondary sources on these philosophers—biographies, interpretations, etc.—are even more numerous, especially
those on Chu Hsi who was hailed by the Ming and the Ch'ing
emperors as the greatest Confucian scholar after Mencius. For a
comprehensive review of the Sung philosophy, the best work is
still *The Ideological Controversy of the Sung-Yüan Period (Sung
Yüan hsüeh-an)* by Huang Tsung-hsi (1610–95). Huang, an intellectual giant in his own right, is primarily known for a collection
of his essays entitled *A Ming Barbarian Waiting for a Visitor
(Ming-yi tai-fang lu)*. But his major contribution to scholarship
remains *The Ideological Controversy*. The sources of vernacular
tales of the Sung period are inadequate and incomplete, largely
because of traditional scholars' contempt for anything written in
the colloquial form. The best available collection, by an anonymous author or authors of an unknown period, is the *Vernacular
Tales of the Capital Edition (Ching-pen t'ung-su hsiao-shuo)*.
For scholars interested in this topic, hopefully some broken
tombs or walls will in the future yield additional treasures.

(32)
Chou Tun-yi / *The Absolute*[1]

The Absolute originates from the Infinite. It generates the *yang*
when it is active. Activity, when maximized, leads to inactivity.
When the Absolute is inactive, it generates the *yin*. When maximized, inactivity in turn leads to activity. Thus, the generation
of the *yang* leads to the generation of the *yin* and vice versa, just
as activity leads to inactivity and vice versa. One is the foundation upon which the other is built. Jointly the *yin* and the *yang*
are referred to as the Two Forces *(Liang yi)*.

The interactions between the *yin* and the *yang* create the
Five Primary Elements, namely, water, fire, wood, metal, and
earth. Their permutations give birth to the physical universe and

also enable it to function in an orderly manner, including the orderly appearance and disappearance of the Four Seasons.

In short, the Five Primary Elements are united in, and trace their origin to, the *yin* and the *yang*. The *yin* and the *yang* are united in, and trace their origin to, the Absolute. The Absolute originates in the Infinite.

As the Infinite is true, each of the Five Primary Elements has its own characteristics. Ingenious and sedulous, they combine with one another to form a multitude of other objects. During the process of formation, the *yin* and the *yang* interact with each other. Males are created when they interact with each other in a positive manner; females are created when they interact with each other in a negative manner. Once an object is created, it changes constantly, in an infinite number of ways.

Of all the substances that come about as a result of the *yin-yang* interactions, man is the finest and the most ingenious. He has not only a form but also a spirit. He possesses the Five Temperaments[2] and knows the difference between right and wrong. To stabilize him, the sages teach him the virtues of moderation, uprightness, love, and righteousness. The motto for man is inactivity and quietude.

A sage reflects the virtue of Heaven and Earth, the brightness of the sun and the moon, and the orderliness of the Four Seasons. He knows what gods have ordained in terms of fortunes and misfortunes. While a small man works against the wishes of gods and thus incurs misfortunes, a gentleman abides by them and brings about good fortunes.

As the *yin* and the *yang* govern the way of Heaven and as hardness and softness govern the way of Earth, love and righteousness should govern the way of man. Once realizing that beginning inevitably leads to end and vice versa, one masters the meaning of life and death. How enormously important change is!

Notes

1. Source: *Sung shih*, roll 427.
2. The Five Temperaments *(wu hsing)* are quietude, nervousness, strength, hardness, and wisdom.

(33)
Lu Chiu-yüan / *On Reading and Other Matters*[1]

Li: What should one read?

Lu: One should read *Historical Records* and *History of the Han.* You cannot be too wrong either if you choose to read the works of such men as Han Yü [768–824], Liu Tsung-yüan [773–819], Ou-yang Hsiu, and Su Shih. There is no better way to acquire knowledge than reading, which enables a student to understand things in a more profound manner. Reading history, for instance, enables him to understand why some succeeded while others failed, or what has been done right and what has been done wrong. Read slowly and carefully and make sure that you digest what you have read. Given time, you will be surprised at what you have learned. Reading in the manner I have suggested, you will learn more in three rolls than you can otherwise learn in thirty thousand rolls. How is your composition?

Li: I have recently read "On Tao" [*Yüan Tao*, by Han Yü] and some other works. But I am confused.

Lu: The *Commentaries of Tso* is much more profound than the works of Han Yü and Liu Tsung-yüan and is very difficult for a beginner. You should start with the works of Su Shih. By the way, what do you intend to do with your life?

Li: I wish to become a good man. I have taken every precaution not to be otherwise.

Lu: What do you mean by "taking every precaution not to be otherwise"?

Li: I do only the right things.

Lu: Even a sage cannot do better. Lately I have noticed that you are not as earnest and energetic as you used to be. Is it because you are overtired or because you have been unduly influenced by unhealthy ideas? Knowledge, to be true, has to be revitalized and regenerated each day, like a piece of iron that needs constant tempering to make it sharp and enduring. A river is dead when no water is pouring into it; a tree is dead when it no longer grows. The same thing can be said about knowledge which has to grow in order to stay alive. You, my friend, cannot remain fixed in one place and say, "This is good enough for me." The acquisition of knowledge contains the following five important steps: broad learning, investigation and inquiry, careful reasoning, clear distinguishing, and finally, forcible implementation. Since broad learning heads the sequence and since obviously your learning has not been broad enough, you cannot be sure that you are doing the right thing when you proceed immediately to action. Taking precaution not to do the wrong thing is of course not original with you, since our ancient sages have said the same thing. But their precaution is somewhat different from yours. Yours is holding obstinately one idea from which you will never deviate. It is a joyless kind which takes much pleasure out of life. I have spoken with you often, and you talk freely about everything under Heaven, including your innermost thoughts. You used to be a happy man, certainly not an obstinate kind. What has happened to you?

Li: I was happy and contented because I knew where I stood and could hold my beliefs without much effort. But I was unable to stay that way for long. As soon as I relaxed my guard, I was tempted by outside influences.

Lu: The fault lies with the lack of constancy which in turn results from forcibly holding one idea in an obstinate manner. You cannot be really happy this way.

Li: I have often thought of this. But I simply do not know how to proceed from here.

Lu: Why did you not speak with me about this before? You have to make up your mind about what you want to do and proceed to do it once you have made up your mind. There is no sense talking about things that you do not intend to follow with action. I presume that you have forgotten everything I said.

Li: I remember everything you said about freedom of mind and determination of will.

Lu: If your mind is free, what you seek will be there by itself. If you had been able to determine your own will, you would not be in such a situation as the one you are in today.

Li: How do I determine my will?

Lu: It is you who have to answer that question for yourself. I cannot answer that for you. In any event, the determination of will has nothing to do with compulsion, either externally or internally imposed. You should make a clear distinction between the basic and the superficial. The basic is what is inside you, and the outward manifestations of yourself, in either a written or an oral form, are really superficial. It is of no consequence whether you know how to write or not, as long as you have the basic within you. In fact, if you have the basic within you, you certainly know how to write. Unfortunately, you have acted as though literature and knowledge were two separate identities, unrelated to each other. How do you feel lately? Are you in good spirits? Do you find happiness inside yourself?

Li: Lately I have not been concerned with anything other than myself. I feel good sometimes.

Lu: The knowledge of oneself is indeed the font of all knowledge. If you tirelessly pursue it, whether in a dark room or underneath a leaking roof, or whatever your worldly fortune is, good or bad, you will eventually achieve your goal. That is what our sages mean when they say that the expression of virtue, as far as a gentleman is concerned, is the expression of oneself. They also say that those who wish to make true virtue prevail throughout the world should begin with the acquisition of knowledge and that knowledge originates with the investigation of objects and things. A truly learned man pursues knowledge for his own use, namely, the expression of the self. Only when one's own virtue has become evident for all to see can one hope to extend it outside oneself and throughout the world. A bell that rings inside a temple can be heard outside; a crane that cries in a pond can carry its sound as far above as the sky. If a person has done his utmost and thus attained his goal, others will notice his accomplishment, even though he might wish to hide it. The difficulty with today's scholars is that they concentrate their effort on the leaves and the branches, rather than the trunk and the roots, of the wisdom tree. Mencius says, "The maximization of the mind is a prerequisite for the knowledge of self, and those who know their selves hold the key to the meaning of Heaven." The most important word in this quotation is "mind," a mind that is shared by you and me and by all the sages in the past and all the men of virtue for centuries to come. The horizon of the mind is infinite and can be as large as the universe. The maximized mind of an individual is indeed the mind of Heaven. Once you understand this, you are on your way to knowledge. Sincerity cannot mean anything other than sincerity with oneself, and virtue originates from within rather than without. None of these has anything to do with making speeches.

Li: How can the mind be maximized? How do you differentiate these four terms: nature, talent, mind, and sentiment?

Lu: Your questions indicate that you are more concerned with leaves and branches than trunks and roots. But I should not blame you for this, since this is a common fault shared by many others. Today's scholars spend much time on the literary aspect of the texts they read, paying little attention to the underlying meanings. Basically, nature, talent, mind, and sentiment are really the same thing.

Li: Can we say that they originate from the same source, even though their names are different?

Lu: If we have to answer this question in words, we are bound to make mistakes. The purpose of using words is communication, namely, to enable others to know one's own ideas. But what we are discussing here has nothing to do with communication; it involves the understanding of oneself for the benefit of oneself. If we have to use words, we may say that nature is the mind existing outside oneself, while mind is the nature that exists within oneself. This definition, which you doubtless approve, is really awkward and is far from indicative of the truth. It is a liability, rather than an asset, if you wish to maximize your mind. The most important thing is whether you are happy with what you are doing; if you are, the rest does not matter. The barrenness of a mountain is no indication that this particular mountain has no "talent" to produce forests; it is of course absurd to assume that since this particular mountain does not produce forests, it is the "nature" of mountains not to produce any forests. As far as man is concerned, it matters not whether it is the "nature" of this particular mountain or mountains in general to produce or not to produce forests; it is his duty not to destroy any forest. To destroy "nature" outside oneself is to destroy the "mind" within oneself.

Nature needs rest; so does man. If a man is restless at night, he must have done something during daytime that causes his conscience to suffer. He may have nightmares, since his mind is in total disarray. He may even act like a beast. But all this has nothing to do with his "talent" or "sentiment"; it originates from a lack of understanding of his own mind. As a popular saying goes, you cannot tell a dream to a fool. Once a lion has got hold of you, it is senseless to fight back with a lump of earth. But you may succeed in warding off your attacker if it happens to be a wild dog instead of a ferocious lion. To be able to understand the situation involved is what really matters. The sages, in their eagerness to teach us, use different terms—sentiment, nature, mind, and talent—under different circumstances, but we should by no means be so stuck with these terms as to forget the essentials. You may, if you want to, use the same terms and tell others the differences between them, as long as you can hold steadfastly the essentials that underlie these terms. Otherwise all the reading you have done will be useless.

Notes

1. Lu and Li in this selection stand for Lu Chiu-yüan and Li Pai-min, respectively. Li, who recorded this conversation, was Lu's student. Source: *The Complete Works of Lu Hsiang-shan (Lu Hsiang-shan ch'üan-chi)*, roll 35.

(34)
Chu Hsi / *On the Observation of the Mind*[1]

Someone asks me to comment on a Buddhist concept called the observation of the mind. Here is my comment.

The mind is the master of the body, indivisible in its organic structure. It initiates rather than responds; it orders rather than being ordered. To view the physical world from the vantage of the mind will enable one to see clearly the reason or reasons behind an object or objects outside of oneself, but to examine one's mind through the use of things outside one's mind is to admit that there is another mind that controls this mind—a proposition that is inadmissible. We have to determine for ourselves whether there are one or two minds, whether the mind is an initiator or a responder, or whether it issues or receives orders. If the mind is indivisible, initiating rather than being initiated, issuing orders rather than receiving them, the Buddhist concept of the observation of the mind, which means the use of another mind to observe this mind, is obviously absurd.

What do our sages mean, then, when they speak of the crystallization of all in one, self-discipline and preservation of goodness, the maximization and the preservation of the mind, the understanding and the nourishment of self, and finally, the application of precedents and the adherence to an objective standard?

These terms, while looking similar, are really different. The difference is a difference between crops and weeds, pink and purple, that may be indistinguishable to a layman but must be recognized by scholars. When a sage speaks of the danger to the human mind, he has in mind the emergence of human desires. When he speaks of the power of the rational mind, he has in mind the ability of that mind to master heavenly reasons. But the mind is the same mind. Whether the mind is "rational" or "human" depends upon whether, at a given time, it is rectified or not. By "the crystallization of all in one" the sage means that we should abide by the rectified mind in order to examine the diversity away from it and that we should dismiss individual differences in order to return to the universally common. Once we can do this, we should be able to hold steadfastly and with faith what is in the middle, deviating neither to the side of excess nor to the side of inadequacy. The sage never means that there are two separate, independent minds—one is human and the other is rational— and that we need a third mind to crystallize these two into one.

Likewise, when a sage speaks of self-discipline and preservation of goodness, he does not mean the dismissal of one mind in order to preserve another mind. What he really means is that if the mind is not disciplined, what should have been preserved will be lost and what should have been lost will be preserved. This discipline of mind involves the close correlation between the conduct of our daily lives and the expression of our inner conscience; it has nothing to do with sitting long hours in a fixed position, like a piece of wood, in order to sink one's mind into a state of semiconsciousness.

When our sages speak of the maximization of the mind, they mean that the objects and the things in the physical world should be observed and investigated so as to comprehend the reason underlying the existence of each of them and that total comprehension of all the reasons and of their interrelationship will lead to the understanding of the reason that exists, *a priori*, in our minds. Likewise, when our sages speak of the preservation of the mind, they mean that we should be reverent within and righteous without—the preservation of the mind, in fact, conveys the same meaning as the crystallization of all in one, as described above. The maximization of the mind—the utilization of the mind to the fullest extent—will lead to the understanding of self as well as of Heaven, since both, self and Heaven, have the same natural reasons underlying their being. The preservation of the mind—the absence of the loss of the mind—enables a person to nourish the self as well as to serve Heaven, since whatever he does always conforms to the natural reasons mentioned above. In short, the maximization of the mind is to use this mind to maximize the same mind; likewise, the preservation of the mind cannot but be the use of this mind to preserve the same mind. There are no two minds standing face to face, as the Buddhists seem to imply, and there is no need to prefer one mind to the other, since there is only one mind.

When the sages speak of the application of precedents and the adherence to an objective standard, they have in mind such virtues as loyalty, faithfulness, honesty, and reverence and the exercise of these virtues according to the dictates of the mind. Without the mind which gives it directions, the exercise of these virtues would be meaningless as well as aimless. This does not mean, of course, that the mind, per se, contains these virtues. The mind dictates wherever the body will be or whatever it will do, but the mind, per se, cannot learn from precedents or adhere to an objective standard. The sages teach us to use the mind as a tool to search for the natural reasons underlying all existences because, once these reasons are mastered, we shall be able to do everything we wish, naturally and in accordance with reason, and as easily as our body directs our arms or our arms direct our fingers. The road ahead of us will be wide and smooth; wherever we happen to be, we shall be comfortable and secure.

The Buddhists, on the other hand, are advocating the use of one mind to search and direct another mind. This is equivalent to the advocacy of using one mouth to eat another mouth, or one eye to see another eye. As the reasoning behind this advocacy is patently absurd, any person who chooses to follow the Buddhist path will find the road ahead of him narrow and dangerous and the situation he is in pressing and precarious. The Buddhist teaching may, in some respects, look similar to the teaching of our sages, but basically they are different. Unless a person is discriminating and careful and is capable of deep thinking, he may indeed be confused.

Notes

1. Source: *Sung Yüan hsüeh-an*, roll 12.

(35)
Huang Tsung-hsi / *Differences between Lu Chiu-yüan and Chu Hsi*[1]

The basic teaching of Lu Chiu-yüan lies in its emphasis on the virtuous self. The most important thing in life, he says, is the establishment of the universal and the merging of the universal with the self. Anything that stands between the universal and the self is by definition minor in nature and should not be allowed to mar the harmonious relationship between the two. Working on things outside the self is like searching for water without a source; the result cannot but be fruitless. The basic teaching of Chu Hsi, on the other hand, lies in its emphasis on worldly knowledge. The investigation of objects and things, he says, will enable a person to master the reasons underlying these objects and things, and such mastery will, in due course, lead one to sagehood. Relying on the mind alone, however hard one works at it, will not get one anywhere since, in this case, the mind has become its own teacher.

As the polemics between the two schools heightened, the followers of Chu Hsi called Lu Chiu-yüan "a mad Buddhist." The followers of Lu Chiu-yüan, in retaliation, referred to the school of Chu Hsi as "vulgar learning of the commonplace." By then the two schools had become so entrenched in their fixed positions that they were as compatible with each other as water and fire. What a pity! It is difficult enough to understand the way of our sages without polemics; it is doubly difficult with it. After the Ch'en brothers had paved the way, the world depended upon these two gentlemen to sustain it, so that the teachings of our sages would continue to flourish. Yet, these two gentlemen chose to quarrel! Even today the quarrel between these two schools is as lively as ever, as they dwell on the slightest excuse in order to disagree. This is indeed a great misfortune.

Nevertheless, the very fact that these two gentlemen did not choose to agree for the sake of agreement indicates clearly that each of them was seeking in his own way a correct and proper interpretation, so that the teachings of our sages would become even clearer to posterity. There was nothing personal involved. The teachings of our sages are the common property of all men, and everyone is indeed entitled to disagreement with others in the way they should be interpreted. This is what Yin Chu [d. ca. 1056][2] means when he says that whenever in doubt argument will help enlighten the issue involved. The argument between Lu Chiu-yüan and Chu Hsi was philosophical and was conducted on the highest level; it was aimed to enlighten rather than to confuse. There is a world of difference between these two gentlemen and later scholars who, without anything original to offer, merely echo whatever other people have already stated. Besides, these two gentlemen were of such high caliber that each, in the conduct of his daily life, practiced the best of the other's teachings. Can anyone accuse Lu Chiu-yüan, who advocated the cultivation of the virtuous self, of not having been engaged in bookish learning or of not having carried out what he had learned? Likewise, can anyone accuse Chu Hsi, who stressed the importance of worldly knowledge, of having failed to devote himself to the cultivation of his inner mind? The difference between the two is a difference in emphasis or priority; it indicates clearly that different roads can indeed lead to the same destination.

In their later years both philosophers seemed to have regretted the extreme positions they took during their younger days. This regret can be seen in the letters and other forms of writing of each during his advanced age. "During the past years I have carefully examined myself and realized that I was once as inconsiderate within as I was rude without," wrote Lu Chiu-yüan in a eulogy to Lü Tung-lai [Lü Tsu-ch'ien, 1137–81] after the latter's death. "Having committed so many errors, how can I say that I truly deserved your friendship?" Doubtless he had in mind the meeting of Ohu[3] when he spoke of himself as being inconsiderate and rude. There is even more evidence that later in his life Chu Hsi came to accept Lu Chiu-yüan's point of view. "Mencius has stated that the purpose of pursuing knowledge is to seek the freedom of the mind," he said in one of his letters to Lü Tzu-yüeh. "Master Ch'eng [Ch'eng Hao] has also stressed the importance of keeping a constant grip on the mind. I, on the other hand, have been deeply buried in a mountain of words from which I do not seem to be able to free myself. The result is that I no longer even realize my own existence and, sadly, have become more and more insensitive to things around me. Even though I have read a great deal, I begin to wonder whether reading has done me any good at all."

"Now I begin to feel that the preservation or loss of the mind is a matter that can go, only too easily, from one side to the other," he wrote to Lü Tzu-yüeh on another occasion. "My studies have been too fragmentary, and consequently I have not been able to build a firm foundation upon which I can stand. Without a firm foundation to stand on, everything else inevitably goes wrong. I have buried myself in books for so long a period and so deep in them that my spirit is now failing me."

From the above quotations we can easily appreciate how humble and generous these two philosophers were. Each did not hesitate to embrace the ideas of the other once he was convinced that they were better than his own. Thus, despite their earlier differences, they eventually came to an agreement. What in the world do the later scholars, invoking the names of these two men, argue about? Furthermore, the purpose of ideological debate is to explore truth as one sees it, and a most important element in this debate is humility and fairness. Whoever happens to be stubborn and combative will appear to be crude and offensive in the eyes of his audience, regardless of the validity or invalidity of his arguments. The purpose of these two philosophers, Lu Chiu-yüan and Chu Hsi, was one and the same, namely, upholding Confucian orthodoxy, even though they did at one time differ on the means of achieving it. But there was nothing wrong in this difference, which they were within their rights to express, as neither of the two had ever voiced any idea opposed to those of the sage [Confucius]. Besides, these two philosophers, later in their years, arrived at the same conclusion about the means, as well as the end, as far as upholding Confucian orthodoxy was concerned.

The scholars of later years, who have never bothered to read the complete works of these two great men and consequently have only a smattering of their differences from a secondary source, are trying hard to elevate their own status by declaring themselves followers of one philosopher or the other. They slander either Chu Hsi or Lu Chiu-yüan, depending on whichever side they happen to choose, little realizing that neither of these two great philosophers need assistance from such mediocre and yet pretentious people as they. They remind me of a friend of my late father's who regarded himself as a true defender of Chu Hsi. "Do you really believe that you can elevate Chu Hsi by downgrading Lu Chiu-yüan?" my father asked him pointedly in a letter. "Have you ever bothered to teach yourself what their philosophies are about? Imagine for a moment that during the Ohu meeting an untutored servant ascended the platform on which the two philosophers were then debating and then grabbed Lu Chiu-yüan and threw him to the floor, on the grounds that he was doing this merely to assist his idol Chu Hsi. Do you think that Chu Hsi would be greatly pleased? I know what Chu Hsi would do. He would beat this servant up and order him out of the room. My friend, the way you have been helping Chu Hsi is identical with the way this servant acted at the Ohu meeting." Today, unfortunately, there are too many scholars who act like my late father's friend.

Notes

1. *Sung Yüan hsüeh-an,* roll 15.
2. A philosopher and historian specializing in the *Spring and Autumn Annals.* A prolific writer, he is best known for the *Annals of the Five Dynasties (Wu-tai ch'un-ch'iu).*
3. This was the famous meeting that never took place. In 1175 Lu Chiu-yüan and Chu Hsi were supposed to stage an open debate at the Ohu Academy (modern Kiangsi province) on their ideological differences. The meeting never took place because each accused the other of having slighted him shortly before the scheduled meeting.

(36)
Su Shih / *Pavilion of Transcendence*[1]

As every object has its attractive aspect, all things can be enjoyable. An enjoyable thing does not have to be unusual, extraordinary, grand, or extremely beautiful. Raw liquor is as good as vintage wine insofar as getting drunk is concerned, and one does not have to eat the choicest meat in order to ward off hunger. Observing this maxim, I have been a most happy person wherever I go.

People seek fortune and avoid its opposite because they believe that fortune is to be rejoiced in while misfortune is something to grieve about. Yet desire is by definition unlimited, while objects and things that can satisfy man's desire are small in number. Forever caught in determining the desirable and the undesirable and steering one's action accordingly, how can one ever be happy in the process?

Thus, in the process of seeking fortunes, we actually become unhappy. Is unhappiness the goal of life? Of course not. Man is unhappy because he has been too willing to be a slave to outward objects and things, when in fact he should have been their master. He should have flown above instead of swimming underneath them.

There is no such thing as a big or small object since, from an object's standpoint, it alone is the most important. As it towers above, we are invariably dazed by its grandeur and brilliance. As it competes with other objects for our attention, they instantly reduce us to a viewer through the keyhole. How can we know which one of them will win? Eventually, of course, we have to side with one or the other. Once the choice is made, happiness or unhappiness comes about. The saddest thing in life is to choose between joy and sorrow.

My transfer from Ch'ient'ang [modern Chekiang province] to Chiaohsi [modern Shantung province] has been a transfer from stately yacht to crude wagon, from sculptured mansion to rustic cabin, from scenic beauty to mulberry wilderness. As crops failed in the year I arrived, banditry mushroomed, litigations followed one another, and jails were filled with prisoners. The kitchen was lifeless, and we had nothing to eat except vegetables that grew wild.

Yet in one year I looked healthier than I had before. Even my hair, which had turned white, became darker and darker. I fell in love with the simplicity and honesty that characterized the people in this district, and these people seemed to be equally fond of my straightforwardness and candor.

As things began to settle down and the future looked brighter, I embarked upon a project of restoring gardens and repairing old buildings. I intended to make life as pleasant as possible under the circumstances. North of the city park and next to the city wall stood an old pavilion that had fallen upon bad times. I had it repaired and painted until it looked almost new. Often I ascend the pavilion and enjoy the panoramic view that stretches far into the distance. There I let my imagination soar and can, in my own mind, do whatever I please.

To the south of the pavilion are Mount Maerh and Mount Ch'ang, which disappear only to reappear, depending upon the conditions of the day. Sometimes they look remote; other times they seem to be close enough to touch. Are there hermits in these mountains? To the east of the pavilion are the Lu Mountains, named after Lu Ao of the Ch'in dynasty [third century B.C.] who abandoned this world in order to live a more secluded life. To the west of the pavilion is the Gate of Muling that looks more like a battlement in the distance. There, I was told, the meritorious deeds of Chiang Tzu-ya [twelfth century B.C.] and Ch'i Huan-kung [686–643 B.C.] can still be traced. Looking downward toward the north I can see the River Wei where Han Hsin [third century B.C.] of Han decisively defeated Lung Ch'i of Ch'u. How great his achievement was! Yet in the end he was put to death on a trumped-up charge. The vicissitudes of life—how uncertain it is!

The pavilion is high and yet secure, large and yet full of light. It is cool in summer and warm in winter. On a rainy or snowy day or on the evening of a bright moon, there I am, accompanied by friends and guests. We bring vegetables from our own garden, fish from our own pond, and wine from our own winery. "How enjoyable life can be!" we remark to one another.

My younger brother Su Ch'e, presently stationed at Tsinan [modern Shantung province], heard about my joys in connection with this pavilion and wrote a poem to commemorate them. He even gave the pavilion a new name, Transcendence. What he meant is that I can find joy wherever I go: that I fly above instead of swimming underneath objects and things.

Notes

1. A copy of the Chinese orginal can be found in *The Most Readable Essays Written in the Ancient Style (Ku-wen kuan-chih)*, edited by Wu Ch'u-ts'ai (ca. 1653–1711), roll 7.

(37)
Anonymous / *A New Bodhisattva*[1]

Worthy audience: The story you are going to hear today occurred in the Shao-hsing period [1131–62] of the great Sung dynasty. The story involves a native of Yüehch'ing, Wenchou prefecture, who, at the age of twenty-three, had already passed the district examination and received a *hsiu-ts'ai* degree. The young man was not only good-looking and highly intelligent but also diligent in his studies. He read extensively and was particularly proficient in history. Everybody expected great things from him; so did he himself. Yet, despite these early promises, he failed three times in the metropolian examination. Worthy audience, you can imagine how disappointed he and his friends were.

After the third failure, Ch'en K'o-ch'ang, as this young man was called, went to see a fortune-teller at Chungan Bridge, Hangchow, hoping to find out what the future had in store for him. The fortune-teller said, "There is a crown on your head, but it is not a worldly one." Then Ch'en K'o-ch'ang began to recall what his mother used to tell him when he was a child: that on the day of his birth she had dreamed of a golden Buddha entering her stomach. Now that he had encountered great difficulties in pursuing worldly fortunes, he might as well, he said to himself, do what the fortune-teller had suggested. He returned to the inn where he had stayed and the next morning, having paid the bill and then hired a man to carry his luggage, went straight to the Lingyin Temple.[2] The abbot of the Lingyin Temple was a man named Yin T'ieh-niu who, being well educated himself, readily accepted the young man as his disciple once he learned about the young man's background. He in fact designated him as his number-two disciple, ahead of eight others.

On the fourth day of the fifth month, in the eleventh year of Shao-hsing [1137], Prince Wu, a maternal uncle of the reigning emperor's and a regular patron of the Lingyin Temple, announced to his retainers that he would repair to the temple to "feed" the monks on the next day. The head retainer, in observance of the prince's order, went to a bank to withdraw the needed cash and, with the money, bought a large quantity of food and other items. After breakfast on the next morning, the prince, having checked the gifts and found them in order, proceeded with his journey and in due course arrived at the Lingyin Temple with his retinue. The abbot had been notified of the prince's visit in advance; when the prince arrived, he quickly ushered him into the main hall where the prince burned incense and made offerings, while the monks beat drums and rang bells. After the worship was over, the abbot presented his monks to the prince one by one. Then they stepped aside and lined up behind the abbot when tea was about to be served.

"As you know," said the prince while drinking his tea, "it is customary for me to distribute dumplings among the monks on the Double Fifth. I shall do the same today."[3] Shortly afterward tray after tray of dumplings were brought before the monks. "Make sure that everyone in this temple has his share," the prince added.

After the tea, the prince took a walk around the temple. In one of the corridors he found a poem inscribed on the wall. The poem read:

> Meng-ch'ang in Ch'i; Chen-oh in Tsin—
> They were not different from what I am.
> But a difference there is.
> Who, pray, can tell me the reason?

"This man is complaining," said the prince to himself. "I wonder who wrote this poem."

Returning to the reception hall, the prince found that a dinner was waiting for him. "Is there a poet in your temple?" the prince asked during the meal.

"All of my disciples know how to write poems," the abbot replied. The prince then asked the abbot to bring all of his disciples before him so he could give them a test, only to be told that eight of them had left the temple on that day to tour the temple estates and that only two were still at home. "Bring both of them here," said the prince.

Once brought before the prince, each of the two monks was asked to write a poem on dumplings. The product of the first monk was good enough to elicit some praise from the prince ("good but lacking refinement"); it was Ch'en K'o-ch'ang's poem, however, that really impressed the prince. "Did you also write that poem on the corridor wall?" asked the prince.

"Yes, I did," Ch'en replied.

"Explain that poem for me," said the prince.

"Prince Meng-ch'ang of Ch'i was born at noon on the Double Fifth; so was General Chen-oh of Tsin. Both were remarkable men and accomplished great deeds in their lives. Your humble servant was also born at noon on the Double Fifth. Yet I have nothing to say for myself."

The prince asked more questions about the young man's background and, satisfied with the answers, decided to help to promote his career. He asked the abbot's permission to bring the young man home as a monk in residence, and the abbot, having been patronized by the prince for so long, readily agreed.

The young monk proved to be very popular in the Wu household, especially with the prince's wife who was impressed with his intelligence, modesty, and, above all, discretion. His duty as a monk in residence was to give advice on worship and other related matters; but, because of his intellectual background, he was also called upon, from time to time, to compose new songs for the prince's musicians to sing. Among the musicians was a slave girl named Hsin-ho, a slender, delicate creature who was as much noted for her beauty as for her voice. Because he had to compose songs for her to sing, Ch'en K'o-ch'ang, regrettably, saw her a little too often.

Time sped like an arrow; quickly one year had passed and another Double Fifth had arrived. The prince had planned to visit the Lingyin Temple on that day but changed his mind when it turned out to be a day of heavy downpour. "Go and fetch Ch'en K'o-ch'ang," said he to his household manager. "You and the young monk should journey to the temple and distribute dumplings on my behalf." The household manager came back and reported that the young monk was sick in his bed. "What is wrong with him?" the prince asked.

"The doctor says that there is nothing wrong with him physically," the household manager replied. "It is a psychological illness of some kind."

Upon further inquiry the prince found out that Hsin-ho, the slave girl with a golden voice, was also ill. "Her eyelids are dropping and her eyeballs move slowly," reported the matron in charge. "Furthermore, her breasts have become bigger and bigger." The prince entrusted his fifth wife, who was close to Hsin-ho, with the duty of ascertaining the young woman's condition, and his fifth wife came back to report that the young woman was indeed pregnant. "Who is this despicable beast?" the prince asked.

"Ch'en K'o-ch'ang, sir," his fifth wife replied.

The prince ordered the young monk to be brought before him immediately. Upon his arrival, the young monk prostrated himself before the prince.

"I have been good to you," said the prince. "Have I not been?"

The young man knocked his head against the floor in agreement.

"How, then, could you do such a despicable thing inside my own house? Besides, you are a monk."

"I did not do it, sir," the monk replied in a barely audible voice.

The prince had expected a ready confession of guilt since the evidence was to him rather obvious. Angered by Ch'en K'o-ch'ang's refusal to confess, he ordered the application of torture. Unable to stand the pain, the young monk finally admitted that he had indeed had an affair with the slave girl. Having secured Ch'en's written confession, the prince ordered him to be confined indefinitely in the city jail of Hangchow.

Worthy audience, our story would have ended here had it not been for abbot Yin's conviction that the young monk was innocent. He, of course, could not offer any proof to substantiate his conviction, but he was, nevertheless, dubious about the validity of the slave girl's testimony. "Whom should we believe, a slave girl with no education to speak of or a Buddhist scholar who has since childhood been taught the importance of propriety and righteousness?" he asked himself. "I have known him for two years—he is not the kind of man who would do such a thing!" However, since Ch'en K'o-ch'ang had already confessed, there was not much the abbot could do except try to convince the prince that the harshness of the punishment should be reduced.

Abbot Yin spoke of his disciple's innocence to abbot Kao of a neighborhood temple and succeeded in convincing the latter that both of them should repair to the prince's mansion to plead mercy on the young man's behalf.

The prince received both abbots with courtesy and, after the exchange of pleasantries, inquired of them the purpose of their visit. The two elderly monks quickly fell upon their knees and reported to the prince the purpose of their visit. "I am as disappointed with him as you are," said the prince. "Nevertheless, I shall notify the magistrate of Hangchow to reduce his sentence." Then he added with a long sigh, "How in the world could a man like him do such a despicable thing as this!"

The magistrate of Hangchow, having been notified of the prince's wishes, sentenced Ch'en K'o-ch'ang and Hsin-ho to one hundred and eighty strokes of beating, respectively, before they were released to whoever wished to accept them "with shame." The monks in the Lingyin Temple did not relish Ch'en K'o-ch'ang's return to their ranks and said so, since the young man had not only brought disgrace to all the monks but had also been officially defrocked by the government.[4] "The real story is not so simple as it appears to be," said abbot Yin. "Truth will in time reveal itself." He ordered a hut to be built in the back of the temple, wherein Ch'en K'o-ch'ang could nurse his wounds and recover before he was returned to his own home at Yüehch'ing.

Meanwhile Hsin-ho had been returned to her parents. Her parents, as we can easily understand, were not happy with this turn of events since their daughter had not only dishonored them but also, according to the law, they had to reimburse the prince one hundred thousand standard coins, for which price he had originally bought her.

"Where can we find this kind of money?" said her parents. "Do you have any savings of your own?"

"I do not have any savings," Hsin-ho replied. "But do not worry. Someone will take care of this."

"You must be out of your mind," her father scolded loudly. "How can that destitute monk take care of this?"

"The monk has nothing to do with my pregnancy," Hsin-ho spoke calmly.

"What?" Her father literally jumped from his chair.

"Yes, the monk is innocent," Hsin-ho repeated. "When Ch'ien, the household treasurer, found out that I was pregnant with his child, he was so frightened that he was totally beside himself. Then he suggested that I should name the monk as the father of the unborn child, on the grounds that because of his great affection for the young man, the prince would not punish me too severely once he found out about my pregnancy. Ch'ien told me that if I cooperated with him in this matter, he would take care of all my financial needs."

Without saying another word, Old Chang, as Hsin-ho's father was called, immediately took off for the prince's mansion and sought out Ch'ien the treasurer. Ch'ien not only denied everything but also accused Old Chang of trying to blackmail him. "You old, shameless scoundrel," he scolded with a loud voice. "Your daughter had an affair with, of all people, a monk, and yet you had the nerve to come down here to blackmail a respectable, law-abiding citizen. Both of them were tried and convicted, weren't they? If you get hold of yourself and request charity, I, out of generosity, might help you with a coin or two. Do you realize what you are accusing me of? Get out of here before I break your old bones."

Disgraced and grieved, Old Chang returned home to report to

his daughter what Ch'ien had said. Upon hearing her father's report, Hsin-ho cried uncontrollably and, holding one hand against the other, vowed revenge. "We shall go to the prince and tell the truth," she concluded.

The prince was still in bed when Old Chang and his daughter arrived early in the morning.

"Injustice, injustice!" Old Chang kept repeating "injustice" as soon as he was brought before the prince.

"Your daughter has committed a crime of unforgivable nature," said the prince. "What do you mean by injustice?"

"I do not mean injustice to my daughter, who deserved the punishment," Old Chang replied. "I mean injustice to the young monk." Then he proceeded to tell the truth as told him by his own daughter.

"Do you have any evidence that treasurer Ch'ien would indeed take care of your daughter's financial needs?"

"Yes, I have," Old Chang replied. He took out from his sleeve a letter in treasurer Ch'ien's own handwriting, in which he promised that he, Ch'ien, would not only take care of Hsin-ho's financial needs but also support her family if she agreed to implicate the monk instead of telling the truth about himself.

The prince was furious. Treasurer Ch'ien was brought to him immediately and, having faced the evidence of his own writing, confessed. He was then handed over to the magistracy of Hangchow for sentencing. The sentence turned out to be one hundred days in jail and one hundred strokes of beating, to be followed by banishment to an island in the South China Sea where he was to remain for the rest of his life. Meanwhile the prince had waived his right to collect any money from Old Chang and his daughter.

Another Double Fifth arrived; it was on this day that Ch'en K'o-ch'ang, having recovered from his wounds, heard the good news. The waiting was over, he said to himself; there was no need to stay in this world even a day longer. He sat down and wrote a note of farewell as follows:

On the Double Fifth I was born, ordained a monk, and implicated in a crime that I did not commit. On the Double Fifth I should also leave this world. A man who has committed an offense in his previous incarnation must pay for it in the present one. Now that I have been cleared of all charges, it is time to return home.

Having written this note, he went to a nearby spring to bathe himself, so that his body, as well as his spirit, would be clean enough for eternity to receive it. He returned to his hut, sat cross-legged, and concentrated. He died shortly afterward.

The prince sighed when he was informed of the young monk's death. To pay his last respects, he and his wife invited all of their friends to the Lingyin Temple to attend the cremation. When the fire was raging and shooting skyward, they saw the young monk standing right on top of the flame. They rubbed their eyes and could not believe what they saw. But any doubt was dispelled when they heard a voice from the flame: "Prince, madame, abbot, and fellow monks: I committed an offense in my previous incarnation and was rightfully punished in this one. Please congratulate me since I am now returning to the land of enlightenment wherefrom I came. If you miss me, go to the temple and take a look at the Merry Buddha of the five hundred Bodhisattvas. It is I!"

Only then did the prince and others know that this young monk called Ch'en K'o-ch'ang was really a reincarnation of the Merry Buddha whom they had worshiped since childhood.

Notes

1. Source: *Ching-pen t'ung-su hsiao-shuo*, roll 11.

2. The Lingyin Temple, famous for its five hundred Bodhisattvas in various postures, is located in the western suburb of Hangchow, Chekiang province. It has been a center of Buddhist worship for the past one thousand years.

3. The dumplings mentioned here are made of glutinous rice wrapped in bamboo leaves. Called *tsung-tzu* in Chinese, they are consumed during the Dragon Boat Festival, which occurs each year on the Double Fifth, namely, on the fifth day of the fifth month.

4. During the Sung dynasty a person had to secure a permit from the government before he or she could be officially accepted by a monastery or nunnery as a monk or nun. The permit could be revoked if the monk or nun had violated the Buddhist code or committed a crime.

CHAPTER

8

Yüan

IF there is any validity to the Taoist saying that one extreme is bound to be followed by another extreme in the opposite direction, it seems only logical that the Sung dynasty, which pampered intellectuals, should be followed by the Yüan dynasty which placed intellectuals, in terms of social status, somewhere between beggars, to whom they were superior, and prostitutes, to whom they were regarded as inferior. The Mongols, who rose from the arid north and, through ruthless application of military might, brought all of China under their control in 1279 and, in due course, created the largest empire the world had ever seen, regarded anything remotely resembling effeminacy as an indication of weakness and had nothing but absolute contempt for those who indulged in sentimentalities or argued over abstractions. Since histories are written mostly by intellectuals, the Yüan dynasty, not surprisingly, has been viewed by Chinese historians as one of the darkest and most deplorable periods in Chinese history.

There are of course heroes even among a group of villains. In searching for heroes, Chinese historians found a man named Yeh-lü Ch'u-ts'ai (1190–1244) who, though a non-Mongol, had served the Mongols most faithfully during the early period of their conquest. It was he who successfully argued against the idea of exterminating all Chinese and turning all of China into empty pasture; it was he who persuaded the Mongols not to put to the sword all the population of Kaifeng, then numbering 1.5 million, after that city was captured in 1233. It is interesting to note that in his arguments against savagery Yeh-lü Ch'u-ts'ai never resorted to ethics or morality which he obviously thought that his Mongol masters could not understand; it was the Mongol self-interest to which he successfully appealed (selection 38).

The Mongols' distrust of their Chinese subjects and Chinese resentment against their Mongol masters account for some of the unique features that mark the Mongol period. Not trusting the Chinese and yet numerically too small to administer a large empire, the Mongols staffed much of their bureaucracy with the so-called men of Western Regions (*Hsi yü jen;* Uighurs, Tibetans, and others), especially in the matter of tax collections. Not until 1315 when the Mongols felt comparatively safe with their Chinese subjects did they revive the civil service examinations whereby more and more Chinese were invited to join the bureaucracy. This gesture, though welcomed by Confucian scholars, was too small and too late as far as most Chinese were concerned. They remained hostile to the Mongol rule throughout the Yüan period.

Perhaps to counterbalance the pervasive influence of such native Chinese ideologies as Confucianism and Taoism, the Mongols singled out Lamaism, a Buddhist sect originating in Tibet, for governmental favors and patronage. In due course Lamaism and its clergy became an integral part of a state apparatus that was created for the continued control of the native population. The record is full of details about the abuse of power on the part of the Lamaist monks who were responsible to no one except their Mongol masters in Peking (selection 39).

One of the most peculiar and yet interesting documents forming part of the Mongol legacy in China is the Yüan Code that describes in great detail the punishment for every conceivable crime. Some of the unique features of this code are more or less expected: for instance, a Chinese who killed a Mongol would automatically be sentenced to death regardless of provocations, while a Mongol who killed a Chinese would be punished only by exile to an expeditionary army. Perhaps reflecting the Mongols' nomadic background, the code downgrades imprisonment as a form of punishment (maximum imprisonment for any crime was three years) but emphasizes corporal punishment. Castration as a form of punishment was abolished; so was hanging. But capital punishment in the form of beheading and slicing was maintained (selection 40).

To be sure, not everything was dark under Mongol rule. The Mongol transportation system, both land and water, was among the most efficient in Chinese history. Though the early Mongol rulers had nothing but contempt for agriculture, their descendants promoted it earnestly once they were convinced that agriculture yielded more tax revenue than nomadism. Even in cultural activities, in which the Mongols were particularly noted for their lack of interest, individual geniuses continued to flourish. The Yüan dramas *(Yüan ch'ü)* are so well written that they have become, in the public mind, almost synonymous with music dramas in general. Two of the greatest novels, *The Marsh Heroes (Shui-hu chuan)* and *The Romance of the Three Kingdoms (San kuo yen-yi)*, were written during the later Yüan and early Ming period, though they are customarily referred to as Ming novels.

As for source materials that cover this period, they are not abundant. In the case of the Sung that precedes this period and the Ming that follows it, there are volumes of collected works by individual scholars and statesmen that shed light on the period in question. This particular source is scarce for the Yüan dynasty, reflecting the anti-intellectual atmosphere of the regime. The major sources covering this period are confined to the two dynastic histories: *History of the Yüan (Yüan shih)* by Sung Lien (1310–81) and *New History of the Yüan (Hsin Yüan shih)* by K'o Shao-min (d. 1933). Though introducing some new material, the *Hsin Yüan shih*, which was not written until the twentieth century, remains basically a reshuffling of the contents of its predecessor.

Interestingly, a most enjoyable book covering this period was not written by a Chinese, but by an Italian named Marco Polo (ca. 1254–1324). While a reader should be cautioned against the author's overenthusiasm for everything Chinese, Polo's description of the Mongol court and its chief occupant, Kublai Khan (who was also the author's employer), remains the most vivid in any language. An excerpt from this book is not included here because the book itself *(Travels of Marco Polo)* is readily available on the market and in most libraries.

(38)
Sung Lien / *Yeh-lü Ch'u-ts'ai*[1]

Yeh-lü Ch'u-ts'ai, a native of Liaotung, was a direct descendant of the royal house of Liao. His father, who had at one time served as a vice-premier under Emperor Chin Shih-tsung [r. 1161–89], died when Ch'u-ts'ai was only two years old; it was his widowed mother who shaped his character during the early formative years. Upon reaching adulthood, he had learned everything his teachers could teach him, including astronomy, geography, mathematics, and law. He was also versed in Taoism, Buddhism, medicine, and divination.

Having heard about Ch'u-ts'ai by reputation, Genghis Khan summoned him for an interview after the Mongol conquerer had brought the territory of Yen [modern Hopeh province] under his control. As soon as the young man was brought in, the Mongol conquerer was most impressed with his appearance. Tall and slender, the visitor sported a long, well-trimmed beard and spoke with a voice that sounded like the ringing of a bell. "Liao and Chin have been traditional enemies," said the great conquerer. "I shall seek revenge against Chin on your behalf."

"Though we are natives of Liao," Ch'u-ts'ai replied, "our family has served Chin for three generations. It is improper for a subject to speak of revenge against his lord." The great conquerer was impressed with this reply and began to refer to Ch'u-ts'ai, affectionately, as Wu-t'u-sa-ho-li which, in Mongol language, means "Long Beard." From then on Yeh-lü Ch'u-ts'ai was addressed by all of the emperor's ministers and retainers as "Long Beard."

As one might expect, Ch'u-ts'ai's influence with the Khan was greatly resented by the Khan's other close advisers. Ch'ang Pa-chin, an expert bow maker and a favorite of the Khan, was particularly vocal in expressing his resentment. "We do not need any scholars," he said, "at a time when military might is all that counts."

"We need an expert bow maker to make bows," Ch'u-ts'ai retorted, "but we also need scholars to govern successfully." Genghis Khan was pleased and became even closer to Ch'u-ts'ai after he had heard about this verbal exchange.

Early in the year of Keng-ch'en [1220] the astronomers in the Western Regions predicted an eclipse of the moon at the full moon of the fifth month. Ch'u-ts'ai disagreed and proved to be right. Early in the next year Ch'u-ts'ai predicted an eclipse of the moon in the tenth month of that year, a prediction that was dismissed as "nonsense" by the astronomers. When the day finally arrived, the moon was indeed eclipsed by 80 percent. From then on Genghis Khan would rarely launch a military campaign without consulting Ch'u-ts'ai in advance about its astrological omens.

When the city of Lingwu [modern Ninghsia province] was captured, all the Mongol generals, as was their custom, went on a rampage, collecting not only worldly treasures such as gold and silk but also men and women to be condemned as slaves. Yeh-lü Ch'u-ts'ai alone collected books and medicine. Shortly afterward an epidemic broke out among the expeditionary army. It was the rhubarb and other drugs that he had collected that saved the lives of many of the Khan's veteran soldiers.

At this time Genghis Khan was too busy conquering one territory after another to pay much attention to administrative details. Local officials, consequently, did whatever they pleased. They killed people at will and robbed them of their wives and daughters. They forcibly took over private properties for their own use, including land and houses. The worst culprit in this regard was the Mongol governor of Yen who beheaded people with as much casualness as a farmer would cut down his ripe crops. With tears in his eyes Yeh-lü Ch'u-ts'ai reported what he had heard to Genghis Khan. As a result of his intervention, a decree was then issued to forbid local officials to carry out a death sentence unless it had been approved in advance by the imperial government.

Upon the death of Genghis Khan [1227], Ogodei, a son of Genghis's and successor to his throne, continued to rely on Yeh-lü Ch'u-ts'ai for advice and counsel on state affairs. As North China was only recently brought under Mongol control, numerous Chinese, unfamiliar with the Mongol law, committed offenses that subjected them to death sentence; yet there was no provision in the Mongol law that called for amnesty, clemency, or reduction of sentence. Yeh-lü Ch'u-ts'ai suggested a general clemency, which was criticized by his Mongol colleagues as too bookish and impractical. Nevertheless he succeeded in persuading Ogodei to issue a decree of general clemency that covered all cases of capital offenses committed before the first day of the first month of Keng-yin [16 January 1230]. Later he drafted a guideline of eighteen articles for all of the local officials to observe. Under the guideline a government of dual structure would be established in each district, headed simultaneously by a magistrate responsible for civil affairs and a military commander in charge of martial duties. With the military and civil officials checking and balancing each other, hopefully the abuse of power by either, which had caused enormous sufferings to the people as a whole, would be somewhat reduced. "Careful attention should be given to the preservation of the people's financial resources," said the guideline. "Any new levies without prior authorization from the imperial government are absolutely forbidden. Moreover, no official is allowed to use governmental funds to engage in trade." Death sentences would be imposed on Mongols, Uighurs, and natives of Hohsi who owned land but refused to pay taxes.[2] Death sentences would be also imposed on those officials who appropriated governmental properties for their own use. Before any death sentence was carried out, however, advance approval had to be secured from the imperial government. Under the guideline all the tributes to the Khan, in the form of goods or treasure, were abolished forthwith since paying these tributes, said Yeh-lü Ch'u-ts'ai, had been a major cause of the people's miseries.

Ogodei accepted all the articles in the guideline except one, namely, the article dealing with paying tributes. "Paying tributes is all right as long as it is voluntary," said the Great Khan.

"No tribute paid to the man in power has ever been characterized otherwise," retorted Yeh-lü Ch'u-ts'ai.

"I have accepted all proposals of yours," said the Great Khan. "Can you not accept only one of mine?" The article dealing with paying tributes was consequently deleted from the guideline.

During the reign of Genghis Khan, the government was in constant war in the Western Regions and consequently had little energy left for the administration of China itself. All officials, high and low, used their official positions to acquire private wealth, at the expense of not only the people they ruled but the government as well. When Ogodei ascended the throne, the treasury was virtually empty. It was at this time that a group of Mongol ministers and generals, headed by Ogodei's close aide Pieh-tieh, recommended the extermination of all Chinese and the transformation of their farmland into empty pastures, on the grounds that the Chinese could not possibly be of any use to the regime. "Now that Your Majesty is planning the conquest of South China," protested Yeh-lü Ch'u-ts'ai, "where will the necessary funds come from if all the Chinese in North China are exterminated? Each year we can take from them, in the form of taxes, five hundred thousand taels of silver, eighty thousand bolts of silk, and four hundred thousand piculs of grain. With this kind of financial resources, we can easily conquer South China. Who is there to say that the Chinese are of no use to the regime?"

"The statistics you cited are indeed impressive," said Ogodei. "I am now charging you with the responsibility of collecting the silver, the silk, and the grain."

To carry out the Great Khan's command, Yeh-lü Ch'u-ts'ai recommended that in those areas of North China then under Mongol control Chinese scholars, such as Ch'en Shih-k'o and Chao Feng who were known for their integrity and enjoyed local confidence, should be employed as tax collectors. After these men were employed, for the first time during Mongol rule there were some officials who could be characterized as incorruptible. In the fall of Hsin-mao [1231] the Great Khan Ogodei, upon his arrival at Yunchung [modern Shansi province], was presented with tax registers as well as the money and the silk that had been collected as taxes. Looking at the massive pile of treasure in his yard, the Great Khan said to Ch'u-ts'ai, jokingly, "If I dismiss you today, I know I still have other men who can collect taxes to meet the nation's needs." Then, in a serious vein, he added: "Is there anybody in South China more able than you are?"

"All the able men have gone to the south," Ch'u-ts'ai replied, "leaving behind only me to serve Your Majesty." Pleased with his modesty, Ogodei ordered wine to be served to him. On the same day Yeh-lü Ch'u-ts'ai was promoted to the presidency of the First Secretariat.

In the spring of Jen-ch'en [1232] Ogodei led his troops southward for the conquest of Chin. When the troops were about to cross the Yellow River, he decreed that all of those refugees who chose to surrender voluntarily would be exempted from death.

"This should not be done," some of the Khan's advisers protested. "These people surrender only when they do not have any other choice. They will revolt against us once they have the opportunity. They cease to be our enemies only when they are dead." Nevertheless, at the insistence of Yeh-lü Ch'u-ts'ai, several hundred flags of surrender were distributed among the refugees, and these flags enabled them to proceed home unmolested. This measure alone saved numerous lives.

According to Mongol law, any city that chose to resist by force after the Mongols had demanded its surrender would be put to the sword once the city was captured. When Kaifeng was about to be captured, General Su-pu-t'ai proposed the extermination of all of its residents in view of its resistance that had caused the loss of many Mongol lives. Having heard about the general's proposal, Yeh-lü Ch'u-ts'ai immediately went to the Great Khan to protest. "Our officers and men have fought for more than a generation," he said. "Their hope is that in victory they will acquire land for themselves. What is the use of land when nobody is there to work on it?" Facing contradictory advice, the Great Khan could not make a decision for the moment. "In this city there are numerous skillful artisans," Ch'u-ts'ai spoke again. "If we kill all the people in the city, we will lose these artisans too." The Great Khan agreed to this reasoning and issued an order to spare the lives of the city residents. At the time when Kaifeng fell to the Mongols, it had a population of 1,470,000, composed largely of refugees.

The Mongols captured a large number of people after their conquest of the areas south of the Yellow River. Most of the captured (70 to 80 percent) chose to flee and head for home once they were conscripted into the Mongol army. According to the Mongol law, anyone who opened his door to a deserter or provided him with financial assistance subjected not only himself but also his relatives, friends, neighbors, and fellow villagers to capital punishment. As this law was strictly enforced, thousands of deserters died of starvation on the road since no one dared offer them any assistance. Deploring this miserable state of affairs, Yeh-lü Ch'u-ts'ai reported to the Great Khan as follows: "Once a territory is conquered, all the people in it are Your Majesty's subjects. It is not a wise policy to force them out of their homes. It is not right, either, to kill one hundred persons on account of one deserter." Despite Ch'u-ts'ai's protest, Ogodei did not change the law governing deserters. Nevertheless he secretly ordered his commanders to relax its enforcement.

During an imperial conference held in the year of Yi-wei [1235] some Mongol generals recommended the employment of Chinese for the conquest of the Western Regions and the employment of Muslims for the conquest of South China. This strategy, said the generals, would enable the Mongols to control both groups easily. Yeh-lü Ch'u-ts'ai disagreed. "An enormous distance exists between China and the Western Regions," he explained. "The employment of Chinese in the Western Regions or the employment of Muslims in China would mean long travels for both; they and their horses would be totally exhausted even before the engagement of battle. Furthermore, the Chinese are not used to the climate of the Western Regions; nor are the Muslims used to the climate of China. Both groups would suffer diseases of epidemic proportions that could not but weaken the army itself." The Great Khan agreed to this reasoning, and the suggestion of using Chinese against the Muslims and vice versa was then dropped.

In the seventh month of the same year [1235] General Hu-tu-hu, with tax registers in his hand, recommended to the Great Khan the division of conquered territories among Mongol princes and generals. Having heard about this recommendation, Yeh-lü Ch'u-ts'ai went to the Great Khan to protest. "This recommendation, if carried out, will generate rivalry and resentment among the prospective recipients," he said. "A better way to reward them is to increase their allotments of gold and silk."

"But I have already promised them," said the Great Khan.

"In that case," said Yeh-lü Ch'u-ts'ai, "officials appointed by and responsible to the imperial government, rather than the princes and the generals themselves, should be charged with the responsibility of collecting taxes. At the end of each year these officials will hand over the collected taxes to each of the princes or generals concerned. Only in this way can overtaxation be avoided."

Having secured the Great Khan's agreement, Yeh-lü Ch'u-ts'ai proceeded to fix tax rates as follows: The yearly household tax was a half-catty of silk for every household that would go to the imperial government, plus one-fifth of a catty of silk that would go to the prince or general to whom the household was assigned as part of his feudal domain. As for taxation on land, the yearly rate was three pints of grain per *mou* for high-quality land, two and one-half pints of grain for medium land, and two pints of grain for poor land. If the land was good enough to grow rice, the tax rate would be then five pints per *mou*. Commercial taxes were fixed at one-thirtieth of the price of the commodity involved, and salt was to be sold by the government at forty catties per ounce of silver. In replying to his colleagues' complaint that the tax rates were too low, Ch'u-ts'ai said: "They are not low in view of the extra amount people have to pay to satisfy corrupt officials. Moreover, tax rates tend to increase with the passage of time. It is a good policy to start them at a low level."

The Great Khan was angry when Yeh-lü Ch'u-ts'ai spoke against the recommendation of T'o-huan, a close adviser of the Khan, that a search for young maidens should be conducted throughout the empire in order to enlarge the imperial harem. Undaunted, Ch'u-ts'ai reasoned as follows: "Only recently twenty-eight maidens have been added to the imperial harem. They seem to be more than adequate to enhance the imperial pleasure. A new search for young maidens will create enormous disturbances among the people, which should be avoided." The Great Khan thought for a long while and then ordered the cancellation of the general search.

In the year of Ting-yu [1237] Yeh-lü Ch'u-ts'ai memorialized the Great Khan as follows: "Just as making vessels requires the skills of an artisan, so building and preserving a nation cannot be attained without the assistance of scholars. The cultivation of scholarship, unfortunately, cannot be achieved overnight." Upon receiving the memorial, the Great Khan said, "If you can find some scholars, I shall make them officials." An examination was then scheduled, and all scholars were invited to participate in it, including those who had been condemned to slavery. "Any owner of a scholarly slave," said an imperial decree, "will be condemned to die if he refuses to yield his scholarly property for examination purposes." Altogether 4,030 scholarly slaves were located, and approximately one-quarter of them were later set free.

The Great Khan loved to drink and intoxicated himself daily with some of his closest advisers, despite repeated remonstrations from Yeh-lü Ch'u-ts'ai. One day Ch'u-ts'ai brought him a ladle of wine and showed him the erosion in the ladle. "If wine can erode a ladle made of iron," said he, "imagine what it can do to Your Majesty's stomach." After Ch'u-ts'ai left, the Great Khan said to his drinking companions, "You all love me, but none loves me more than my Long Beard." He ordered gold and silk to be awarded to Ch'u-ts'ai and instructed his drinking companions to limit their daily presentation to him to three goblets only.

The tax revenue for Honan was fixed in the year of Keng-yin [1230], but was repeatedly increased from then on. By the year of Wu-hsü [1238] it had reached a grand total of 1.1 million taels of silver. Yet, in that year, the government decided to double it to 2.2 million taels of silver. Yeh-lü Ch'u-ts'ai protested this increase vigorously, to the point of shedding tears. "Are you going to have a physical fight with me on account of this?" said the Great Khan. "Taking into consideration the fact that you have shed tears for those miserable taxpayers, I am making you this promise: If the increase does not work, I will revoke it." Unable to change the Khan's mind, Ch'u-ts'ai sighed with resignation. "The misery of our people begins today," said he.

Though in power for a long period of time, Yeh-lü Ch'u-ts'ai never used that power to recommend any of his relatives to an important position. Urged by his friend Liu Min to be more considerate toward his relatives, he replied: "It is one thing to present your relatives with gifts; it is a different thing to elevate them to a position of power. I do not want to be placed in a position whereby I have to prosecute and punish my own relatives." None of his relatives, consequently, was ever elevated to a position of power.

On the third day of the second month, in the year of Hsin-ch'u [1241], Great Khan Ogodei was seriously ill, as the attending physician reported that the patient's pulse had been too weak to be discernible. Not knowing what to do, the empress summoned Yeh-lü Ch'u-ts'ai to her presence to seek advice. "There are many innocent men in jail," said Ch'u-ts'ai. "A little mercy on our part may inspire Heaven to show mercy on us. I am recommending a general clemency." The empress wanted to issue an order of general clemency right away, but Ch'u-ts'ai objected, on the grounds that only the Great Khan could issue such an order. A little while later the Great Khan awakened, and the empress and

Ch'u-ts'ai went into his room to request an order of general clemency. The Khan, having already lost his speech, nodded his head. On that night, while the order of general clemency was read aloud and thus officially became the law, the Great Khan's pulse became stronger and stronger until it was as normal as that of a healthy man. He completely recovered on the next day.

Nine months later the Great Khan, as was his wont, was planning a hunting trip. Yeh-lü Ch'u-ts'ai, having consulted his books, declared that the trip was inauspicious. The Khan's other advisers said, "How could the Great Khan amuse himself without the chase?" On the fifth day of the eleventh month [8 December 1241] Great Khan Ogodei died in a hunting lodge.

After the death of Ogodei, his empress, Ma-chen, served as regent and entrusted some of the most unprincipled Muslims with the management of state affairs. The power of the government fell into the hands of a man named Ao-tu-la-ho-man who had been primarily known for his ability to collect the largest amount of taxes possible. As the new man in power, he was feared by everyone. The empress regent trusted him so much that she gave him blank papers bearing the imperial seal; whatever Ao-tu-la-ho-man chose to write on them would automatically assume the authority of an imperial decree. Only because of Yeh-lü Ch'u-ts'ai's vigorous protest did this practice later stop. At another time the empress regent instructed the royal historian to record anything Ao-tu-la-ho-man wanted to say, at the pain of losing his right hand if he refused to record it. "If anybody's hand has to be sundered, it should be mine," said Yeh-lü Ch'u-ts'ai, "since it is I who have been charged by the late Khan with the responsibility of preserving this dynasty's institutions. To preserve them, I am willing to risk my life—never mind my hand!" During the ensuing verbal exchange, the empress regent became angrier and angrier while Yeh-lü Ch'u-ts'ai's voice became louder and louder. "I have served two Great Khans consecutively for thirty years, and none of them found any fault with me," he shouted. "You cannot kill me without a valid reason." From then on the empress regent learned to respect him, though resenting him intensely.

After Yeh-lü Ch'u-ts'ai's death in the fifth month of Chia-ch'en [1244] at the age of fifty-four, someone reported to the empress regent that the man from Liao, before his death, had accumulated an enormous amount of wealth that was presently hidden inside his house. The empress regent ordered an investigation, and the investigator, having searched the house thoroughly, found a dozen lutes, some paintings and bronzes, and several thousand rolls of the dead man's own writing. The man from Liao left behind no worldly fortunes.

Notes

1. *Yüan shih,* roll 146.
2. Contrary to the Chinese, the Mongols, Uighurs, and natives of Hohsi (modern Kansu province) had enjoyed special privileges, descending in that order, under the Mongol rule. The natives of Hohsi were the former subjects of Hsia, a kingdom in western China that was conquered by Genghis Khan in 1227.

(39)
Sung Lien / *Lamaism*[1]

The Mongols originated in the Northern Grassland and had embraced Lamaism before they conquered China. When the Western Regions were brought under control, Emperor Yüan Shih-tsu [Kublai Khan, 1216–94] decided to promote Lamaism in these regions, for the purpose of weakening the militancy and warlike spirit of the native population and thus enabling the government to exercise control over this vast, remote, and sparsely populated area. The area was divided into provinces and districts, with officials appointed by and responsible to the Grand Lama in the capital. Assisting the Grand Lama in the governance of this area was the Council of Public Policies *(Hsüan cheng yüan),* the vice-president of which, who actually ran the daily administration, was always a Lamaist monk, appointed by the emperor upon the recommendation of the Grand Lama. Local officials, however, could be either Lamaist monks or civilians. Whether monks or civilians, they had absolute authority, in military as well as civilian matters, over the districts or provinces under their jurisdiction. They were responsible to no one except the Grand Lama, whose orders bore the same authority as imperial decrees, as far as the Western Regions were concerned.

For more than one hundred years during the Yüan dynasty the imperial court went to great extremes to honor Lamaism and its representatives. Even empresses and princesses took Lamaist vows and worshiped Lamaist gods. During the imperial conference, while other high-ranking officials lined up on both sides of the audience hall, the Grand Lama had a special seat next to the throne. Whenever a new emperor was installed, one of his first items of business was to issue a decree eulogizing the Grand Lama and granting him such symbols of respect as new seals and scrolls, with inlaid words made of mother-of-pearl. Whenever the Grand Lama returned to the capital from a trip in the provinces, the emperor would order high-ranking officials, accompanied by a hundred or more cavalrymen, to serve as official escorts; their duty was to see that every need of the Grand Lama was well taken care of. Once inside the capital area, he was escorted to his residence by a long procession of honor guards bearing the proper insignia.

From time to time expensive gifts were showered upon the Grand Lama as a way of showing imperial appreciation. In the ninth year of Ta-teh [1305], for instance, the gift consisted of five hundred taels of gold, five thousand taels of silver, ten thousand bolts of silk, and paper currency equivalent to three thousand taels of silver. The gift for the second year of Huang-ch'ing [1313] was composed of five thousand taels of gold, fifteen thousand taels of silver, and seventeen thousand bolts of silk. Even the Grand Lama's brothers were provided with expensive food and lodging by local officials wherever they went; one of them was even married to a royal princess. They were titled dukes and counts, bearing seals fashioned from gold and jade. Their followers, together with those of the Grand Lama, acted like bullies wherever they happened to be; the harm they caused to the people was immeasurable. Sadly, as days passed by, their power continued to increase; with increased power, they did even greater harm.

Yang-lien-chen-chia, who served as superintentent of lamas in the Lower Yangtze during the reign of Yüan Shih-tsu, proceeded to dig graves and unearth hidden treasures the moment he assumed office. Altogether he opened up 101 mausoleums that entombed the bodies of the late Sung emperors and some of their chief ministers, in Shaohsing as well as in Hangchow,[2] and killed four civilians in the process. During his tenure of office, he openly accepted bribes that consisted of beautiful women as well as treasure and, in one way or another, robbed people of valuable possessions. A partial list of his loot would include 1,700 taels of gold, 6,800 taels of silver, 152 curios, 50 taels of pearls, a large amount of paper currency equivalent to 116,200 taels of silver, and 23,000 *mou* [2,950 acres] of paddy fields. He also saw to it that 23,000 households under his protection did not have to pay any taxes.

In the first year of Chih-ta [1308] the lamas of the K'aiyüan Temple in the capital, having bought a large quantity of firewood, refused to pay for it. The seller lodged a complaint in the magistrate's court, and the magistrate, whose name was Li Pi, proceeded to conduct a hearing on this case. During the hearings the lamas, accompanied by a large group of muscled men, burst into the courtroom with long sticks. They dragged down the magistrate by his hair, threw him to the floor, and beat him up. Then they locked him inside an empty room. Having finally succeeded in escaping from his confinement, the magistrate appealed his case to the imperial court. The imperial court, after hearing his presentation, decided to forgive him for having offended the lamas.

In the second year of Chih-ta [1309] the Council of Public Policies proposed that any civilian who beat a lama should have his hands cut off and any civilian who orally abused a lama should have his tongue cut out. Only through the vigorous intervention of the crown prince, later known as Emperor Yüan Jen-tsung [r. 1312–20], did the proposal not become a law.

In the second year of T'ai-ting [1325] Censor Li Ch'ang reported that he had recently toured such districts as P'ingliang, Chinghui, and Tinghsi[3] and had personally witnessed the outrageous behavior of some of the western lamas.[4] Wearing prominently "labels of preference" with words stitched in golden threads, said Li, these lamas roamed on horses from one town to another, sometimes in groups of a hundred or more. If government hostels were not large enough to accommodate them, they would force their way into civilian houses where only too often they chased out male residents so they could spend an evening alone with their wives and daughters. The postal station of Fengyüan, for instance, was visited 185 times from the first to the seventh month by these lamas, who requisitioned 840 horses for their personal use, 60 percent more than Mongol princes requisitioned for official duties during the same period. The horse owners had no place to lodge their complaints, since the court was totally powerless insofar as law violations by lamas were concerned. "The government is supposed to issue the 'labels of preference' only to those involved with national defense," continued Li. "What justification is there for the monks to wear them?" Li proposed that Lamaist monks should be denied the free use of postal horses and that local courts should be given jurisdiction over them, at least in cases where there was an obvious abuse of privileges. The imperial government, however, chose not to reply to Li's proposal.

The expenses involved in Lamaist worship were no less than staggering. In the fourth year of Chia-yu [1317] it was reported that Lamaist worship of the royal house alone, for each and every year, involved the consumption of 439,500 catties of noodles, 79,000 catties of vegetable oil, 21,870 catties of cheese, and 27,300 catties of honey. For more than thirty years early in the Yüan dynasty the number of occasions calling for Lamaist worship was only 102 per year; it was increased to more than 500 after the seventh year of Ta-teh [1306]. Knowing no limit to their greed, the Lamaist leaders, in close collaboration with their allies around the emperor, requested and received an annual grant of millions of taels of silver in the name of charity, at the taxpayers' expense, of course. The amount was several times greater beginning with the Ta-teh period [1297–1307].

Whenever a Lamaist festival occurred, the Lamaist hierarchy would request the government to declare a general clemency as a means to please the gods and accumulate Lamaist deeds in Heaven. Many notorious thieves became free in this manner. Li Liang-p'i, a former counselor in the Council of Public Policies who had been convicted of a crime of accepting bribes and selling offices, was immediately set free after the Grand Lama had intervened on his behalf. The popular reaction was that a crime ceased to be a crime so long as the criminal had some connection with the Lamaist religion. To reward its followers, the Lamaist hierarchy often persuaded the government, only too successfully, to start a nationwide charity campaign, so these followers would be lucratively employed as campaign managers.

In summary, whatever political abuse one could think of, the Yüan dynasty had it.

Notes

1. *Yüan shih*, roll 202.
2. Both were located in modern Chekiang province.
3. All these districts were located in modern Kansu province.
4. Tibetan and Turkestan lamas.

(40)
The Yüan Code / *Homicide*[1]

1. A person who kills another person is punishable by death. The family of the victim is entitled to receive from the family of the killer fifty taels of silver for funeral expenses.[2] The amount could be reduced if the family of the killer is too poor, but under no circumstances should it be less than ten taels of silver in paper currency. If a general clemency is declared before the death sentence is carried out, the payment to the injured family will be doubled.

2. When more than one person conspire to kill an official and succeed in their attempt, all persons involved, the leader or leaders who plan the killing as well as their followers who execute the killing, are punishable by death. If injury rather than death is the result, all persons involved are to be punished by 107 blows and then be exiled to a distant region. The families of the guilty must pay funeral expenses for the dead official.

3. A person who, after having killed another person, chooses to commit suicide but fails in his attempt is punishable by death nevertheless.

4. A person who kills another person is eligible for clemency if he has accumulated good deeds after the killing, provided that the killing is accidental rather than intentional.

5. In a physical fight between two persons, the person who has no intention to kill at the beginning but acquires such intention during the process of fighting is regarded as having harbored the

intention to kill, if the physical fight ends with the death of the other person.

6. In a physical fight between two or more persons, the person who has used a weapon, such as a knife, in the fight and thus caused the death of a person or persons against whom he has been fighting is regarded as having harbored the intention to kill.

7. In the situation as described in article 6 the offending person will be punished by 107 blows, instead of being sentenced to death, if his victim or victims suffer injury rather than death as a result of his offense.

8. If a person wielding a knife intends to kill another person but is unsuccessful in his attempt after his intended victim has managed to escape and if, subsequent to this escape, he shifts his anger to those bystanders who have tried to stop him, he is regarded as having harbored the intention to kill, if he kills one or more of these bystanders.

9. A person who kills a tax collector is regarded as having harbored the intention to kill, even though the tax collector has used high-pressure methods to collect the taxes due and the taxpayer, out of desperation, decides to kill him.

10. If a man while intoxicated with liquor attempts to kill his wife and, having failed in his attempt, shifts his anger to those bystanders who have tried to stop him, the man is regarded as having harbored the intention to kill and will be sentenced to death if he kills one or more of these bystanders.

11. If a man kills a prostitute who has refused to elope with him, the man will be regarded as guilty as if he had killed a person other than a prostitute.

12. All cases that have to do with physical fights and subsequent death or deaths of the parties involved must be reported to higher authorities before sentences are carried out.

13. A person who beats to death the person who has killed his father is regarded as guiltless. The family of the person who has killed his father is responsible for the payment of fifty taels of silver for his father's funeral expenses.

14. If a Mongol, in a physical fight or in a state of drunkenness, kills a Chinese, the Mongol will be punished by exile to an expeditionary army, in addition to the payment of funeral expenses for the dead person.

15. In a physical fight involving a number of persons, the per-

son who accidentally tramples to death a child or infant will be punished by 107 blows, in addition to the payment of funeral expenses for the dead child or infant. The person who causes death to an adult in this physical fight will be punished in a manner as provided elsewhere in this statute.

16. If a man beats to death another man who has been flirting with his wife, he will receive a punishment one degree lower than the death sentence. He will be responsible for the dead man's funeral expenses.

17. If a person beats to death a notorious outlaw who would have been sentenced to death if captured by governmental authorities, he is guiltless. He is not responsible for the dead man's funeral expenses.

18. If a person with an object other than a knife causes injury to another person who subsequently dies as a result of this injury, he will receive a punishment three degrees lower than the death sentence.

19. In a quarrel between two persons, if one person smashes his head into the chest of the other and, in the process of falling down, accidentally causes death by damaging the other person's heart with his elbow, the offending person will be punished by 107 blows, in addition to the payment of the dead person's funeral expenses.

20. The retainer of an official who beats to death a laborer in the inn where the official stays will be punished in the same manner as any other person who has caused death by beating.

21. In a physical fight resulting from one person's violent response to another person's joke, the person who causes injury and subsequent death to the other person will be punished by 107 blows.

22. The man who marries a widow becomes the foster father of the widow's offspring by her first marriage. He will not be responsible, however, for any crime committed by any of his adopted sons if the latter has been evicted by him from his house and lives in a separate residence. In this case the son alone is responsible for any injury he causes to others.

23. A convicted criminal who kills another convicted criminal will be punished in the same manner as if he had killed any other person. A tax collector who beats a person to death in the process of exacting tax payment will be sentenced to death.

24. If an official beats to death a civilian who has accused him in the court of justice of having accepted bribery, the official will be regarded as having harbored the intention to kill and be punished accordingly.

25. If a military officer, in a moment of fury, orders his soldiers to beat a civilian who subsequently dies as a result of injury, the military officer will be punished by 87 blows and will be discharged from his post for a period of one year. When reinstated after the one-year period, he will be demoted by one rank. He is responsible for the dead person's funeral expenses.

26. If a garrison commander, in a moment of fury, orders the murder of one of his subordinates who has exposed him for the theft of public treasure, the garrison commander will be regarded as having harbored the intention to kill. He will be permanently barred from further service, and the punishment he receives will not be reduced by a general clemency. He is responsible for the payment of a cash equivalent of twice the amount of the standard funeral expenses.

27. An official in a bureau or commission who inexcusably beats an artisan to death will be sentenced to death.

28. A father who inexcusably kills his son with a knife will be punished by 77 blows.

29. A father is guiltless if the son he kills has been undutiful toward him. However, any of his brothers or nephews who have collaborated in, or given assistance to, this killing will be punished by 107 blows.

30. If a father kills his married daughter after having discovered a serious offense committed by her, the father will be punished by 57 blows. The husband of his deceased daughter is entitled to receive from him the full amount of money which he paid for his daughter, so the husband can marry someone else.

31. If a father, with valid reason, beats a son or daughter of his and accidentally causes his or her death, the father is guiltless.

32. A man who kills the son of his wife by her first marriage is punishable by death.

33. A wife who kills a son of her husband's concubine will be punished by 97 blows. Her husband can either marry her off or sell her as a slave.

34. A man or woman who mistreats his or her daughter-in-law and causes her death will be punished by 107 blows, despite the

fact that the woman, before her death, has not been a good daughter-in-law.

35. If a man kills not only his son who has been undutiful toward him but also his daughter-in-law, for no other reason than the fact that she happens to be his son's wife, the man will be punished by 77 blows. Her dowry and all of her other belongings shall be returned to her parents.

36. A man who, for flimsy reasons, kills his younger brother is punishable by death.

37. If adopted sons plan and carry out the murder of their younger brother who was born to the family and therefore its legitimate heir, the planners as well as the executors of the murder will be sentenced to death. All their properties, including land and houses, will from then on belong to the murdered person's wife and sons. The sons of the murdered person will be regarded as heirs to the family.

38. If a man kills his younger brother who has struck him first, the man will be regarded as having killed a guilty person. He will not be punished in the same manner as a murderer would be.

39. If a man, in a quarrel, accidentally kills his younger brother who has lived in a separate residence, the man will be punished by 77 blows. He shall pay half of his younger brother's funeral expenses.

40. A man who kills his cousin in a quarrel will be punished in a manner as if he had killed an unrelated person.

41. If a man kills his younger sister who, though a nun, has had illicit sexual relations with some other man, the man is regarded as having killed a guilty person and will not be punished in the same manner as a murderer would be, provided that before the killing he has warned her about her improper conduct and that his sister, instead of heeding his advice, has verbally abused him in return and physically wrestled with him.

42. If a man beats his younger brother's wife who subsequently dies as a result of injury, the man will be punished by 107 blows. He shall pay for the dead woman's funeral expenses.

43. If a woman causes death by drowning her husband's younger sister, the woman will be regarded as having harbored the intention to kill.

44. If a man kills a son of his cousin in a quarrel, the man will be punished by 107 blows. If a knife is used in the killing, the man

will be punished by death. He shall also pay for the dead man's funeral expenses.

45. If a man beats to death a son of his brother for the purpose of acquiring the latter's properties, the man will be punished by death.

46. If a man accidentally beats to death a member of the younger generation in his family, the man will be punished by 77 blows. He shall also pay for the funeral expenses if the dead person, before his death, has lived in a separate residence.

47. A man who kills his wife for flimsy reasons will be punished by death.

48. If a man hates his wife and subsequently causes her death by poisoning, the man will be regarded as having killed an unrelated person.

49. If a man beats his wife and subsequently causes her death for her arrogant attitude toward his parents, the man will be punished by 77 blows.

50. If a man beats his wife and accidentally causes her death after his wife has refused to attend to his needs during his illness and if, in the meantime, she has been verbally abusing his parents and has caused him to lose all affection for her, the man is guiltless.

51. If a man who hates his wife and loves his concubine chooses to kill his wife by citing some minor faults of hers, the man will be punished by death.

52. If a man, having heard some rumor of a derogatory nature about his fiancée, kills her, the man will be regarded as having killed an unrelated person.

53. A woman who cruelly beats to death her husband's concubine will be punished by 107 blows. She shall be stripped before the beatings are inflicted upon her body.

54. If a man, without valid reason, kills a son of his sister, the man will be regarded as having killed an unrelated person.

55. If a man kills his son-in-law for some grudge of his own, the man will be regarded as having killed an unrelated person.

56. If a man beats to death his slave who has verbally and physically abused him, the man is guiltless.

57. If a person kills his or her slave who has been faultless, he or she will be punished by 87 blows. If he or she is in a state of drunkenness when the killing takes place, the punishment will be reduced by one degree [i.e., 77 blows].

58. If a person beats to death a slave who is about to gain his or her freedom, the offending person will be punished by 77 blows.

59. If a person plans and then carries out the killing of a former slave, he or she will be regarded as having killed a free person.

60. If a free person, in a physical fight, beats to death a slave, the person will be punished by 107 blows. He or she shall pay fifty taels of silver for the dead person's funeral expenses.

61. If a free person, without malice, accidentally kills somebody else's slave, the person will be punished by 77 blows. He or she shall pay fifty taels of silver for the dead person's funeral expenses.

62. If a slave beats to death his younger brother who is also a slave of the same owner, the slave will not be punished if the owner requests exemption from penalty on his behalf.

63. If a slave of one owner kills a slave of a different owner, the crime thus committed will be regarded as a crime committed by one free man against another. If the slaves involved belong to the same owner, the punishment is provided elsewhere in this statute.

64. A landlord who beats to death his tenant will be punished by 107 blows. He shall pay fifty taels of silver for the dead man's funeral expenses.

65. If a man in a state of drunkenness mistakes another man for his enemy and kills him, the man will be regarded as having killed a man who is not his enemy.

66. If a slave acts according to his owner's command by killing another man who is his owner's enemy, the slave will be punished by exile instead of death.

67. A convicted murderer who has planned and executed the killing of another person will not be pardoned even though there is a general clemency. His accomplice or accomplices, on the other hand, will have their death sentences reduced to one-year imprisonment.

68. A killer cannot escape punishment simply because he is old and sick.

69. A person seventy years old or older who has maliciously killed another person will be shackled and thrown into jail, where he shall remain until he dies.

70. If two men run into each other in total darkness and if one accidentally knocks the other down and causes his death, the man is guiltless. However, he shall pay fifty taels of silver for the dead man's funeral expenses.

71. A killer under the age of fourteen is guiltless if the killing is accidental rather than intentional. However, the killer and his family are responsible for the dead person's funeral expenses.

72. If a person under the age of fourteen, in a physical fight, injures another person who subsequently dies, the family of the offending person must pay an indemnity to the family of the dead, the amount of which is subject to negotiation between the parties involved. In addition, the offending person and his family are responsible for the dead person's funeral expenses.

73. If a blind person beats another person who subsequently dies as a result of injury, the blind person will be punished by 107 blows. He is responsible for the dead person's funeral expenses.

74. If a person in a state of insanity beats another person who subsequently dies as a result of injury, the person is guiltless. He is responsible, however, for the dead person's funeral expenses.

75. If a physician, because of his insufficient knowledge, kills a patient with his needle or medicine, the physician will be punished by 107 blows. He shall pay for the dead person's funeral expenses.

76. If a construction worker throws a rock or brick and accidentally hits a person who subsequently dies, the construction worker will be punished by 87 blows. He shall pay for the dead person's funeral expenses.

77. If a soldier, while practicing archery, accidentally hits a person with his arrow, the soldier is guiltless, even though the injured person subsequently dies. He is responsible, however, for the dead person's funeral expenses.

78. A person who accidentally tramples a child or infant to death will be punished by 77 blows. He is responsible for the dead child's funeral expenses.

79. If a person, in the darkness of the night, accidentally runs into another person with his mount and causes the latter's death, the person will be punished by 77 blows. He is responsible for the dead person's funeral expenses.

80. If a carriage driver injures another person with his carriage and the injured person subsequently dies, the carriage driver will

be punished by 77 blows. He is responsible for the dead person's funeral expenses.

81. If a carriage driver, in the darkness of the night, tramples another person to death with his moving carriage and if it is established that he cannot possibly see the victim on the road because of the darkness, the carriage driver will be punished by 37 blows. He is responsible for one-half of the dead person's funeral expenses.

82. If a small child, while playing with other small children, accidentally injures one of them who subsequently dies, the small child is guiltless.

83. The law shall not intervene if the parties involved in an accidental death decide to settle the dispute by themselves.

84. If an adult, while playing a game of gymnastic exercise, accidentally loses his grip and causes his partner, another adult, to fall down on the floor or ground, the man is guiltless, even though his partner subsequently dies of injury.

85. In a game between an adult and a child, if the child subsequently dies of fright, the adult will be punished by 67 blows. He shall pay fifty taels of silver for the dead child's funeral expenses.

86. In a game of chase, if one person, being chased by another, stumbles, injures himself, and subsequently dies, the person who does the chasing will be punished by a prison term. He is responsible for the dead person's funeral expenses.

87. If a camel, while being pastured, bites a person and causes his death, its keeper will be punished by 17 blows. The family of the dead person will acquire the ownership of the camel.

88. If a horse, while being hired by a postal station, bites a person and causes his death, the family of the dead person will acquire the ownership of the horse. The original owner of the horse shall buy another horse with his own money, so he can continue his service to the postal station.

89. A slave who intentionally kills one of his children for the purpose of blackmailing his owner will be punished by 107 blows.

90. If a man as a result of a quarrel with his wife deliberately drowns, and consequently causes the death of, a child of his wife's by her first marriage, for the purpose of blackmailing someone else, the man will be regarded as having harbored the intention to kill and will be punished accordingly.

91. If a man places poison in the food of his wife's child by her

first marriage and causes the child's death, the man will be regarded as having poisoned, and thus having caused the death of, an unrelated person and will be punished accordingly.

92. If a man kills a guiltless son or grandson for the purpose of blackmailing some enemy of his, the man will be regarded as having killed an unrelated person and be punished accordingly.

93. A killer does not have to pay a standard sum, called funeral expenses, if his victim has no close relatives to receive it. After conviction, the ownership of his properties will be transferred to his wife and children. He shall work for his own keep before the implementation of his sentence.

94. A person who kills a convicted criminal will not have to pay for the dead person's funeral expenses.

95. If a bandit kills two or more persons in the process of practicing his trade, the bandit will be punished by slicing. The family of each of his victims is entitled to receive funeral expenses from him.

96. If a person in a physical fight kills another person of the same residence and subsequently dies before his guilt can clearly be established, the family of the offending person is not responsible for the other person's funeral expenses. Nor is the family of his victim responsible for his funeral expenses.

97. If a killer and his victim happen to live in areas other than the place where the killing occurs, the government shall see that funeral expenses are collected from the family responsible for these expenses.

98. If a convicted killer is too poor to pay for his victim's funeral expenses and if in the meantime no relative of his can be located for shouldering these expenses, the government will be responsible for these expenses.

99. The maximum amount of funeral expenses, in all cases of death resulting from injury, is limited to one hundred taels of silver in paper currency.

100. In the case of a general clemency when the sentence of a convicted criminal is reduced but the amount of funeral expenses he has to pay for his victim is doubled, let the doubled amount be fixed at one hundred taels of silver in paper currency, for himself as well as his accomplice, if any.

101. A killer who confesses the killing is obligated to pay for his victim's funeral expenses, even though the body of his victim has not been, or may never be, located.

102. A monk or priest who has been convicted of killing will be assessed the same amount of funeral expenses as a layman.

103. An employer is not obligated to pay for the funeral expenses of a victim of his employee.

104. If a slave kills a person in his owner's house, the owner will be responsible for the dead person's funeral expenses. The owner will not be responsible for the dead person's funeral expenses if the killing takes place outside his house.

Notes

1. The Yüan Code is a lengthy document, and the section dealing with homicide is only part of it. The English translation of some other sections of the same code can be found in Dun J. Li, *The Essence of Chinese Civilization* (New York: Van Nostrand, 1967). Source: *Yüan shih*, roll 105.

2. The term "funeral expenses" in this statute should be construed more as "financial compensation" than as "funeral expenses" per se.

CHAPTER

9

Ming

HISTORIANS have debated for centuries which of the two groups, men of thought or men of action, are more instrumental in the development of history. Whatever the verdict is, extensive debate can quickly be set aside as far as political history is concerned, since political leaders are almost by definition men of action. In China the founder of a major dynasty was supposed to have possessed a political acumen none of his contemporaries could match, as his goal, the achievement of supreme power, was the same as that of his numerous rivals. Most founders of Chinese dynasties were members of nobility and inherited a political base from which they sprang to supreme power, but there were a few exceptions. The most notable exceptions were Liu Pang (d. 195 B.C.), a former village chief and later founder of the Han dynasty, and Chu Yüan-chang (1328–98), an ex-monk, a former beggar, and later founder of the Ming dynasty. Both were of course men of action and shared a common contempt for all of those who, they said, only knew how to play with words (selection 41).

The Ming dynasty, like every major dynasty before it, passed through what historians often refer to as a dynastic cycle—from peace and prosperity to war and depression. During the early period of the dynasty the country was energetic and often exorbitant, accompanied by a self-confidence that was too frequently expressed in acts of chauvinism. The most exorbitant acts, on all accounts, were the so-called Cheng Ho's Seven Voyages to the Western Ocean in which Chinese ships, then the largest and perhaps the best constructed anywhere in the world, sailed to such remote places as the Persian Gulf, the Red Sea, and the eastern coast of Africa (selection 42). Cheng Ho (ca. 1373–1435), the Chinese admiral, brought back dozens of alien kings and their envoys to Peking to pay tribute, at enormous expense to China itself. By 1430 when Cheng Ho made his last voyage, the dynasty's fortune had already begun to decline, and his adventure remains until this day the most ambitious that a Chinese government ever undertook overseas.

At a time when Cheng Ho was the best-known Chinese overseas, few foreigners realized that his legal position inside China was among the lowest. He, in fact, was a eunuch, castrated during childhood so he could serve his imperial master with undivided attention. The eunuch institution, which began in China as early as the eighth century B.C. and did not officially end until 1911, cannot be understood fully without a close examination of the autocratic nature of Chinese government. Chinese emperors, as Sons of Heaven, were entitled to the best amenities in life that the world could offer, and the best amenities, in a preindustrial society like China, consisted primarily of enjoyment of food and sex and their various aspects. This was especially true for a Chinese emperor who lived a secluded existence in his Forbidden Palace. In sex most men mistake quantity for quality; and Chinese emperors, being no exceptions, had harems that varied in size from a few dozen to a few thousand women carefully chosen for their beauty, intelligence, and charm. Due to the size of the harem, most of these women never had the opportunity to meet their supposed spouse, let alone consort with him. What would have happened to their chaste virtue, to which traditional China attached great importance, if the servants in the Forbidden Palace were natural or uncastrated men?

It is easy to condemn the eunuch institution by invoking modern standards. Interestingly, few Chinese ever advocated its abolition before the twentieth century. Whenever debate occurred involving the eunuchs, it was their abuse of power, rather than eunuchs as an institution, that occupied Chinese scholars' attention. Legally the humblest among servants, eunuchs were often entrusted with great power by their imperial masters. A strong emperor could take that power away from them as easily as he had granted it, but a weak emperor often found himself a mere puppet of his supposed servants. Sometimes their power became so great that they installed or deposed emperors as they pleased.

As autocratic power increased with each succeeding dynasty, the power of eunuchs also increased proportionally, since, basically speaking, it was an extension of the autocratic power of the emperors. The autocratic power of Chinese emperors reached an all-time high during the Ming dynasty; not surprisingly, the abuse of power by eunuchs during this period was also the worst in Chinese history. A strong emperor like Yung-lo (r. 1403–24) could use Cheng Ho's special talent to advance Chinese prestige abroad; a weak emperor, such as Ming Hsi-tsung (r. 1621–27) quickly became a convenient tool whereby an unprincipled, ambitious eunuch like Wei Chung-hsien (1568–1627) could destroy the very fabric of a legitimate government. A study of Wei Chung-hsien's career sheds much light on the Chinese government at its darkest moment (selection 43); it indicates, among other things, that even normally decent men can succumb to their worst instincts whenever power is involved.

Denied such modern concepts as democracy and representative government, even the most learned Chinese scholars could not find a proper solution to the abuse of power by Chinese monarchs. The Chinese were of course entitled to stage a rebellion against an oppressive government, according to the Confucian theory of the mandate of Heaven; but rebellion, whether successful or not, involved the loss of lives and property to millions—a prospect in which few responsible men wished to indulge. The alternative was to plead and to remonstrate, reminding the tyrants that the Son of Heaven was also the Father of Men and that in the remote years of China's past good emperors such as Yao and Shun served their subjects' interest rather than their own (selection 44). If a tyrant refused to entertain a change of heart, the only hope was his early and untimely death—not exactly a vain hope, in fact, when one took into consideration the kind of life (heavy drinking, debauchery, etc.) that most tyrants were famous for.

The Ming dynasty, though more productive culturally compared with the Yüan, lagged behind other great dynasties of the past such as the Han, the T'ang, and the Sung. The greatest thinker of the Ming dynasty was Wang Shou-jen (also known as Wang Yang-ming, 1472–1529), but even he could not but plow familiar ground (selection 45). In the fine arts the Ming Chinese definitely did better, especially in painting and ceramics.

As for source material covering this period, the *History of the Ming (Ming shih)*, compiled by a committee headed by Chang

T'ing-yü (1672–1755) and completed in 1739, is regarded as one of the better-written dynastic histories. Yet, by following a rigid format common to all dynastic histories, it has its obvious short-comings. It describes in great detail what we today might call trifles (e.g., ceremonial clothing), but gives only a sketch of sub-jects about which we wish to learn more (e.g., Cheng Ho's voy-ages abroad). Nevertheless, it is the standard reference book for this period. Another book covering the same period but much smaller in volume (80 rolls as compared with 336 rolls for the *Ming shih*) is *Events in the History of the Ming (Ming shih chih-shih pen-mo)* by Ku Ying-t'ai (eighteenth century), which has more colorful details dismissed by the authors of the *Ming shih* as "rumor and hearsay." As far as Ming institutions are concerned, a definitive work is the *Ming hui-tien (Institutions of the Ming Dynasty)*, consisting of 228 rolls and completed in 1576. It is also known as *Ta Ming hui-tien (Institutions of the Great Ming Dynasty)*.

In philosophy a comprehensive but introductory work is the *Ideological Controversy of the Ming Dynasty (Ming yü hsüeh-an)* by Huang Tsung-hsi, whose name has been mentioned in an earlier chapter. For details one has to read the complete works of individual philosophers, such as the *Complete Works of Wang Shou-jen (Wang Wen-ch'eng ch'üan-chi)*.

Other than those mentioned above, the books that have been recommended most often for the Ming period are *A Ming Bar-barian Waiting for a Visitor* (which has been mentioned earlier) by Huang Tsung-hsi and the *Daily Accumulated Knowledge (Jih-chih lu)* by Ku Yen-wu (1613–82). Huang, Ku, and another man named Wang Fu-chih (1619–92) are often referred to as the last intellectual trio of the Ming dynasty, though, in terms of their life-spans, they belonged more to the Ch'ing than to the Ming dynasty.

Should one wish to read primarily for pleasure, he cannot choose a better book than *Strange Spectacles of Ancient and Modern Times (Chin-ku ch'i-kuan)*, compiled and edited by an anonymous author who lived around 1600 and called himself Pao-wen Lao-jen, or "Old Man Who Holds an Earthen Jar." The book contains forty stories, and a rewritten version of one of these appears here as selection 46.

(41)

Chao Yi / *A Comparison of Two Emperors*[1]

Like Liu Pang, who founded the Han dynasty, Chu Yüan-chang, founder of the Ming dynasty, began his career as a commoner. Before the achievement of absolute power, he was often reminded by his advisers of the words and deeds of the Han emperor, after whom he consciously modeled himself. At the very beginning of the uprising, he was urged by Li Shan-ch'ang, a top lieutenant, to follow Liu Pang's example. "Though coming from a humble background, the founder of the Han dynasty was broad-minded and easy to reach," said Li. "He knew whom he could trust, and trust he did once they won his confidence. In five years he, a commoner, established himself as the emperor of China. You, sir, hail from Hao, which is not far from P'ei where he began his career.[2] If you decide to follow his example, the pacification of China should not be too difficult a task to complete." On another occasion Chu Yüan-chang spoke to K'ung An-jen, another lieutenant, as follows: "Realizing that the fall of the Ch'in resulted from an exercise in tyranny, Liu Pang was more than generous in dealing with his competitors. It was this generosity that enabled him to unify all of China. Now, once again China has become a battleground for all of those who wish to be its unifier. They will fail, of course, since none of them is enlightened enough, as Liu Pang once was, to introduce new programs that could make his success inevitable." The above quotations indicate clearly that Chu Yüan-chang intended to follow Liu Pang's example at the very beginning of the uprising.

As soon as the capital was settled at Nanking, the founder of the Ming dynasty proceeded to build a palace that was as grand in size as it was elegant in style, even though the new emperor would rarely reside in it, since he was still fighting all over China. Liu Pang, as one recalls, also built the Weiyang Palace at a time when China was yet to be pacified.

(The construction of the Weiyang Palace had cost so much treasure that Liu Pang scolded Hsiao Ho, the initiator of this construction, for its unnecessary luxury. "At a time when China has yet to be pacified," he said, "how can we enjoy ourselves at the people's expense?"

"This palace is modest enough for a new emperor when China has yet to be pacified," replied Hsiao Ho. "It will be more elegant when China is unified." Liu Pang was very pleased with this reply and decided to move to the new palace.)

After Nanking was designated as the capital, the founder of the Ming dynasty ordered the move of 140,000 wealthy households from areas south of the Yangtze River to it. As one recalls, the founder of the Han dynasty moved as many as 100,000 wealthy households from all regions of China to his new capital at Ch'angan. Chu Yüan-chang established feudatories, governed by his close relatives, as a means of protecting the royal house; Liu Pang, previously, had done the same. Chu Yüan-chang titled as village squires all wealthy men eighty years old or older, communal squires if they were ninety years old or older. A similar measure, as one recalls, was also adopted by Liu Pang.

Imitation, of course, could sometimes be overdone. When the founder of the Ming dynasty decided to purge or physically eliminate many of those who had made his success possible, in the same manner as the founder of the Han dynasty used to do, imitation had indeed become a vice instead of a virtue.

Notes

1. *Erh-shih-erh shih tsa-chi,* roll 32.
2. Hao and P'ei were located in northern Anhwei and northern Kiangsu, respectively. Northern Anhwei and northern Kiangsu are geographically contiguous.

(42)
Chang T'ing-yü et al. / *Cheng Ho's Voyages*[1]

Cheng Ho, a native of Yunnan, was popularly known as San-pao the Grand Eunuch *(San-pao t'ai-chien).* At one time he served as a staff member in the feudatory of King Ch'eng; later he was promoted to the position of grand eunuch in recognition of his contribution to King Ch'eng's successful revolt against Emperor Ming Hui-ti [r. 1399–1402]. After his accession to the throne, Emperor Yung-lo, the former King Ch'eng, suspected that his defeated predecessor Hui-ti might have escaped from Nanking and be residing somewhere in the South Seas and wanted very much to know his whereabouts. Besides, he wished to glorify Chinese arms in the remote regions and show off the wealth and power of the Central Kingdom. It was this combination of motives that prompted him to launch Cheng Ho's voyages.

In the sixth month of the third year of Yung-lo [1405] Cheng Ho and his deputy Wang Ching-hung, as ordered by the emperor, proceeded with their journey to the Western Ocean.[2] Well furnished with treasure and accompanied by more than 27,800 officers and men, they sailed in sixty-two giant ships, each of which measured forty-four *chang* [ca. 517 feet] in length and eighteen *chang* [ca. 212 feet] in width. The ships left the Liuchia River [near modern Shanghai] for the sea and then sailed southward to Fukien wherefrom they proceeded with sails full-blown to Champa. From Champa the Chinese envoys visited one country after another. They read the imperial decree that demanded the submission of the kingdoms they visited and rewarded generously those rulers who agreed to submit. As for those who chose not to obey, force was used to assure their compliance.

In the ninth month of the fifth year of Yung-lo [1407] Cheng Ho returned to the capital and presented to the emperor tribute-bearing envoys from the kingdoms he had visited. The emperor was greatly pleased and granted titles and financial rewards to all of those who had been presented to him. Cheng Ho also brought back many prisoners of war, including the captured king of Palembang.

Palembang was formally known as Sanfuch'i whose ruler, a Chinese named Ch'en Tsu-yi, had been active as a pirate in the South Seas before he was captured by Cheng Ho. When Cheng Ho demanded his surrender, he said he would, but in secret he was planning to launch an attack upon Cheng Ho's ships. Once the perfidy was recognized, Cheng Ho attacked and won a decisive victory. Ch'en Tsu-yi was captured alive and later brought to Peking. He was executed shortly afterward.

In the ninth month of the sixth year of Yung-lo [1408] Cheng

Ho sailed again for Ceylon. Upon his arrival, the king of Ceylon, a man named Alagakkonara, invited him to visit his city with fine promises. Once inside the city, Cheng Ho was presented with a demand for gold and silk; moreover, Alagakkonara had already ordered an attack on the Chinese ships. Taking advantage of the fact that practically all the Ceylonese troops had been out of the city for this attack, Cheng Ho personally led two thousand soldiers to attack the city itself. The surprise worked, and Alagakkonara and his family, together with many high-ranking officials, were captured alive. The Ceylonese troops hurried back to rescue their king, only to be routed by the Chinese. In the sixth month of the ninth year of Yung-lo [1411] the captured Ceylonese, including their king, were presented to the Chinese emperor for a determination of their fate. The emperor decided to forgive them and ordered them to be returned to Ceylon. By then all of Indochina had been pacified and brought under Chinese jurisdiction. Frightened by Chinese might, more and more kingdoms sent envoys to China to pay their tribute.

In the eleventh month of the tenth year of Yung-lo [1412] the emperor again ordered Cheng Ho to proceed to Sumatra. Cheng Ho arrived at a time when Sekander, son of a former ruler of that kingdom, was plotting the overthrow of the reigning prince so as to establish himself as the king. Resenting Cheng Ho for having failed to give him any gold or silk, he ordered his men to attack Chinese troops. Cheng Ho responded vigorously, defeated his army, and pursued him until he, together with his family, was captured at Lambri. The Chinese envoy returned to Peking in the seventh month of the thirteenth year [1415], to be welcomed by a pleased emperor who rewarded all the officers and men for their efforts.

In the winter of the fourteenth year of Yung-lo [1416] Malacca, Calicut, and seventeen other nations sent envoys to China to pay their tribute. The emperor ordered Cheng Ho to accompany them on their return trip after they had successfully completed their own mission in China. Having granted gifts, in the name of the emperor, to each of the kings who had sent tribute missions to China, Cheng Ho returned to Peking in the seventh month of the seventeenth year [1419].

In the spring of the nineteenth year of Yung-lo [1421] Cheng Ho again visited the kingdoms that had sent tribute missions to

China. He returned in the eighth month of the following year [1422].

In the first month of the twenty-second year of Yung-lo [1424] Shih Chi-sun, king of Palembang, requested the honor of being appointed a pacification commissioner. The emperor granted the request and ordered Cheng Ho to bring to him the appropriate seal to make the appointment official. The emperor died before Cheng Ho's return to China.

In the sixth month of the fifth year of Hsüan-teh [1430] the reigning emperor, Hsüan-teh, was greatly annoyed that many of China's tributary states had so far failed to pay tribute to him. He, consequently, dispatched Cheng Ho and Wang Ching-hung to these states for an inquiry. The Chinese envoys visited Hormus and sixteen other states before returning home.

Cheng Ho served three emperors with distinction and conducted seven voyages altogether. Among the more than thirty kingdoms he had visited were the following: Champa, Java, Camboja, Palembang, Siam, Calicut, Malacca, Borneo, Sumatra, Aru, Cochin, Quilon, Chola, Cail, Jurfattan, Koyampadi, Ceylon, Lambri, Pahang, Kelantan, Hormus, Brawa, Maldives, Sunda, Mogedoxu, Malinde, Sana, Zufar, Juba, Bengal, Mecca, Lide, and Battak.[3] The amount of treasure he brought to China from these kingdoms was of course enormous, but the expense to China herself was even more staggering. Beginning in the Hsüan-teh period [1426–35] these kingdoms, occasionally, still sent tribute missions to China, but they could not be compared with the tribute missions of the Yung-lo period [1403–24] that were not only more sumptuous but also more frequent. By then Cheng Ho had become too old to undertake any strenuous task. Long after his death, however, his achievement was still so highly regarded that Chinese generals and admirals, whenever serving abroad, kept mentioning it as a way to impress foreigners. Even laymen spoke of the Seven Voyages of the Grand Eunuch as a most outstanding event of the Ming dynasty.

Notes

1. *Ming shih*, roll 304.

2. A term used during this period to cover the general area of South and Southeast Asia.

3. Champa is part of modern Vietnam. Java, Palembang, Borneo, Sumatra,

Aru, Lambri, Sunda, Lide, and Battak form part of modern Indonesia. Camboja is modern Cambodia; Siam is modern Thailand. Calicut, Cochin, Quilon, Chola, Cail, Jurfattan, Koyampadi, Maldives, and Bengal are located on the coast of modern India. Malacca, Pahang, and Kelantan are located in the Malay Peninsula. Hormus is located at the head of the Persian Gulf; Sana, Zufar, and Mecca are located on the Arabian Peninsula. Brawa, Mogedoxu, Malinde, and Juba are located on the eastern coast of Africa.

(43)
Chang T'ing-yü et al. / *Grand Eunuch Wei*[1]

As a young man, Wei Chung-hsien was known to be irresponsible and shiftless. Pressed by other gamblers for payment after heavy losses in a game of chance, he castrated himself in a moment of frustration and anger. He changed his name to Li Chin-chung. Only later was his original name restored.

Selected as a palace eunuch in the Wan-li period [1573–1619], Wei Chung-hsien moved quickly to ingratiate himself with those who could help his cause. An excellent cook, he was particularly patronized by Princess Wang, mother of the crown prince designate, later known as Emperor Ming Hsi-tsung. Subsequently he became a lover to the prince's wet nurse named K'e, who had abandoned an earlier lover on his behalf. As later events proved, this alliance between a eunuch and a wet nurse, based upon a relationship of illicit love, formed the basis of Wei Chung-hsien's emergence to power.

Within a month after Ming Hsi-tsung's accession to the throne, wet nurse K'e was titled Madame Feng-sheng and eunuch Wei received three simultaneous appointments, including the appointment as administrator of rites *(ssu li)*. Normally only a man of great learning could be privileged to occupy that post; eunuch Wei acquired that post only because of K'e's insistence. Meanwhile the close relatives of both, including an elder brother of the eunuch, were promoted to lucrative positions and titled accordingly. The increasing influence of K'e alarmed many members of the censorate who, noting the forthcoming royal marriage, maintained that the emperor had no more need of his wet nurse and that she, indeed, should be ousted from the palace. The emperor, in reply, stated that he could no more dispense with the service of his wet nurse than he could with that of his own mother. In view of the love and protection that the wet nurse had provided for him when he was a child, he, the emperor, could not but be eternally grateful.

As long as K'e's influence over the emperor continued, Wei Chung-hsien could do whatever he pleased with his rivals or enemies inside the palace. All of them, one after another, were ousted from positions of power and influence, including K'e's former lover previously mentioned. Having thus secured his own position inside the palace, Wei Chung-hsien received permission from the emperor to train the eunuchs under his control in the use of military weapons and other martial arts. To keep the emperor busy, he led the young man to a variety of dissipations, such as sex, music, hunting, and gambling. The emperor was furious when a group of officials, led by Liu Tsung-chou, recommended proceedings of indictment against eunuch Wei. Only through the intervention of Grand Councillor Yeh Hsiang-kao was Liu's life spared.

So far the power of eunuch Wei was confined to the palace. To explain its extension to the imperial government and eventually the country as a whole, we have to review the development of events toward the end of the Wan-li period. Later in his life Emperor Wan-li [r. 1573–1619] increasingly lost interest in the management of state affairs and seldom bothered to read the memorials that had been presented to him. As he gradually moved away from political activities, factions began to develop among his ministers, each of whom resorted to the expression of radical ideas to gain attention and influence. Many ministers of state resigned from their respective posts, ostensibly for health reasons, whenever they were attacked by their rivals or enemies. Among them was a man named Ku Hsüan-ch'eng [d. 1612] who, after resignation, assumed a post as head of the Tung-lin Academy, to which were attracted many like-minded scholars and statesmen interested in the maintenance of Confucian orthodoxy. From then on these people were known as members of the Tung-lin Group, who regarded anyone opposing them, ideologically or politically, as a man of the Wicked Group. The Tung-lin Group soon came to power and, by the beginning of the T'ien-chi period [1621–27], had succeeded in deposing all of its opponents from positions of influence. Many predicted then that by being so rigid and uncompromising toward its political opponents it would in due course be boomeranged.

However, it took the emergence of Grand Eunuch Wei as the new man of power to fulfill this prediction. The enemies of Tung-lin, having sensed that a new base of power was being developed, quickly congregated around it, thus helping to broaden as well as strengthen it. Those who opposed the Grand Eunuch were dismissed from their posts, while those who supported him were either appointed to new positions or promoted to greater responsibility. To impress others with his own importance, the Grand Eunuch increased his personal retainers to ten thousand and was always escorted by armed guards, whether inside or outside the palace. Meanwhile his palace ally K'e was doing her utmost to make sure that the royal weakling could not produce a legitimate heir. Concubine Chang was executed in secret when it was learned that she had become pregnant; when the empress was also found to have become pregnant, K'e made sure that a miscarriage would occur. Thus the boy emperor, despite the size of his harem, was never able to produce an heir.

In the fourth year of T'ien-chi [1624] Censor Yang Lien, incensed by the Grand Eunuch's increasing abuse of power, indicted him on twenty-four counts of "unforgivable crime." As the crimes were itemized and elaborated in detail, the Grand Eunuch, for the first time, was frightened. He defended himself, tearfully, in the presence of the emperor, even suggesting willingness to give up his supervision over the Eastern Chamber.[2] Thanks to the intervention of K'e and his other allies and friends, the Grand Eunuch was not only forgiven for whatever crimes he had allegedly committed, but Yang Lien himself was reprimanded for having made false charges against the emperor's loyal minister.

The day after the emperor had made his decision known, more than seventy ministers, headed by Minister of Rites Ong Cheng-ch'un and Minister of War Ch'en Tao-heng, jointly petitioned the emperor to "retire Wei Chung-hsien to his private residence" so as to stop, once and for all, all the scandals originating in the palace. As later events proved, this petition, which was rejected by the emperor, provided the strongest incentive for the Grand Eunuch to purge or physically eliminate all of his opponents. Ku Ping-ch'ien, a political ally, proceeded to compile a list of disloyal elements; Wang T'i-ch'ien, another political ally, recommended the use of corporal punishment to bring the recalcitrant ministers into line. Shortly afterward Wan Ching, a senior adviser then serving in the Ministry of Public Works, was beaten to death after he had satirized the Grand Eunuch in a petition to the emperor. Those whose names appeared in the list of disloyal elements were dismissed from their respective posts one after another, including Minister of Personnel Chao Nan-hsin, Censor Kao P'an-lung, and also, of course, Yang Lien. Their vacant posts were taken over by the Grand Eunuch's loyal followers, such as Ts'ui Ch'eng-hsiu and Wang Shao-hui.

Later Ts'ui Ch'eng-hsiu compiled a new list of disloyal elements entitled "Heaven-condemned Comrades" and Wang Shao-hui, not to be outdone, had his own list entitled "Disgraced Generals." On both lists appeared the names of Chou Yüan-piao, Ku Hsüan-ch'eng, Yeh Hsiang-kao, and Liu Yi-ching, all of whom were denounced as Tung-lin chieftains. Not satisfied with mere dismissals, Grand Eunuch Wei ordered more severe punishments for those he called ringleaders. Some were exiled; others were either beaten to death or thrown into jail. When the dust finally settled, all the important positions in the imperial government had been taken over by the Grand Eunuch's sycophants. Meanwhile the Eastern Chamber had intensified its investigatory activities, throwing into jail anyone who was suspected of having been engaged in disloyal activities or expressing disloyal thoughts.

By the sixth year of T'ien-chi [1626] not only the officials in the imperial government but also those on the local level had become devoted followers of the Grand Eunuch. In the sixth month of that year Pan Ju-chen, Governor of Chekiang, petitioned for the erection of a living shrine in honor of the Grand Eunuch. Other governors, trying to show that they were no less loyal to the Grand Eunuch than the governor of Chekiang, petitioned for the same. Before long living shrines in honor of the Grand Eunuch mushroomed all over the empire. From every corner of the empire came eulogies, the writers of which competed with one another in extolling the Grand Eunuch's virtues. Those who disagreed openly were arrested on trumped-up charges and punished accordingly.

A political machine was thus established, which functioned effectively, though ruthlessly, throughout the empire. Its top echelon consisted of a military as well as a civilian group. The civilian group, nicknamed Five Tigers, was headed by Ts'ui Ch'eng-hsiu, the Grand Eunuch's confidant and early supporter. The military group, nicknamed Five Cougars, was headed by General T'ien Erh-keng. Beneath the Tigers and the Cougars were the Ten Dogs (headed by Minister of Personnel Chou Ying-ch'iu), the Ten Children, and the Forty Grandchildren. Each of them, in turn, had his own following. The political machine was so pervasive that none of the cabinet ministers and governors-general, or any other high-ranking official, could hold his post for a single day without being a staunch member of the Grand Eunuch's clique.

By the spring of the seventh year of T'ien-chi [1627] the construction of living shrines had become so fashionable that not only governors-general and governors but also ordinary citizens, including ruffians and scoundrels, were anxious to join the act. Each shrine in honor of the Grand Eunuch was as elaborate as money could buy or ingenuity could conceive, and the promotors of these shrines, to acquire land and material for construction, often took over people's farms, forests, and houses by force. No victim dared complain, let alone start a suit for redress. In an atmosphere of universal adulation even the most bizarre events could take place. For example, Lu Wan-ling, a candidate for the provincial examination, petitioned the government to have the Grand Eunuch worshiped side by side with Confucius. One scholar who refused to compose a eulogy on the opening of a new shrine was immediately sentenced to death; so was another scholar who declined to prostrate himself after entering a living shrine in honor of the Grand Eunuch. After dissent had been totally suppressed, there was not a single petition to the imperial government, whatever its main purpose, that did not contain some adulatory words for the Grand Eunuch.

Though politically inept, Emperor Ming Hsi-tsung was most ingenious as a cabinetmaker. He could spend days and nights, without ever feeling tired, on different types of wood, varnish, and lacquer and he made with his own hands some of the most beautiful furniture. Whenever the Grand Eunuch made a report to him on state affairs, he inevitably became annoyed or irritated, saying, "Can you not do the best you can without bothering me?" It was this kind of imperial permissiveness that enabled the Grand Eunuch to do whatever he pleased. Accompanied by retainers, guards, grooms, cooks, and entertainers who sometimes numbered ten thousand or more, the Grand Eunuch and his lieutenants often went to the countryside for amusement. He loved to ride his carriage at full speed, bypassing swiftly and without even giving a nod to all the officials and squires who had come a long distance to line up on both sides of the road to pay their respects. Nevertheless, they shouted aloud: "Long live the Nine-thousand-years!"[3] Whenever an important document arrived that required his immediate attention, the courier had to spur his mount to its best effort in order to catch up with him.

Great though it was, the power of the Grand Eunuch fell as precipitously as it had risen. In the eighth month of the seventh year of T'ien-chi [1627] Emperor Ming Hsi-tsung died and was succeeded by Prince Hsing who, after accession, was known as Emperor Ming Ch'ung-chen [r. 1627–44]. When serving as a crown prince, Ch'ung-chen detested Grand Eunuch Wei for his evil ways but was careful enough not to offend him until he, upon becoming an emperor, could do something about his misgivings. Indictments against the Grand Eunuch soon appeared on his desk, but the new emperor, being unsure about the timing, decided not to act upon them. Later Ch'ien Chia-cheng, an examination candidate, indicted Grand Eunuch Wei on ten counts of "unforgivable crime": first, deceiving the emperor; second, insulting the empress; third, abusing the armed forces; fourth, being irreverent toward the imperial ancestors; fifth, eliminating feudatories without authorization; sixth, being irreverent toward Confucius; seventh, selling titles; eighth, concealing the achievements of the generals on the frontier; ninth, exploiting the people; and tenth, engaging in unethical and illegal dealings. Having received the petition of indictment, the emperor summoned the Grand Eunuch to his presence and asked one of the officials to read the indictment aloud. Realizing that the walls had finally closed in on him, the Grand Eunuch offered heavy bribes to Hsü Ying-yüan, the emperor's own eunuch and confidant and the

Grand Eunuch's one-time gambling partner, hoping to ease the pressure. The emperor learned about the bribe and reprimanded Hsü Ying-yüan for accepting it. In the eleventh month of the same year [1627] the Grand Eunuch was exiled to Fengyang [modern Anhwei province].

Shortly after the Grand Eunuch's exile, the emperor ordered a special prosecutor to proceed to Fengyang to question him about the crimes he had allegedly committed. Hearing about the impending arrival of the prosecutor, Grand Eunuch Wei, together with a close associate named Li Ch'ao-ch'in, hanged himself. The emperor ordered his head to be severed from his body and his body sliced as a posthumous punishment. K'e, the Grand Eunuch's long time ally and friend, had already been executed. By the second year of Ch'ung-chen [1629] all of the Grand Eunuch's former followers had been dismissed from their respective posts, and members of the Tung-lin Group, who had been blacklisted during the T'ien-hsi period, were once again in the government's good graces.

Notes

1. *Ming shih,* roll 305.

2. *Tung ch'ang,* here translated as Eastern Chamber, was an extralegal apparatus, supervised and staffed by eunuchs, for the prosecution and trial of what the eunuchs regarded as disloyal elements to the emperor. Time and again the Eastern Chamber was used to intimidate or punish the eunuchs' enemies. Only the emperor could reverse its decisions.

3. The emperor was customarily addressed as *Wan sui,* or "Ten-thousand-years."

(44)
Huang Tsung-hsi / *On Law*[1]

Governance by law existed before and during the Three Dynasties [i.e., Hsia, Shang, and West Chou] but has been absent since. How is this statement to be explained? The Two Emperors and the Three Kings[2] regarded the world as the common domain of all men; they, therefore, provided land for people to grow their food, as well as materials for their clothing, so no one in the world would suffer from hunger or cold. Knowing that civilized men needed education, they established schools; knowing that sexual activities without restraint were synonymous with license, they promoted the sanctity of marriage; knowing that man's instinct for aggression, if not properly channeled, would lead to lawless violence, they taught people the art of peaceful competition, such as tournaments in archery and chariot riding. These were laws existing before and during the Three Dynasties, the purpose of which was to advance the welfare of all men, rather than that of a particular individual or a specific group.

The kings of later ages changed this ancient concept. Being afraid that they or their descendants might not be able to hold the empire indefinitely, they formulated laws to reduce that fear. In other words, their laws were private laws aimed at the maintenance of their control of the empire which they regarded as their private possession, rather than public laws that were adopted to advance the interest of all the people in the empire. Called laws of the empire, they were actually laws of the royal household. When the royal house of the Ch'in abolished the feudal system and replaced it with a centralized administration, it obviously believed that its own interest could be better served by the latter form of organization. Likewise, when the royal house of the Han decided to create many feudatories to be governed by its own members, it had in mind building a bulwark for its own protection. Needless to say, the royal house of the Sung wanted to reduce the threat to its own security when it proceeded to deprive provincial authorities of military commandership. In short, all the basic laws of the nation were formulated in such a way as to enable the royal house to continue to control the empire; the welfare of the people was never considered. Hence this question: How can a law be legitimately called a law if its primary purpose is to advance the interests of one individual or one household at the expense of all other individuals or all other households?

The spirit of law during the Three Dynasties was that everything in the world belonged to everyone in the world. Natural resources were carefully conserved instead of being ruthlessly exploited; justice was administered with fairness and impartiality; and a man was not judged by his station in society, but by his worth as an individual. Laws formulated on this basis were viewed by people of later ages as too simplistic, but they were beneficial nevertheless. As the law shows no bias against, or favor for, anyone in the nation, no one regarded high station in society as particularly desirable or low station in society as particularly dishonorable. As the law was simple and easy to understand, few people violated it. This is what I would call a lawless law[3]—the best kind of law in the world.

The spirit of law after the Three Dynasties was totally different, since it was no longer related to the welfare of all men. It was related instead, colloquially speaking, to the filling of individual suitcases. No longer was the law meant to benefit the people; it was meant to strengthen the government. Whenever a person was employed, the government took for granted that the person would use his position to advance his own selfish interest; it therefore had to employ another person to watch him. Whenever an act was to be performed, the government had to initiate another act to make sure that the first act would not fail on account of personal deception and chicanery. Everyone knew where his suitcase was and worried day and night about its possible disappearance. One law was piled upon another for the prevention of wrongdoing, only to create more wrongdoings. This is what I would call an unlawful law, the enactment of which merely generates more laws instead of preventing wrongdoing.

Some say that as dutiful sons of our forebears we must observe the laws of previous generations, and certainly we should not abolish them. When saying this, they fail to recognize that these laws were unlawful to begin with, since their sole purpose was to advance the interest of their initiators, namely, the kings who were in power. When the kings of later ages decided to abandon them, they obviously concluded that circumstances had changed in such a way that their interests could be better served without these laws. We deplore the abandonment of these laws on the grounds that ordinary citizens would suffer, but we neglect to point out that when they were enacted, their purpose was not to bring benefit to the people either. As long as the law itself remains unlawful, those who defend or promote one set of laws against another only find themselves caught between rationalizations. They may pride themselves, or be referred to by others, as legal experts; but basically they merely repeat familiar arguments. The presence or absence of the kind of law they advocate or criticize has nothing to do with good government.

As we look back, it seems clear that the spirit of a lawless law, which prevailed before and during the Three Dynasties, has suffered two severe and irreparable injuries. The first injury occurred during the Ch'in dynasty; what remained was destroyed altogether during the Yüan dynasty. Compassion and love, which formed the basis of the way of ancient sages, are conspicuously absent in our present concept of law. Acknowledgedly it is difficult to restore all the sound institutions of ancient times; nevertheless, men of foresight must think seriously of revising those that are feasible at the present time, such as the well-field system,[4] the feudatory system, the nationwide school system, and finally the channeling of people's aggression through organized sports, including archery and chariot riding. Reform of this nature, small though it may seem, would go a long way toward improving the quality of life for all of our citizens.

Some say that good government comes about as a result of the availability of good men rather than good laws. I would say, however, that good laws precede good men and that shackled by unlawful laws, the best a good man can do is to reduce their harmful effect; whatever he can achieve positively has to be extralegal by definition. In most cases he merely drifts along, thinking little of achieving anything in particular. If, on the other hand, we have in force the law of our ancient sage kings that contains concepts above and beyond the ordinary concept of law, a good man who enforces the law will be able to do his best to the benefit of all, and even a bad man will not be in a position to employ legal jargon to practice government-sanctioned brutality. Let me repeat: good laws are more important than good men.

Notes

1. *Ming-yi tai-fang lu*, essay 3.

2. The Two Emperors were Yao and Shun. The Three Kings were Yü of the Hsia dynasty, T'ang of the Shang dynasty, and King Wen and King Wu of the West Chou dynasty—actually four kings.

3. The author tries to make a distinction between lawless law *(wu fa)* and unlawful law *(fei fa)*. Lawless laws are customary and mostly unwritten laws that have an ethical content and are formulated to advance the interests of all men, while unlawful laws do not have an ethical content and are enacted to protect the special interests of men in power.

4. A land distribution system which, according to tradition, was enforced early in the West Chou dynasty.

(45)
Wang Shou-jen / *Innate Knowledge*[1]

Innate knowledge is the same as what Mencius refers to as the knowledge to distinguish right from wrong—a knowledge that is inherent in and common to all men. Since it does not require much thought, nor does it demand learning, to distinguish right from wrong, innate knowledge is in fact the nature of Heaven reflected in the mind of man, namely, the mind of man in its natural and unadulterated state. Whenever a wish emerges, the mind is immediately aware of it; and, because of the existence of innate knowledge, the mind can instantly tell whether such a wish is morally right or wrong. An honest man does not need outside assistance to distinguish right from wrong, because he knows the distinction all the time. Even an evil person can be persuaded to abandon his evil ways by a morally superior man, after the latter has pointed out to him where goodness is. This shows that innate knowledge, the knowledge to distinguish right from wrong, is present even among the so-called morally degenerate.

Why is it, then, that sincerity of intention is most essential to the expression of innate knowledge? Though a wish, once emerging from our consciousness, can be immediately recognized as being of a moral nature, we may actually run away from it and pursue its opposite instead if we do not have the sincerity of intention to follow it by action. We, in this case, have betrayed what our innate knowledge has taught us. By the same token, a wish that emerges from our consciousness may be immediately recognized as being of an evil nature; but, without the sincerity of intention to avoid evil, we may actually practice it. Once again we have betrayed what our innate knowledge has taught us. In short, without sincerity of intention, we may practice evil while knowing that it is evil and run away from goodness while knowing that it is good. When this happens, knowledge has indeed become non-knowledge. With sincerity of intention, on the other hand, we should be able to pursue goodness and avoid evil, as soon as our innate knowledge reveals to us the nature of our wish, good or evil, that emerges from our consciousness.

By no means should innate knowledge be regarded as something abstract and abstruse—something that hangs in the air and lacks substance. On the contrary, innate knowledge has as its foundation the conduct of our daily lives. To know is to observe and investigate objects and things, since all wishes that emerge from consciousness have a factual content. The purpose of investigation is to rectify, namely, to restore things to what they should normally be. This is another way of saying that the purpose of rectifying the nonrectified is to eliminate evil and that the purpose of restoring things to their rectified status is to advance goodness. This is what investigation is all about. The word "investigate" appears often in the *Book of History*, in such statements as "Investigate high and low" and "Investigate the evil within oneself." The "investigation of objects and things" in the *Great Learning* carries the same meaning as the word "investigate" carries in the *Book of History.*

The recognition of good or evil through the use of innate knowledge and the sincerity of intention to avoid evil and adhere to goodness—all of this is meaningless if it is not followed by concrete action. Only through positive action can innate knowledge be put into full use and can sincerity of intention be truly tested. Anyone who follows this course of action will become the happiest among men, since he has no apology to make and no regrets to be sorrowful about.

Notes

1. *Wang Wen-ch'eng ch'üan-chi.*

(46)
Pao-wen Lao-jen and Li Dun-jen / *A Broken Lute*[1]

On his way home from the state of Ch'u where he had served as a special envoy on behalf of the king of Tsin, Yü Pai-ya decided to take the river route, the beauty of which he had heard about but had never seen. Entering the Yangtze, he found the river more enchanting than he had thought possible. The undulating hills against the blue sky, the vertical cliffs that appeared from nowhere, the evergreen forests that pushed their way to the edge of the river, and the crystal water that shone under the sun like a sheet of fine silk—all of this provided an endless variety of nature's magnificence. At night the peaceful silence was occasionally broken by a sharp, shrieking sound from the shore. "This is the cry of the monkey," said the boatmen, "as monkeys are most numerous in this part of China."

Several days after the journey had begun and on the fifteenth day of the eighth month, the day of the Moon Festival, the boat reached the mouth of the Han River. As the evening drew near, dark clouds began to gather; soon there was a heavy downpour. Unable to move forward, the boatmen anchored the boat inside a cove underneath a towering cliff. The storm quickly moved away, however; soon a full moon appeared on the eastern horizon. It seemed to be brighter than ever, having been washed clean by the heavy storm.

Deeply moved by the scene, Yü Pai-ya ordered incense to be burned and preparations to be made for him to play the lute. Hardly had he completed one song, however, when a string suddenly snapped. Astonished beyond belief, he jumped to his feet. "This is very strange," said he. "How can there be anyone in this wilderness intelligent enough to understand my music and, by listening to it without my knowledge, cause the string to snap?" Was the stranger a political enemy who would try to assassinate him? Could he be the head of a group of bandits who only waited for the right moment to board the ship to rob him? Not willing to take a chance, Yü Pai-ya ordered the boatmen to search for the stranger or strangers on the shore.

When the boatmen were about to leave the boat for the shore, Yü Pai-ya heard a man speaking aloud across the water. "I am neither a bandit nor an assassin," said the man. "I am a woodcutter. While on my way home, the sky suddenly broke open, and I had to seek protection underneath this cliff. By the way, you are not a bad musician."

"Haha!" Yü Pai-ya laughed in total disbelief. "A woodcutter understands music!"

"If the gentleman in the boat has read Confucius," said the woodcutter, "he must remember the sage's saying that 'in every ten households there must be a man as virtuous as I am.' If no one in this wilderness can understand music, how is it possible that someone here knows how to play it?"

Yü Pai-ya was surprised at the way the woodcutter retorted. A woodcutter he might be, but certainly he was not an ordinary one. "If the gentleman on the shore understands music, may I ask him to name the song that I have played?"

"It is a song of remembrance," the woodcutter replied. "It describes Confucius's mourning for his disciple Yen Hui and goes as follows:

> Sadly he died so young;
> Remembering him is to enhance my own sorrow.
> Poor though he was in life. . . .

It was at this moment, sir, that the string snapped, and you were unable to finish the song. If my memory is correct, the last line should read:

> In death he will forever live.

Yü Pai-ya was as surprised as he was pleased when he heard the reply. "My apology to the gentleman on the shore," he cried aloud. "May I have the pleasure of his company so we can talk more about music?" He ordered the boatmen to help the stranger to board the ship. But the stranger, a rugged young man, did not need much help.

The stranger had a bamboo hat on his head and a straw cape over his shoulders. His trousers, rolled up, revealed a pair of muddy legs. His sandals, made of straw, were soaked with water.

He wore a wide belt around his waist, on which hung a woodcutter's knife. "You need some wine to warm you up," said Yü Pai-ya.

After wine was brought in, Yü Pai-ya, none too subtly, began to question the woodcutter's knowledge about music. "If you appreciate lute music," he said, "you must know something about the history of the lute. Who invented the lute? What qualities must a good lute have?"

"The lute was invented by Fu-hsi," said the woodcutter. "Walking in a forest one day, Fu-hsi saw a meteor speed across the sky and then mysteriously disappear into a tung tree. Soon he saw a phoenix land on the same tree. Here I must say a few words about the phoenix. As the queen of the feathered animals, it eats only bamboo fruits, drinks water only from the sweetest spring, and will not rest anywhere except a tung tree. Convinced of the superior quality of the tung tree referred to above, Fu-hsi felled it to make a musical instrument. The tree, thirty-three feet in length, was sawed into three parts of eleven feet each. Taking the upper part and testing it, Fu-hsi found it too light and yielding a sound too treble. Taking the lower part and testing it, he found it too heavy and yielding a sound too bass. He decided to use the middle part since it yielded a sound neither too bass nor too treble. After soaking the wood in running water for a period of seventy-two days, or one-fifth of a year, he dried it slowly in the shade. Then he commissioned Liu Tzu-ch'i, a great artisan of ancient China, to fashion it into a musical instrument. This was the jasper lute, the first lute in China.

"This lute measured thirty-six inches in length, which corresponded to the 360 degrees of a circle. Its width was eight inches in the front and four inches in the rear, corresponding to the eight festivals and the four seasons. It had a uniform height of two inches that corresponded to the two generating forces in the universe, *yin* and *yang*. Its head was shaped like that of a man and its waist like that of a woman. It had twelve stops that corresponded to the twelve months of the year; an extra stop was later added, however, to represent the extra month of a leap year. It had five strings that represented the five primary elements, namely, metal, wood, water, fire, and earth, as well as the five pitches, namely, *kung, shang, chüeh, cheng,* and *yü.* It was this kind of lute that Yao and Shun played when they sang the *Psalm of the Southern Wind* during a period of universal peace.

"When King Wen of Chou was imprisoned at Chiangli, his son Pai-yi-k'ao was so grieved that he added a new string to his own lute in protest of his father's undeserved fate. This string was known as the Wen string which yielded a melancholy sound. When King Wu launched a military campaign against King Cheo, his joy was so great that he added another string to the lute. This was the Wu string which, when strummed, produced a loud and heroic response. This instrument of seven strings was later known as the Wen-Wu lute.

"The Wen-Wu lute will suffer damage in tone under any of the six climatic conditions: bitter cold, extreme heat, strong wind, heavy storm, noisy thunder, and heavy snow. It should not be played under any of the seven circumstances: mourning the dead, simultaneous playing with an orchestra, preoccupation with wordly matters, uncleanliness in body, untidiness in costume, failure to burn incense in advance, and finally, lack of an appreciative audience. Its tone possesses eight unique qualities: clarity, wonder, remoteness, eloquence, sadness, manliness, softness, and extensibility. In the hands of an accomplished player, it can tame even the most ferocious beast."

Though greatly impressed, Yü Pai-ya thought that the woodcutter might have memorized the details without much understanding. He decided to test him further. "When Yen Hui stepped into a room where Confucius was playing the lute," said Yü Pai-ya, "he was shocked to find that the Master was contemplating an act of murder. 'Master!' he shouted. 'Do not be alarmed,' Confucius calmly replied. 'I saw a cat chasing a mouse, and I was hoping that the cat would succeed in catching it.' From this story we know that a piece of music will not only tell what is obviously expressed in words but also reveal the sentiments and emotions of the player. I shall play some music, and I would like you to tell me what I am thinking about."

"I would like to try," said the woodcutter.

Yü Pai-ya connected the broken string, thought for a while, and began to play.

"How lofty and majestic are the mountains!" the woodcutter exclaimed. "You, sir, are thinking of the high mountains."

Yü Pai-ya did not reply. Then, concentrating, he played another tune.

"Rolling on and on, the water moves forward in an endless

fashion," said the woodcutter. "You, sir, are thinking of the running current."

Astonished beyond belief, Yü Pai-ya pushed the lute aside and stood up. He saluted the woodcutter and apologized profusely for his rudeness. "An ordinary rock may contain the most precious gem," he mused. "He is not wise who judges a person according to his station in life or the kind of clothes he wears." Having introduced himself, he learned that the woodcutter's name was Chung Hui, also known as Chung Tzu-ch'i, that he lived not far from the river, and that his sole means of support was cutting and collecting firewood. "Why should a man of your talent be satisfied with anonymity in a remote village?" he asked.

"I have aged parents whom I must support," Chung Tzu-ch'i replied, "since I do not have any brothers. Besides, I like the way I live. I do not want any change."

Yü Pai-ya was impressed. The woodcutter was not only a good musician but also, most importantly, a good man. Right then he decided that he wanted this encounter to be the beginning of a more permanent relationship. "How old are you?" he asked.

"I am twenty-seven," Chung Tzu-ch'i replied.

"I am ten years older than you are. If you do not deem me unworthy, I would suggest that we become sworn brothers."

"I appreciate your kindness," said Chung Tzu-ch'i. "But you are a minister of state in a great country, while I am a woodcutter in a remote village."

"You do not understand me," said Yü Pai-ya. "It is easy to make a thousand acquaintances, but it is difficult to find a friend. I have met all kinds of people in my life; but let me say that I have never met a more worthy person than the person I met today."

Hearing no more objections, Yü Pai-ya ordered the servants to bring in candles, incense, wine, and food so the ceremony of sworn brotherhood could properly take place. The two men prostrated themselves before Heaven and Earth and pledged that, as sworn brothers, they would never desert each other. After the ceremony, they resumed the conversation. Yü Pai-ya quickly learned that the woodcutter was knowledgeable not only in music but also in philosophy, literature, and the arts.

Time sped by, and the moon lost more and more of its brightness as it descended westward. As the boatmen hoisted the sails and prepared for another day's journey, Yü Pai-ya knew that it was time to say good-bye. "Can you visit me in the capital?" he asked.

"I would like to," Chung Tzu-ch'i replied. "But my parents are very advanced in age. They need me every day."

"I understand," said Yü Pai-ya. "In that case I shall come here to see you."

"When?"

"We met for the first time on the day of the Moon Festival," Yü Pai-ya replied. "We shall meet again on the same day. Next year at this time I shall pay my respects to your parents in person. Meanwhile it is a great honor to me if you would accept this little present on their behalf." He presented his friend with ten pieces of gold, and the latter accepted.

Returning to the capital, Yü Pai-ya reported to the king the successful completion of his mission and then, as an aside, mentioned the fact that he had met a very unusual person by the name of Chung Tzu-ch'i. "By law and custom the king cannot command a hermit to his presence," said the king. "But this does not mean that he has no right of persuasion. When you see him next year, say that the king will be delighted to have his company."

With the king's blessing, Yü Pai-ya had no difficulty in obtaining leave to visit his friend. He arrived on the fifteenth day of the eighth month as previously agreed upon. Having anchored the boat underneath the same cliff where the two men had met for the first time, he cried aloud the name of his friend. The moon was as bright as the moon of one year earlier, but there was no response except his own echoes. "He is not the kind of man who would break a promise," Yü Pai-ya said to himself. "Is he ill?" He called his friend's name again, and again there was no response. "I met him by the lute; I shall meet him again by the lute," he finally concluded. He ordered his servant to bring the lute to the deck and to place incense in the burner. When the incense began to burn, he adjusted the strings and started to play. Surprisingly, the *shang* string yielded a sound more than melancholy; it was a mourning and grievous sound. He stopped playing immediately. "A tragedy has happened to my friend," he said to himself. "Possibly one of his parents has passed away. Tomorrow I shall repair to his village and visit him at his home." He ordered his servant to pack his lute and then went to sleep.

He did not sleep well that evening and got up as soon as the day broke. Before starting the journey he changed into a commoner's costume so that his presence would not attract too much attention among the villagers. Accompanied by one of his servants who carried the lute, he left the boat and walked away from the shore.

Emerging from the mountains three miles later, they encountered a vast expanse crisscrossed by two roads. Not knowing which one of the two roads would lead to his friend's village, Yü Pai-ya decided to wait for a passerby to provide him with the direction. He chose a large rock to sit on, while his servant stood behind.

A moment later, Yü Pai-ya saw a man walk slowly toward the place where he sat. As he came closer and closer, the man seemed to become older and older, so old in fact that his white beard reached as far as his chest and that he walked haltingly and with great difficulty. He held a cane in his left hand and a bamboo basket in his right hand. In the basket were wine, incense sticks, and candles.

As he approached, Yü Pai-ya stood up, walked toward him, and saluted. The old man put down his basket, raised his cane with both hands, and saluted in return. "Please tell me," said Yü Pai-ya, "which one of these two roads leads to the Chung family?"

"There are many Chungs around here," the old man replied. "Which one of the Chungs do you wish to see?"

Upon hearing that the visitor wished to see Chung Tzu-ch'i, the old man suddenly burst into tears. "He was my son," he explained. "One year ago my son met Yü Pai-ya, a senior minister from the state of Tsin. The two liked each other and became great friends. The minister gave my son ten pieces of gold before he left, and my son used this money to buy more books. He cut wood during daytime and studied books in the evening. He died of exhaustion three months ago."

Yü Pai-ya cried and cried until he collapsed on the roadside. By then the old man already knew who he was. Finally regaining his composure, Yü Pai-ya saluted the old man again and inquired where his friend's grave was. "When my son knew that he was not going to recover," said the old man, "he asked his mother and me to bury him near the river bank and next to the cliff, should he die. He said that he had promised the Tsin minister to wait for him on the river bank and that he was going to keep that promise. The new grave which you must have seen on your way here is my son's last resting place."

Before the grave Yü Pai-ya lit the incense sticks and spread wine on the ground. He stood silently for a moment and then kowtowed to pay his last respects. His servant brought the lute to him, and, sitting on the ground in a cross-legged fashion, he began to play. Tears continued to stream down from his eyes until they covered all of his face and began to drip down on his clothes. Once he finished playing, he took a sharp knife from his pocket and cut all seven strings. Then, raising the lute above his head, he smashed it, with all of his might, against a rock in front of the grave. "I shall never play again," he explained. "Who, from now on, can understand me anyway?"

Notes

1. This is a rewritten version of the Chinese original. The Chinese original appears in *Chin-ku ch'i-kuan*, roll 19.

CHAPTER

10

Ch'ing

HOW could the Manchus, a numerically small and culturally backward people, succeed in conquering the largest nation and one of the most sophisticated peoples on earth? To answer this question, one may wish to expound upon the brilliant leadership and organizational ability of Nurhachi (also known as Ch'ing T'ai-tsu, 1559–1626) and Abahai (also known as Ch'ing T'ai-tsung, 1592–1643) who led the Manchus during the early stage of their conquest, or, better still, dwell in detail upon the weight of decline of the Ming regime which the Manchus replaced. The nature of this book precludes elaboration of this decline; one illustration might be more than sufficient. Toward the end of the Ming dynasty, while millions of starving peasants rose angrily in revolt, the imperial household had in its employ one hundred thousand eunuchs and nine thousand court women—the cost of cosmetics for these women alone was budgeted at four hundred thousand taels of silver per year. Before committing suicide, the last Ming emperor, Ch'ung-chen, complained bitterly that his ministers had failed to inform him about the true nature of state affairs and that he did not deserve the fate that was awaiting him. Well, as a Chinese proverb says, those inside a mountain are most unlikely to know what shape the mountain is.

Upon entering China proper, the Manchus adopted what one may call a "carrot and stick" policy. Those Chinese who chose to cooperate with them could expect rewards: promotions for generals and bureaucrats and tax deductions for all others. As for those who resisted them, punishment was harsh and swift: the massive killings at Yangchow and Chiating (both in the Lower Yangtze) have been described as among the most atrocious in history. To differentiate "loyal" from "rebellious" Chinese, the new regime issued a series of head-shaving decrees (selection 47) which demanded that all male Chinese shave their heads in a doughnut fashion, with the hair in the middle to be braided into a pigtail. The head-shaving decrees were vigorously enforced: literally, "either one's hair or one's head has to come off." The staunch Ming loyalists preserved their hair by continuing the fight, but most Chinese complied. In short, the "carrot and stick" policy worked beautifully.

Once all of China was pacified, the early Ch'ing emperors went all out to prove that they were conscientious rulers worthy of Chinese support, and in many respects they succeeded remarkably well in this endeavor. Taxes were reduced; cultural activities were promoted; and well-educated Chinese were invited to join the government through a competitive examination system. The most conscientious of the Ch'ing rulers was K'ang-hsi whose reign of sixty years (1662–1722) has been characterized as among the most enlightened in Chinese history. He regarded himself as a model Confucian monarch and deservedly so (selection 48).

The reigns of K'ang-hsi, Yung-cheng (r. 1723–35), and Ch'ien-lung (r. 1736–95) were the golden era of the Ch'ing, in terms of domestic peace and prosperity as well as international prestige. In February 1796, Ch'ien-lung abdicated in favor of his son Chia-ch'ing on the grounds that no mortal, however wise, had the right to rule China longer than his grandfather K'ang-hsi. Doubtless sincere when he expressed this reason for his abdication, possibly he also sensed that the empire was not what it used to be and did not want his name to be associated with the impending disaster. At the time of his abdication an open revolt led by a secret society called the White Lotus had already begun; and, five days after his death in February 1799, Ho-shen (1750–99), his most trusted minister for more than twenty years, was indicted for grand larceny and other crimes (selection 49). The golden era had ended and the empire was in serious difficulties.

The White Lotus was merely one of many secret societies in China that rose from time to time to challenge established authority. By the middle decades of the seventeenth century, long after most Chinese had accepted the new regime and cooperated fully with it, whatever resistance there was went underground and became the rallying point of many secret societies. As the government was Confucian in outlook, the secret societies, almost without an exception, associated themselves with Buddhist or Taoist ideology. To avoid detection and therefore persecution, they passed their tradition from one generation to the next in oral rather than written form. This poses great problems for historians who try to differentiate facts from myths, as myths are inextricable from facts in the tradition of all the secret societies. This is true even for the better known, such as the Hungmen Society (selection 50). We do know, however, that the Hungmen later branched out into a variety of other secret societies, including the Triad Society *(San-ho hui),* the Heaven and Earth Society *(T'ien-ti hui),* and several others that played an important role in the overthrow of the Manchu regime in 1911.

The secret societies were able to exploit Chinese nationalism only after the Ch'ing dynasty had reached the stage of decline. As challengers to established authority, they were ineffective during the dynasty's golden era when discontent was limited and protest less conspicuous. Intellectuals certainly wished to have nothing to do with them when, under the enlightened rule of K'ang-hsi and Ch'ien-lung, they were encouraged in their scholarly pursuits and were generously rewarded in the process. An enormous amount of literature was produced as a result, especially on Confucian ideology. By then the ideologists had debated the comparative merits of the Han and Sung schools for several hundred years, millions of words had been written, and no ground remained that had not been plowed many times over. Basically, the Han school emphasized the literary and textual aspects of Confucian classics as a means to ascertain the meanings of the sages; the Sung school, on the other hand, wanted, to use its own phraseology, "to go into the heart of the matter" by examining in detail certain passages and sentences that, to its own thinking, crystallized the teachings of all of the sages. Led by such men as Lu Chiu-yüan and Chu Hsi of the Sung dynasty and Wang Shou-jen of the Ming dynasty, the scholars of the Sung school commented voluminously on such concepts as nature, mind, and self. The Sung scholars criticized their opponents as too pedantic and bookish, and the Han scholars, in retaliation, regarded the Sung learning as too abstruse and redundant. Besides, said the Han scholars, the Sung school was not really Confucian since it was imbued with Buddhist and Taoist influences.

The question inevitably arose of what the debate had to do

with individual welfare or the good of the nation. Stunned by the easy conquest of China by the Manchus, many scholars in the seventeenth century began to wonder aloud about the usefulness, or the lack of it, of the mountains of verbiage produced by the Han and the Sung schools and advocated instead that a scholar's true contribution to society was contingent upon how he could serve it in a more practical or concrete manner. This utilitarian approach led Yen Yüan (Yen Hsi-chai, 1635–1704) to condemn bookish learning and to advise his learned colleagues to specialize in one of the following fields: military affairs, agriculture, or rites and music. On the surface Yen Yüan seems to have been able to break through the narrow confines of traditional Confucian learning, but even he did not venture very far. Of the three fields of learning, he placed rites and music far above the two others in terms of importance: he thus ended where he had begun (selection 51). Not until the second half of the nineteenth century, after China had repeatedly been defeated by Western powers, was serious attention given to the study of science and technology.

Since the Ch'ing is the last of Chinese dynasties and closest to the present in terms of time, there are more materials on the Ch'ing period than there are on any of the previous periods. Some of the basic sources covering the first half of the Ch'ing period appear below:

The Tung-hua Records (Tung-hua lu), edited by Chiang Liang-yi (eighteenth century). This is a collection of documentary materials that covers the first six reigns of the Ch'ing dynasty. Tung-hua was the name of a city gate in Peking, behind which the cabinet was then located.

A Record of Saintly Might (Sheng-wu chi), edited by Wei Yüan (nineteenth century). This is a record of wars for the first eight reigns of the Ch'ing dynasty—a definitive work in its field.

The Tung-hua Records of the First Eleven Reigns (Shih-yi ch'ao Tung-hua lu), edited by Wang Hsien-ch'ien (nineteenth century). A corollary to the *Tung-hua lu,* it covers five more reigns, from Emperor Ch'ien-lung to Emperor Tao-kuang (r. 1821–50) inclusive.

Institutions of the Ch'ing Dynasty (Ch'ing hui-tien). Compiled in a similar manner to *Ming hui-tien* (p. 276), this work, having as many as 1,220 rolls, is by far the most complete in its field.

A Sequel to the Study of Cultural Heritage (Hsü wen-hsien t'ung-k'ao), compiled in 1747. As its title implies, this work is organized in the same manner as Ma Tuan-lin's *Wen-hsien t'ung-k'ao* (p. 187). It contains documents relating to major policy decisions and is particularly detailed for the K'ang-hsi period.

For each Ch'ing scholar or statesman, there is usually a chronological biography *(nien p'u)* authored by his admirer or admirers, besides a collection of his own works. In a chronological biography, the author enters into each "age heading" all the major events relating to the subject. For instance, "Age 25: passed the metropolitan examination and received the *chin-shih* degree. Wrote an essay on flood control which reads in part as follows. . . ." A chronological biography begins with the birth of the subject and ends with his death. It is the most popular biographical form in China.

All the works listed above are of a serious vein, understood little and cared about even less by anyone other than a member of the intellectual elite. An average reader, in China as well as elsewhere, wishes to be entertained. Fortunately there is a massive assemblage of literature created during the Ch'ing period to satisfy his needs. *The Dream of the Red Chamber (Hung-lou meng,* by Ts'ao Hsüeh-ch'in of the eighteenth century) has been hailed by many as the greatest novel of China, and many other works, though less well known, prove to be equally entertaining. The authors of these works never enjoyed the same prestige as that accorded to great philosophers and historians, and some of them were "discovered," long after their deaths, only by accident. *The Six Chapters of a Floating Life (Fou-sheng liu-chi,* by Shen Fu, b. 1763), for instance, is perhaps one of the most charming books ever written, but it was not "discovered" until the 1880s, then only by accident. A condensed version of one of the *Six Chapters* appears here as selection 52.

(47)
Shun-chih / *The Head-shaving Decree*[1]

The various decrees relating to head shaving have been purposefully inconsistent in some respects in order to meet a variety of situations that might arise. There has never been any doubt that once all of China is pacified, a decree will be issued to end all the inconsistencies. Now that all of China has become one family, it is mandatory that the king and his subjects be united as one, as a subject's disloyalty to his king can no more be tolerated than that of a son to his own father. To be otherwise is to regard the king and his subjects as strangers to each other—an absurdity so obvious that you must know it fully well without any of my elaborations.

It is therefore decreed that within ten days after this public announcement all the men in the capital and its adjacent areas must shave their heads and that all the men in the provinces must shave their heads within ten days after the arrival of this announcement in their respective provinces. Only those who shave their heads are to be considered loyal subjects of this nation; those who hesitate or refuse to do it are to be regarded as traitors and will be punished severely. No excuses for evasion, however cunning or clever, are to be tolerated.

It is further decreed that all the local officials, civilian as well as military, must see to it that the above order relating to head shaving is to be implemented without fail and that any official who is impudent enough to petition the government to delay or relax the enforcement of this order will be condemned to death without mercy. The same penalty will also be imposed upon those officials who are impudent enough to petition the government for the maintenance of those Ming customs that are at variance with those of the present dynasty. However, a reasonable length of time will be allowed for people to change from their old Ming costume to that of the present dynasty. From now on all people in China must obey the laws of this dynasty, and defiance in whatever form is not to be tolerated.

The Ministry of Rites is hereby ordered to proclaim this decree in all the provinces, districts, and other administrative units, as well as the capital and its adjacent areas, to assure its observance by all officials, civilian as well as military, teachers and students, and all other people in the empire.

Notes

1. This decree, in the form of an internal order to the Ministry of Rites, was actually issued by Dorgon (1612–50), regent for the boy emperor Shun-chih (r. 1644–61), in July 1644. Source: *Tung-hua lu*, the sixth month of the first year of Shun-chih.

(48)
K'ang-hsi / *On Good Government and Other Matters*[1]

Good government depends upon the employment of good men, and good government cannot come about if eunuchs are employed as responsible officials. The validity of this statement has been proved by events in each and every dynasty of China's past. The harm is even greater if the eunuchs are allowed not only to enjoy power but also to build a large following who do the eunuchs' bidding for their own avarice and greed. It is for this reason that my imperial ancestors, T'ai-tsu and T'ai-tsung, knowing as they did about the eunuchs' abuse of power in the past, did not introduce in the imperial court the institution of eunuchs. It was also for this reason that my immediate predecessor [Shun-chih] confined the duties of the eunuchs to those of a servile nature and that when they were occasionally entrusted with positions of authority he did not forget for a moment that they were evil and conspiratorial as a group. In one of his last decrees before his death he reminded us that the downfall of the Ming dynasty was caused primarily by the employment of eunuchs in positions of power and that the founder of this dynasty had no use for eunuchs. In observing the wishes of my predecessors, I shall be most diligent insofar as the observation of the eunuchs' behavior is concerned.

*   *   *   *   *

There is no better way to good government than to follow the rules of one's forebears and to abide by the precedents that have been sanctified as law. Only in this way can one hope to avoid serious errors.

Emperor T'ai-tsu, in observing the wishes of Heaven, founded this dynasty and thus completed a task sanctioned by tradition. Emperor T'ai-tsung, by extending the dynasty's territory far and wide, brought happiness to a great multitude. Since my ascension to the throne, I have often pondered their great achievements and wished to be worthy of them as their successor. My immediate predecessor Chang-tsung [Shun-chih] had at one time ordered scholars to compile and edit all the decrees issued during the reigns of T'ai-tsu and T'ai-tsung, but somehow the work was never completed.

It is hereby decreed that the writers and editors currently employed in the imperial archives and libraries should proceed with the uncompleted work and classify and catalog all the decrees mentioned above, so a complete work will in the end materialize. I shall read it from time to time for my own benefit. My children and grandchildren also shall do likewise.

*   *   *   *   *

Yesterday I was instructed by Her Ladyship the Dowager Grandmother as follows:

Though confined in the palace, I knew, more or less, the way my late husband, Emperor T'ai-tsung, ran the government. The dynasty was then only newly established, and the emperor, consequently, stressed the importance of martial arts. Though the country has long been pacified, it should be constantly remembered, nevertheless, that the feeling of security engenders the prospect of danger and only the fear of danger can assure one of some degree of security. Military preparedness should not be neglected by any means.

There are of course loyal and upright ministers in the court who report to the emperor what they honestly believe. There are others, too, who advance their selfish ends via the official position they occupy and upgrade or downgrade their subordinates in accordance with their likes or dislikes, rather than the true merit of the persons involved. Keep in mind that whenever a difference of opinion occurs, it is the duty of the emperor to render a fair and impartial judgment. Only in this way can he expect not to commit too many errors.

I have studied this instruction carefully and shall always remind myself that an emperor should always be fair and impartial in rendering judgment.

*   *   *   *   *

When reading history, one cannot but be impressed with the openness with which the king and his ministers discussed national issues during the reigns of Yao and Shun. Likewise, one cannot but admire the willingness of T'ang T'ai-tsung to accept sound advice, though this advice may have been initially repellent to him. In the case of T'ang T'ai-tsung as well as that of Yao and Shun, the king and his ministers acted toward each other like members of one family; the king, consequently, was able to suppress evil and elevate goodness. Most naturally the reigns of Yao, Shun, and T'ang T'ai-tsung have been remembered with satisfaction and pride as the best in Chinese history. The situation was totally different toward the end of the Ming dynasty when a wide gap existed between the king and his ministers and the king, therefore, had no way of knowing how much the people really suffered.

Since the establishment of this dynasty by T'ai-tsu and T'ai-tsung, all officials in the empire—civilian as well as military, Chinese as well as Manchus—have been cooperating fully not only in informing one another about their respective tasks but also in reporting to the government the true condition of the people. They act as if they shared one body, one mind. They are sympathetic to people's wishes and do whatever they can to improve their living conditions, sometimes under very difficult circumstances. Let this attitude of theirs be an abiding and inviolable rule for thousands of generations to come!

Admiring the great achievements of our ancient sage kings and wishing, respectfully, to abide by the laws of my imperial ancestors, I am opening the door to all the talented men in the empire, with whom I wish to discuss the best ways to attain the goal of good government. If a king treats his ministers in the same way as a father treats his children, the ministers will certainly do their utmost to carry out the tasks assigned to them. The validity of this statement has been proved beyond any doubt in the course of Chinese history.

*   *   *   *   *

In the economic sufficiency of the people lies the peace and security of the nation. This has been true throughout history.

Reading the *Rules Governing the Reclamation of Abandoned Fields,* I was surprised to learn that peasants who volunteer to cultivate abandoned fields can enjoy tax exemption for only a six-year period and have to pay taxes beginning with the seventh year. The peasants cultivating abandoned fields are usually among the poorest in the nation and have a most difficult time earning a livelihood. Having to pay taxes that increase their burden, they may decide to abandon the fields they have cultivated and thus become unemployed. About this I am deeply concerned.

Let it be known that peasants in all the provinces who volunteer to cultivate abandoned fields will not be taxed for a ten-year period.

*   *   *   *   *

Since we have had bumper crops in recent years, many peasants, who have no concept of savings, tend to become extravagant. Last year the harvests in Shantung and Honan were less than abundant, and the authorities in these two provinces immediately reported the condition of famine and petitioned the imperial government for tax exemption and emergency relief. Had these authorities lived up to their responsibility by encouraging and promoting savings during the good years, the deplorable situation as described in their reports would have been avoided.

Recent reports from the provinces indicate that precipitation has been very good this year and that a bumper crop is expected. Lest the people become extravagant again, I am instructing all the officials, from governors-general to village chiefs, to urge people in their jurisdiction to be thrifty, so that enough grain can be stored away for relief in some future years when harvests may not be so abundant. Knowing how much I love my people, the officials cannot do less than I have instructed.

Having traveled extensively in seven provinces, I think I know the people's economic conditions. The reason that people are less affluent than they should be stems from the simple fact that as peace has prevailed for a long time, population increases enormously, while total cultivated acreage remains substantially the same. It is no wonder that people have become less well-to-do today.

Next year will mark the fiftieth year of my reign, and I have pondered the possibility of canceling all tax payments for that year. I was told, however, that such a sudden and drastic reduction of revenue would adversely affect our ability to maintain our armed forces at the present strength and may indeed damage the smooth operation of the postal system. Nevertheless, let it be known that in a three-year period beginning with next year all areas in China will take turns having one year's exemption of all taxes, so that all the people in China will receive this tax benefit, without in the meantime causing a sudden drop in governmental revenue.

* * * * *

About to reach the age of seventy, I realize that I have been the sovereign ruler of this great empire for more than fifty years. Though I have not been able to lead all my subjects to goodness, peace has indeed prevailed for a long time and all households have been more or less economically sufficient.

For the past fifty years I have done my utmost to advance the well-being of all of my subjects. Not a single day elapses without my thinking about the best way to serve them. To say that I have toiled hard and long is indeed an understatement.

I realize the importance of the position I hold. A little carelessness on my part will not only cause millions of people to suffer but also create a bad precedent, the evil effects of which will bring harm to people of generations to come. A man who is casual about small things will in some future time commit a serious offense. That is why I have been most careful and diligent whenever a decision is to be made, regardless of how important or insignificant the matter at hand seems to be.

Notes

1. The Chinese original of this translation is excerpted from various sections of the *Tung-hua lu*.

(49)
Chia-ch'ing / *Ho-shen's Twenty Crimes*[1]

As a special favorite of His Majesty the Late Emperor [Ch'ien-lung], Ho-shen, the accused, was promoted from the ranks of Imperial Guards to the high position of Grand Councillor. For many years he worked in the Privy Council. During the Late Emperor's reign none had received more favors than this man.

Having been entrusted with the burden of the state, I had the great misfortune to be suddenly confronted with the death of His Majesty the Late Emperor.[2] In my grief I kept reminding myself that "a dutiful son does not change his father's way of doing things for three years after his father's death,"[3] particularly having in mind that the Late Emperor had always been most reluctant to dismiss his important ministers. However, the crimes committed by Ho-shen were of such gravity and of such unforgivable nature that I could not but act immediately. Having received the report of these crimes which were elaborated in detail by responsible officials, I, on the day of making public the Late Emperor's will, ordered the indictment and arrest of the accused. These crimes, in summary, are as follows:

1. On the third day of the ninth month, in the sixtieth year of Ch'ien-lung [15 October 1795], His Majesty the Late Emperor formally designated me as the crown prince and heir apparent. But the designation was not yet made public. However, on the day before the designation, namely, on the second day of the ninth month, Ho-shen chose to leak this information, thus violating the law governing state secrets. Unquestionably he wished to create the impression that he had something to do with the designation and thus ingratiate himself with the new emperor.

2. In the first month of the third year of Chia-ch'ing [1798] Ho-shen, having been summoned by His Majesty the Late Emperor for an audience at Yüan Ming Yüan,[4] rode his horse straight to the Chung-tso Gate, passed by the Palace of Uprightness and Enlightenment, and eventually reached Shushank'ou. He never bothered to dismount. This lack of respect for the Late Emperor constitutes crime number two.

3. Besides, under the pretext of suffering from a leg injury,

Ho-shen often went into and came out of the Forbidden City, usually by the way of the Shen-wu Gate, in a sedan chair. He seemed to be not in the least concerned with prudence and propriety.

4. He took as his concubines women who had been released from their palace duties. This shows his total disregard for proper conduct.

5. He deliberately delayed forwarding to me confidential reports submitted by field commanders, the field commanders who were then fighting religious bandits in Szechuan and Hupeh.[5] He doubtless intended to deceive me.

6. He showed no grief when His Majesty the Late Emperor was seriously ill. In fact, he talked and laughed as usual after each time he visited the patient.

7. He not only took over all the power in the Ministries of Personnel and Justice but also interfered with the administration of the Interior Ministry. He in fact wanted to be a dictator in all the ministries.

8. In the winter of the third year of Chia-ch'ing [1798] when the Late Emperor was ill and could not be meticulously accurate in his comments on calligraphies and paintings, Ho-shen was impudent enough to make changes in these comments without the Late Emperor's knowledge.

9. Upon hearing the report from General K'uei-shu that more than one thousand bandits had ravaged the districts of Shunhua and Kueiteh and killed two persons and stolen a number of cattle in the process, Ho-shen dismissed the report as inaccurate and chose not to take any action, even though he knew in advance that the same group of bandits had also been engaged in lawless activities in Tsingtao and its adjacent areas.

10. After the death of His Majesty the Late Emperor, I issued an order that those Mongol princes who had not suffered smallpox during their childhood should not bother to come to the capital to pay their last respects. Ho-shen changed the order by saying that all Mongol princes should not bother to come to the capital, whether they had or had not suffered smallpox during their childhood.

11. Ho-shen concealed from me the fact that Su-ling-ah continued as a Grand Councillor even though he was old, deaf, and sick, for no other reason than the fact that Su-ling-ah was related

to Ho-lin, Ho-shen's younger brother, by marriage. Besides, the same Ho-shen appointed Wu Shen-lan, Li Huang, and Li Kuang-yün for posts on the Board of Education when these three persons were actually employed by him as tutors in teaching his own children.

12. He added or dismissed personnel in the Privy Council as he pleased and without valid reason.

13. An investigation of Ho-shen's properties has revealed that the houses in his residence compound were constructed with cedar wood, that his Topao Pavilion has the same architectural style as that of the royal Ningshan Hall, and that the landscaping of his residence compound is similar to that in the Summer Palace. All these luxuries far exceed the limit permitted by custom and law.

14. The tomb for Ho-shen's ancestors at Chichou has been built in such a way as to contain a sacrifice hall, linked to the entrance by a long underground tunnel. Local people in Chichou refer to it as the "Imperial Mausoleum of Ho."

15. The investigation reveals that he owned two hundred bracelets made of high-quality pearls. Some of the pearls found in his residence are larger than those on the imperial crown.

16. Numerous precious stones were found in his residence. Some of these stones are so rare and valuable that even the imperial household does not own any of them.

17. The various items found in his residence, such as silverware, furs, and furniture, are assessed at a value of 10 million taels of silver.

18. The investigation further reveals that he had twenty-six thousand taels of gold hidden inside his residence walls, six thousand taels of gold in his private vault, and 1 million taels of silver buried underneath the ground.

19. Ho-shen owned banks in Chichou and T'ungchou [modern Hopeh province], capitalized at one hundred thousand taels of silver each. Thus he unfairly competed with bona fide merchants for profits.

20. He impressed more than a thousand soldiers from the armed forces to serve as servants in his household.

I am ordering a tribunal of princes and ministers to be formed for the trial of the accused. I am also ordering all governors-general to report to me crimes that have been committed by the accused which are not listed above. Report to me any suggestion you may have in terms of punishment if the accused is convicted.[6]

Notes

1. Source: *Sheng-wu chi*, the Chia-ch'ing period, roll 4.
2. Ch'ien-lung abdicated in favor of his son, known by his reigning title as Chia-ch'ing, on 9 February 1796. Ch'ien-lung died on 7 February 1799, three years after his abdication. Five days after his death, Ho-shen was indicted for having committed twenty cardinal crimes.
3. A Confucian adage that appears in the *Analects of Confucius*.
4. The emperor's Summer Palace that was burned by the British in 1860.
5. This refers to the armed revolt led by the White Lotus Society.
6. Subsequently Ho-shen was convicted and sentenced to death.

(50)
Li Dun-jen / *Origin of the Hungmen Society*[1]

In the eleventh year of K'ang-hsi (1672) the Tibetans invaded China's border provinces. The expeditionary army, which had been sent to repel them, was repeatedly defeated. Alarmed, the Ch'ing government pasted recruiting posters everywhere, in the hope that men of unusual talent might be induced to join its army. Having read one of the posters, Cheng Chün-ta, a monk in the Shaolin Temple,[2] spoke with his colleagues about enlisting so that, as he put it, the Ming loyalists (as these monks were) could penetrate deep into the Ch'ing government and topple it from within. One hundred twenty-eight of his fellow monks agreed with his reasoning and joined the Ch'ing army as new recruits.

The reputation of Shaolin monks as superior warriors was well known to all, including Emperor K'ang-hsi who was as surprised as he was pleased when he learned that these monks had volunteered their service on his behalf. During an audience he granted, the monks informed him that they wanted no soldiers to be placed under their command and that all they needed were feed for their horses and food for themselves. The emperor, happily surprised, gave each of them a sword with words of authorization engraved on it so that from then on they could legally act on his behalf.

The Tibetans proved to be no match for these Shaolin monks who defeated them in every battle. In less than three months the king of Tibet was forced to surrender and personally appeared before the Shaolin monks to sue for peace. The monks triumphantly returned to the capital without suffering a single casualty and were received with pomp by a gratified emperor. The emperor ordered that ranks and titles be awarded to them, but the monks, with the exception of Cheng Chün-ta, declined the honor, on the grounds that as men dedicated to Buddha they preferred to return to a life of meditation in the temple. Not wishing to impose his will on them, the emperor ordered a banquet to be given in their honor, besides showering them with such valuables as gold, silver, and silk. From then on, said the emperor, these monks were to be known as "jade monastics," as each of them received a jade incense burner as a farewell present. Their temple was to be decorated with tablets inscribed with the emperor's own handwriting, and on the fifteenth day of the eighth month of each year, said the emperor, he himself was to journey to the Shaolin Temple to worship Buddha with them. Meanwhile the temple was to be renovated at the government's expense. On the day of their departure, the emperor, accompanied by all the dignitaries in the government, personally escorted them several *li* to bid them farewell.

There is a black sheep even among the best group of men; and the Shaolin monks, soon after their return to the temple, found one among themselves. His name was Ma Fu-yi who, taking advantage of Cheng Chün-ta's absence, attempted to seduce Cheng's young wife and also his equally beautiful young sister. The attempt was discovered before it yielded any fruit; and Ma, in accordance with the Shaolin law, was ostracized from the temple by a unanimous decision. Little did these monks realize that by dismissing one colleague they would in due course bring disaster to themselves.

After his dismissal, Ma Fu-yi actively sought revenge. He quickly reported to the governor of Fukien, within whose jurisdiction the Shaolin Temple was located, that the ultimate goal of the Shaolin monks was to overthrow the Ch'ing government and to replace it with a rejuvenated Ming regime. The governor, having always had a healthy regard for the monks' military prowess, hesitated in his response and certainly would not have initiated any action had two of his lieutenants not insisted. These two lieutenants, named Ch'en Wen-yao and Chang Chin-ch'iu, had been jealous of the monks' martial reputation and, being military men themselves, had been waiting for the opportunity to demonstrate their own superiority. They, therefore, reported directly to the emperor what they had learned from Ma Fu-yi and recommended immediate action, saying specifically that if this conspiracy were not crushed in its infant stage, it would snowball and eventually pose a threat to the security of the crown. The emperor was reluctant to take action against a group of people whom he had only recently showered with favors. But, facing the incontestable testimony of Ma Fu-yi, he finally approved a plan which, when carried out, would mean the destruction of the Shaolin Temple and the extermination of all its monks.

On the night when the plan was to be carried out, Ch'en Wen-yao and Chang Chin-ch'iu, at the head of three thousand troops and with Ma Fu-yi as an advance guard, quickly arrived at the Chiulien Mountain, in the P'ut'ien district of Fukien, where the Shaolin Temple was located. By midnight, when the monks were soundly asleep, they had surrounded the temple with several rows of soldiers. Secretly and without making a sound, the soldiers of the innermost layer set the temple afire with saltpeter and other inflammable materials. Suddenly finding themselves in an inferno, the monks rushed out to flee, only to be cut down, one by one, by the surrounding soldiers. The order of the day was to kill all the monks on the spot; nevertheless, eighteen monks managed to escape.

Led by Ma Fu-yi, the soldiers began a hot pursuit of the fleeing monks. Outnumbered and outequipped, the monks lost more men as they fled southward, though they themselves had killed a large number of soldiers. By early morning only five monks remained, and these five monks, led by Ts'ai Teh-chung, were later referred to as the First Five Patriarchs of the Hungmen Society.[3] Finally they arrived at the village of Shawank'ou where they felt comparatively safe. Then each of the monks ritualistically broke a branch from a nearby tree, snapped it, and vowed "eternal revenge." "Heaven and Earth may crumble," they swore, "but this debt of blood must be paid." If any comfort existed at all, it was the fact that Ma Fu-yi, the traitor, had been killed by them with a piercing arrow. Ever since the name of Ma Fu-yi has been taboo among the Hungmen members. Since Ma Fu-yi, before his dismissal, had been ranked seventh in martial skill among the Shaolin monks, no Hungmen member, from that day on, would ever mention the number seven or use it.

The five monks left Fukien for Kwangtung where their presence was soon detected by the Ch'ing forces. Saved at the last moment by a group of woodcutters, they journeyed northward to Kiangsi where they learned that Cheng Chün-ta's wife and sister had escaped to Mount Ting of Hsiangyang, Hupeh province. At Mount Ting, they were told by Cheng's wife that her husband had been executed by the Ch'ing government and that she and her sister-in-law had with great difficulty transported his body to Mount Ting to be buried. The monks went to the grave site to pay their respects and once again vowed revenge.

Before long the Ch'ing government, once again, discovered the monks' whereabouts. As Mount Ting was surrounded on all sides by the Ch'ing forces, Cheng's widow and sister volunteered to fight as a rear guard so as to give the five monks enough time to engineer their escape. In the ensuing battle, the outnumbered rear guard were defeated, but they did fight long enough to enable the monks to flee. After the defeat the two women, having successfully completed their assigned duties, committed suicide by drowning themselves in a river. Ever since their death, Kuo Hsiu-ying and Cheng Yü-lan, as Cheng's widow and sister were called respectively, have been remembered as two of the greatest Hungmen heroines.

Shortly after the destruction of the Shaolin Temple and the killing or dispersion of its monks, Ch'en Chin-nan, a native of Hupeh who then served the Ch'ing government as a Hanlin academician, remonstrated the emperor on the injustice of his course. The emperor, consumed with anger, summarily dismissed him from office, on the grounds that he had unjustifiably sided with the rebels. Having lost his means of livelihood, Ch'en Chin-nan traveled from place to place and earned a living as a geomancer and diviner. Eventually he settled at the Cave of White Swans near his birthplace in Hupeh and devoted himself to the study of Taoism. It was in his capacity as a Taoist priest that he met many Ming loyalists, including the five Buddhist monks previously described. As more and more Ming loyalists came and went, Ch'en Chin-nan quickly learned that the Cave of White Swans had become too small for meeting purposes. Subsequently he moved his headquarters to the Pavilion of Red Flowers which, being more spacious, could hold large gatherings. Day and night he and his compatriots voiced their nationalistic sentiments and discussed the best way to overthrow the Ch'ing regime and reestablish the Ming dynasty.

One beautiful morning, while taking a walk along a river near the Pavilion of Red Flowers, the five monks found an incense burner made of white stone. The base of the incense burner was inscribed with not only the admonition "Overthrow the Ch'ing and Restore the Ming," but also the weight of the incense burner, namely, "fifty-two catties and thirteen taels." The monks were overwhelmed by this find and quickly brought it to Ch'en Chin-nan for an evaluation of its significance. The admonition of "overthrowing the Ch'ing and restoring the Ming" did not require much explanation, but the words involving the weight of the incense burner remained a puzzle. "The 'five' in the 'fifty' represents the five lakes in China," said Ch'en Chin-nan the Taoist diviner after much thought. "The 'two' in the 'fifty-two' refers to the two capitals, namely, Peking and Nanking. Needless to say, the 'thirteen' in the 'thirteen taels' means the thirteen provinces of China." The Ming loyalists were jubilant upon hearing this interpretation. "The mandate of Heaven is loud and clear," they declared. "The Ch'ing dynasty has been destined to die, and we shall not lose a moment to speed up its demise."

On this optimistic note, the Ming loyalists at the Pavilion of Red Flowers began to invite like-minded leaders all over China to attend a meeting. More than one thousand fellow loyalists arrived, mostly from Kwangtung, Fukien, and Kiangsi. Among them was Chu Hung-chu, a grandson of Ch'ung-chen, the last Ming emperor. The Ming loyalists unanimously elected him their leader, thus assuring the legitimacy of their own revolt.

On the evening of the twenty-fifth day of the seventh month, in the thirteenth year of K'ang-hsi (26 August 1674), the Ming loyalists held a general meeting at the Pavilion of Red Flowers to mark the beginning of their organization. It was a foggy night, shadowed by a starless sky. While the meeting was in progress, a red light suddenly appeared in the distance, brightening the sky as far as one's eyes could see. Interpreting the red light as a good omen, the Ming loyalists decided to name their organization "Hung" which, in Chinese character, means "red." Then they realized that the second character of Chu Hung-chu's name was also pronounced "Hung," though in a different Chinese character which carries the meaning of "great" or "grand" rather than "red." It was the character that means "great" or "grand" that they eventually adopted for the name of their organization, as this character, unlike the character that means "red," could also be properly regarded as a surname. Thus, *Hungmen Hui*, which was the full name of their organization, means, literally, the Association of the Hung Family. In this family, as dictated by tradition, those who joined earlier were regarded as elder brothers to those who joined later, regardless of age differences.

Notes

1. This story, written by this author with information drawn primarily from *Chung-kuo pang-hui shih (History of Chinese Secret Societies)* (Hong Kong: Modern Publishers, n.d.) by Shuai Hsüeh-fu, should be read more as folklore than as historical fact. It is written in such a way as to reflect the tenor of Chinese folklore which, as a child, this author used to hear in his native village.

2. There were at least two Shaolin Temples in China. The better-known one was the Shaolin Temple in Tunfeng, Honan province, which was constructed in 496 during the Later Wei dynasty when Buddhism reached the height of its popularity. Northwest of the temple was a stone wall before which the Indian missionary Bodhidharma (sixth century), founder of Ch'an (Zen) Buddhism, was supposed to have meditated for nine years before reaching nirvana. The lesser-known one was located on Mount Chiulien, in the P'ut'ien district of Fukien. The Shaolin Temple referred to here was the lesser-known one.

3. The other four monks were Fang Ta-hung, Ma Ch'ao-hsing, Hu Teh-ti, and Li Shih-k'ai.

(51)
Yen Yüan / *On Learning*[1]

A sage regards Heaven, Earth, and everything in between as one grand unity and regards all men under Heaven, whether they be far or near, as his own brothers. He wishes to feed them, educate them, and make them secure since in his view he and all other men spring from the same origin.

Basically no difference exists between a sage's mind and the minds of all others; in theory, every man can become a sage. The difference lies in the fact that while an ordinary person places the individual "I" above the collective "we," thus confusing the important with the comparatively insignificant and, furthermore, blocking the communication between the individual "I" and the collective "we," a sage does exactly the opposite. In the case of an ordinary person the situation has sometimes so deteriorated that he regards as his enemies not only unrelated persons but his own parents, brothers, and sisters as well. Nothing can be more deplorable than this! Deeply concerned, the sages teach us the principle of grand unity: that all the things in the universe, including human beings, are manifestations of a single, inseparable organ and that the force that holds this unity together is love *(jen)*. They want us to be more strict with ourselves and more generous toward others.

This principle of grand unity is by no means purely academic; during the time of Yao, Shun, and the Three Dynasties people actually lived by it. Those who lived by it were called sages or virtuous men, and those who did not were referred to as scoundrels, no matter how learned they were. All the people—from scholars to farmers, artisans, and merchants—had been taught this principle at home and in schools and guided their conduct in accordance with it. They did not occupy themselves with ideologies or literature, let alone the pursuit of fame, power, or wealth. Their primary concern was how they could best serve as dutiful sons to their parents, respectful juniors to their elders, and trustworthy friends to all others. They served well because their conduct and behavior were natural and spontaneous, as their bodies and minds were united in this matter. Furthermore, it never occurred to them that they would not do their best to serve others. In their view the capacity to love was inherent in all men; it was merely a simple matter to put it into practice.

Now let us examine what their schools taught. The basic discipline that formed the foundation of all curricula was the cultivation of virtue, and all the specializations, whatever they happened to be (rites and music, government and education, agriculture, irrigation and water control, etc.), were developed in accordance with the students' natural inclinations and talents. The purpose of this education was to create a morally superior man with a special skill of his own choice. Since his personal ethics would never be in doubt and since his occupation corresponded to his natural talent and special skill, he would be happy and content with the same position for the rest of his life. Believing firmly in the principle of grand unity as described above, he did not regard his position as either superior or inferior, leisurely or burdensome, as long as he could best serve others. Whenever in a position to hire the service of others, he considered their ability and specialization the only criteria, since he had no doubt about other people's ethics as they had no doubt about his. There were no such things as noble tasks or menial jobs, as they were all equal in importance. All of this was possible because all the people regarded one another as members of one family, working diligently to bring benefit to all. Those unusually talented and able were entrusted with the duty of government, while all the others served as farmers, artisans, and merchants. None aspired to a position other than the one he already had, since no position was higher or lower than any other one. It was a simple matter of the division of labor.

Looking back at this golden era, today's scholars regret deeply that the way of our ancient sages is no longer with us and spend much of their time tracing the good customs and sound institutions of the past and trying to put together whatever fragments still remain. They deserve our praise since they want to restore the way of our ancient sages. Unfortunately, the way of the sages was replaced by the way of the power brokers for such a long time that these scholars, however wise, tend to be influenced by the latter rather than the former and that, despite their sincerity insofar as the restoration of ancient institutions is concerned, actually strengthens the argument of the power brokers.

At the moment these scholars keep themselves busy as commentators on Confucian classics, as memorizers of ancient literature, and as writers of a variety of forms of poetry. This is the way they seek fame; this is the way they seek beauty. In each of their so-called disciplines there are several schools, each of which competes with others for recognition and influence. Each school is like a maze, or better still, an amusement park, where some jump and run, while others laugh and flirt with one another. Each person tries to impress others as to how important or, really, how "cute" he is. It is no wonder that those who spend their lifetime in this never-never land have lost the right sense of values and, in many cases, become totally neurotic and irresponsible. Sadly enough, emperors and kings are supposed to be impressed with their so-called erudition. What is their advice to the emperors and the kings? "Power and wealth"—that is their advice.

As the way of the sages slowly disappears in the distance, we become more and more used to the concept of power and wealth. Many of us have been influenced by Buddhism and Taoism, but Buddhist and Taoist teachings have in no way reduced our yearning for power and wealth. Prominent scholars have warned us against the evil consequences of this worldly obsession, but these warnings have unfortunately fallen upon deaf ears. For several thousand years power and wealth have been the primary goals for nations and individuals—long enough to enable their poison to seep deep into the marrow of our bones. To seek power and wealth, people fight among themselves to become more influential, more famous, and to acquire greater ability to push other people around. A clerk would like to have a division of soldiers under his command or to decide other people's fate by becoming a criminal judge. A magistrate wishes to become a governor, a governor wishes to become a governor-general, and there is no limit.

To justify their claims, people need eloquence and sophistry which they devote much of their lifetime to acquiring. Reading extensively and memorizing a great deal, they want to impress others with how much they know. They use this knowledge to cover their own misdeeds and to make plausible what cannot be justified. They write well, and the richness of their rhetoric is aimed to deceive rather than to reveal. When you ask them about their life goal, they reply without hesitation that they want to serve the people. They realize that had they told the truth, they would not be able so easily to serve their own selfish ends. With this kind of attitude to pursue this kind of learning, is it really surprising that they find themselves at odds with the sages of ancient times?

Notes

1. A copy of the Chinese original can be found in Ch'ien Mu, *Chung-kuo chin san-pai nien hsüeh-shu shih (A History of Chinese Thought: The Last Three Hundred Years)* (Taipei: Commercial Press, n.d.), vol. 1, pp. 187–91.

(52)
Shen Fu / *My Wife*[1]

As a child I was betrothed to a girl of the Yü family, but unfortunately she died at the age of seven. Upon reaching adulthood I was married to Yün, a maternal cousin of mine from the Ch'en family.[2] Yün, born with high intelligence, was able to recite the *Song of P'i-p'a*[3] almost as soon as she learned how to speak. At the age of three her father died, and the family, from then on, was plagued with financial difficulties. Fortunately Yün, even in her teens, proved to be an expert tailor; her earnings not only provided a livelihood for all the members of the family but also enabled her younger brother to continue his schooling. As far as her own schooling was concerned, she taught herself.

At the age of twelve, as I recall, I accompanied my mother to visit the Ch'en family and, being totally innocent as far as romance was concerned, was shown some of Yün's writings. I was impressed with what I read but somehow felt that a girl of such talent might not enjoy good fortune in the long run. Yet, how can one's mind deny what one's heart truly desires? "If you wish to find a wife for me," I said to my mother, "there is only one woman for me." My mother, greatly pleased with Yün's gentleness and modesty, agreed and presented her mother with a golden ring to seal the engagement. This event occurred on the sixteenth day of the seventh month, in the fiftieth year of Ch'ien-lung [11 August 1775].

Sometime later my mother and I again visited the Ch'en family when one of Yün's cousins was about to be married. On the wedding day when all the women wore the brightest clothes they owned, Yün alone chose to dress in a subdued manner. Only her shoes were new. When questioned, she admitted that the shoes were her own creation. Looking at the intricate embroidery that graced her feet, I knew for the first time that her talent was not confined to literature alone.

Yün had a long neck, but narrow shoulders. She was slender, but not skinny. Underneath her long, curved eyebrows were two bright, gentle eyes. The only thing that might be regarded as inauspicious was her partially opened mouth that revealed, though only slightly, her teeth. Lovely though she looked, the most attractive part about her was still her personality, so beguiling and inviting that I simply found it irresistible.

I asked her about the poetry she had been writing and was surprised to learn that some of her poems were never completed. "Why the incompletion?" I asked.

"Sometime in the future there must be someone understanding and knowledgeable enough to help me to complete them."

Jokingly I wrote on her booklet: "Beautiful Words in a Silk Bag." Little did I realize then that the incompletion in her poetry was an inauspicious omen for the shortness of her life.

On the evening of her cousin's wedding we did not return to Yün's house until midnight, having escorted the bride and her party outside the city gate. I was very hungry, and the maid presented me with dried dates. While complaining that the dates were too sweet, I noticed that Yün was gently pulling my sleeve. Following her to her room, I, to my happy surprise, found on her table a bowl of rice pudding, together with a dish of pickled vegetables. Before I had time to enjoy it, I heard one of her cousins calling her outside the door. "I am awfully tired," she replied. "I am already in bed." Before she had time to close the door, however, her cousin was already in. Noticing that I was eating pudding, he said to her, teasingly, "A moment a go I was asking you for some pudding, and you said it was all gone. Now I see that you were saving it for your fiancé." Yün felt greatly embarrassed and left the room without a word. All the people in the family laughed with merriment when they heard about this incident. From then on Yün scrupulously avoided me whenever

I returned to the Ch'en house, being fearful that others might poke fun at her again.

I was married to Yün on the twenty-second day of the first month, in the forty-fifth year of Ch'ien-lung [26 February 1780]. She was the same slender girl I used to know, and we smiled knowingly at each other once the wedding veil was lifted from her face. Upon drinking from the nuptial cup and thus pledging eternal love to each other, we were then left alone. Under the light of wedding candles, we sat side by side and dined together. Gingerly I sneaked one of my hands underneath the table and held her wrist. It was smooth and warm, and my heart began to pound. I urged her to eat but was told that she had been fasting for a long time. Counting the days she had been fasting, I suddenly realized that the beginning of her fast corresponded to the day I contracted smallpox and that she had been fasting for me. "Now that I am as healthy as a man can possibly be," I said to her, "you can break your fast." She smiled at me with her eyes and nodded in agreement.

As a newly married woman, Yün was very quiet and only smiled when I spoke to her. Never for a single moment did she become irritated or angry. She was respectful toward my parents and kind to those socially below her. She managed the household expertly and rarely committed an error. She quickly got up when the morning light began to appear in the window, as if someone in authority had commanded her to be present. "The pudding days have long passed," I said. "Nobody will laugh at you even if you stayed with me a little longer."

"I do remember how I became a laughingstock as a result of the pudding incident," she replied. "No, I am not afraid that people might tease me again. I am afraid that the lady above might think that her newly married daughter-in-law is too lazy." Though I would have liked her to stay in bed with me a little longer, I got up the moment she got up, being convinced that she was right and I was wrong. From morning to night we were as inseparable as an object and its shadow. The enjoyment of love was so great that words are inadequate to describe it.

Time moved fast because it was enjoyable; a month passed quickly after our marriage. My father, who was then a government official at Kueichi [modern Chekiang province] sent a man to fetch me so I could resume my studies with the famous scholar

Chao Sheng-chai. (Chao was a conscientious, persuasive teacher. If I can write reasonably well today, the credit should rightly belong to him.) I was disappointed when I received my father's command because, at the time when I left my teacher for the wedding, I thought I had more time to stay at home. Fearful that Yün might not be able to control her emotions in front of other family members, I forced myself to be cheerful. But the fear proved to be unfounded, as Yün, instead of showing her emotions, actually tried to cheer me up. Only at night when I was alone with her did I detect a sense of sadness. "Take care of yourself," she whispered in my ear, "since nobody over there is going to take care of you."

Three months away from my wife seemed like ten years. Though she wrote from time to time, the letters consisted mostly of words of encouragement, plus a few clichés. Furthermore, I received only one letter for every two letters I wrote her. I felt disappointed. Whenever wind blew across the bamboo yard or the moon slowly made its appearance in the window, I thought of her and sighed. Having sensed how I felt, my teacher wrote a letter to my father requesting permission to send me home for a vacation. He gave me an assignment of ten themes which I had to complete during my stay at home. I did not think much about the themes: the moment I left his presence, I felt like a bird flying away from a cage.

The boat moved slowly, so slowly in fact that every minute seemed like a year. Arriving at home, I first went to my mother's room to pay my respects. Repairing to my own room, I found Yün standing there to receive me. Without exchanging a word, I took her hands into mine. As soon as our hands touched, we melted into each other. Our spirits left our bodies, and our bodies wafted into the thin air.

This was the sixth month of the year, and it was very hot inside the house. Fortunately there was a little structure west of the main residence and next to a brook, which my father had previously used as a guest house. Having a huge tree in front that shadowed the windows as well as the door, it was noticeably cooler inside. I requested and received my mother's permission to spend a summer in it, and Yün, my wife, agreed to suspend her embroidery work in order to spend the time with me. Day and night we read together and discussed, and sometimes criticized, what we had read. Yün was not a good drinker, however. When pressed, she might consume as many as three cups. Reading and drinking with the woman I loved, I thought that I was the happiest man in the world.

By nature I did not particularly care for so-called proper manners. I was sometimes annoyed by Yün's strict adherence to etiquette. Whenever I helped her with her clothes, she always said, "Thanks, thanks"; whenever I handed something to her, such as a towel, she always stood up to receive it. "Are you going to tie me up, hand and foot, with your so-called proper manners?" I asked brusquely at one time. "Do you realize that, as our ancients say, deception lurks behind overpoliteness?"

"How can you confuse respectfulness with deception?" she retorted with a reddened face.

"Respectfulness exists within and has nothing to do with overpoliteness which is superficial and unnecessary," I responded.

"No person in the world is dearer than one's parents," she continued. "Can a son be casual with his parents in his outward behavior while claiming that he is reverent toward them inside? Frictions of a personal nature often begin with jests intended to be harmless. But these jests are only too often taken seriously by the other side. I cannot live a single day if anything of this nature ever happens between you and me."

Then I knew how wrong I was and quickly apologized. I pulled her into my arms and caressed and comforted her until she finally smiled. From then on and for the remainder of our married life I never raised an objection when she murmured "Sorry" or "Thanks."

Not far from our house was a Taoist temple called Tungt'ing, popularly known as the Narcissus. The temple compound had in it a large garden, intersected by curving colonnades and zigzagging corridors. During a Taoist festival each wealthy clan in the city followed an ancient tradition by installing its own altar inside the garden. The altar was elaborately decorated; above it hung a glass lamp of beautiful designs and around it were vases of different shapes, in which fresh flowers were arranged in various forms. The competition was intense, as each clan tried to outdo the others in its display of beauty or, perhaps more correctly, vanity. At night, while plays were staged in the theater in honor of the gods, thousands of candles of various heights were lit around the flowers, creating a phenomenon known locally as "beauties that reflect one another." There were tables across the vast garden, and around them people played music or listened to it, chatted over a cup of tea, or did nothing in particular except enjoy the sight. During a Taoist festival thousands came and went each night.

I told Yün how much I enjoyed it after seeing it with some of my friends. "Unfortunately I am not a man and cannot go there myself," she said disappointedly.

"Why, if you wear my hat and change into my clothes," I responded, "who knows that you are not a man?" Taking my suggestion seriously, she quickly loosened her hair band and braided it into a queue, washed off her makeup, and put my hat on. My gown proved to be two inches too long and somewhat too wide. But this did not pose much of a problem, as she altered it to her own size. Having put the gown on, she covered the upper part of it with a jacket, which further camouflaged her femininity. "All this is fine," she said, while looking at herself in the mirror, "but what am I going to do with my feet?"

"There are in the market the so-called butterfly boots that have a variety of sizes," I responded. "I shall fetch a pair for you, and you shall wear them outside your regular shoes."

After supper when she was dressed as a man, I coached her on how to walk and act like a man. She learned diligently and then suddenly decided that she was not going after all. "If people ever find out about my impersonation or if my parents-in-law ever hear about it," she reasoned, "what would become of me?"

"People in charge of the temple know me well," I assured her. "If the impersonation is discovered, they would probably have a good laugh, and that is about all. My mother is currently visiting one of her daughters far away and will never find out if we do not tell her. We go there in secret and come back in secret. Nobody in the world will ever know."

Yün took a last look at herself in the mirror and burst into laughter again. I pulled her by the arm, and without anybody's knowledge she and I went on with our nighttime excursion. We moved up and down the temple ground; happily no one discovered her true identity. When we encountered an acquaintance, I just introduced her as one of my younger cousins, making sure that she merely bowed and never uttered a single word. Yün enjoyed the sight thoroughly, as we visited one altar after another. At one of the last altars we visited, Yün accidentally brushed a young woman's shoulder with her elbow. The woman's attendant, who sat nearby, jumped from her seat and spoke in great anger, "What kind of scoundrel are you who dare to be so impudent?" I quickly apologized, but in vain. In desperation Yün took off her boots, showing that she, too, was a woman. I can still remember their surprise, as they had never heard of a woman impersonating a man before. Their anger disappeared instantly, and they invited us to share their refreshments. After a pleasant chat of some length, they sent for their sedan chairs to bring us home.

One summer when I was again at home, I requested and received my mother's permission to rent a cottage east of the Chinmu Bridge. In front of the cottage was a fish pond and behind it was a vegetable garden. To the west of it rose a hill that provided a broad view of the wilderness farther beyond. Underneath the shade trees and next to the pond Yün and I often angled together. As the evening drew near, we climbed the hill to view the sunset. At night when the moon made its appearance in the pond, we moved chaise longues to the water's edge. We drank toasts to the moon as well as to each other, and the gardener's wife, who often joined us, had stories of ghosts to tell. "Someday you and I will build a cottage here, surrounded by a vegetable garden," said Yün. "The income from the garden, plus your painting and my embroidery, will enable us to live reasonably well. We do not have to go anywhere else: right here we shall find our paradise."

Today the vegetable garden is still there. Even if I could purchase it, who will be there to share it with me?

Notes

1. This is a condensed version of the Chinese original. Source: *Fou-sheng liu-chi*, roll 1.

2. The author was married to a daughter of his mother's brother. According to Chinese custom, it was permissible, and in fact quite common, to marry one's maternal cousin, but one could not marry one's paternal cousin, since in this case the cousins shared the same surname. Only in the twentieth century was this custom abolished.

3. The *Song of P'i-p'a*, or *P'i-p'a hsing*, was written by the T'ang poet Po Chü-yi (772–846).

Chronological Chart

Chronological Chart

Dynasties	Government and Politics
Hsia (ca. 2205–ca. 1766 B.C.)	Yü, founder of the Hsia dynasty The Great Flood (legend?) Chieh, last Hsia ruler
Shang (ca. 1766–ca. 1122 B.C.)	T'ang, founder of the Shang dynasty Frequent shift of capital until it was settled at Yin (modern Honan province) in 1401 B.C. P'an-keng (ca. 1401–1374 B.C.)
Chou (ca. 1122–249 B.C.) West Chou (ca. 1122–771 B.C.) East Chou (770–249 B.C.) Spring and Autumn period (722–481 B.C.) Warring States period (403–221 B.C.)	King Wen, King Wu, and Duke Chou Feudalism established, ca. 1122 B.C. Feudal states: Lu, Ch'i, Tsin, etc. Interstate warfare after 771 B.C.; interstate conferences; decline of feudalism Duke Huan of Ch'i and Duke Wen of Tsin Rise of Ch'u Warring States: Ch'in, Ch'i, Ch'u, Chao, Han, Wei, and Yen
Ch'in (221–207 B.C.)	Shih Huang-ti, Li Ssu China unified, 221 B.C. Legalism adopted as the state philosophy: the burning of books Central control and bureaucratic administration over all parts of China
Han (202 B.C.–A.D. 220) Former Han (202 B.C.–A.D. 9) Hsin dynasty (A.D. 9–23) Later Han (A.D. 25–220)	Liu Pang (Han Kao-tsu) Han Wu-ti Defeat of Hsiung-nu and conquest of Korea Usurpation of the Han throne by Wang Mang Liu Hsiu, founder of the Later Han Usurpation of power by eunuchs Massacre of eunuchs, A.D. 189 Ts'ao Ts'ao

Socioeconomic Developments	Culture
Domestication of animals Cultivation of wheat and millet Sericulture	Black pottery Animism
Trade; cowrie shells used as medium of exchange	White incised pottery Bronze vessels and weapons Carved ivory and jade Written language *(chia-ku wen)* Ancestor worship Oracle bones
The "well-field" system *(ching-t'ien chih)* The rise of the merchant class and the growth of cities after the eighth century B.C. Sinicization of South China Iron Age Introduction of metallic coins Shang Yang's social and economic reforms Roaming scholars	*Book of Odes* Confucius Mo Ti *Book of Taoist Virtue* Chuang Chou Mencius Ch'ü Yüan and Sung Yü Han Fei *Chou-pi Mathematics*
Standardization of weights and measures *The Ch'in Code* Irrigation projects and public works	*Small Script* declared as standard for all writing
Persecution of merchants Wang Mang's reforms Resurgence of the landed class under the Later Han regime Personal loyalty	Tung Chung-shu Confucianism declared as the state philosophy Ssu-ma Ch'ien Ssu-ma Hsiang-yü Alchemy Compass Pan Ku, Pan Chao Invention of paper Introduction of Buddhism Wang Ch'ung *The Peacock Flies Southeast*

Dynasties	Government and Politics
Three Kingdoms	Ts'ao P'i, Liu Pei, Sun Ch'üan
Wei (220–65) Shu (221–65) Wu (222–80)	
Tsin (265–420)	Tsin Wu-ti
	Barbarian invasions
West Tsin (265–317)	Sack of Loyang, 311 and 316
East Tsin (317–420)	Tsin Yüan-ti
Southern and Northern Dynasties	China divided
	Liu Yü
South: Liu Sung, 420–79; Ch'i,	Shih Hu, Wei Hsiao-wen-ti
479–502; Liang, 502–57; Ch'en,	Liang Wu-ti
557–89	
North: Later (North) Wei, 386– 535; East Wei, 534–50; West Wei, 535–56; North Ch'i, 550– 77; North Chou, 557–81	
Sui (590–618)	Sui Wen-ti
	Sui Yang-ti
	Civil service examination intro- duced
	War with Korea
T'ang (618–906)	Li Shih-min (T'ang T'ai-tsung)
	T'ang Kao-tsung: conquest of Central Asia and Korea
	Empress Wu
	The Three Secretariat System; Six Ministries
	T'ang Hsüan-tsung
	An Lu-shan's revolt
	Hui-heh, T'u-fan
Five Dynasties (907–60)	Warlordism
	Loss of the Sixteen Yen-Yün Districts
Later Liang, 907–23 Later T'ang, 923–36 Later Tsin, 936–47 Later Han, 947–50 Later Chou, 951–60	Chou Shih-tsu

Socioeconomic Development	Culture
The nine-rank system introduced	Decline of Confucianism Taoism; Buddhism

Mass migration to the Yangtze region, fourth century Clans Moral decline of the gentry class Invaders Sinicized Hsiao-wen-ti's land reform Elite families	Pilgrimage to India: Fa-hsien Calligraphy: Wang Hsi-chih T'ao Ch'ien Seven Sages of the Bamboo Grove "Parallel form" Buddhism: popularity and persecution

Ever-ready granaries Grand Canal	Block printing

Land distribution *Liang-shui fa* (semiannual tax system) Arab and Persian traders	Hsüan-tsang Buddhism: Ch'an and Pure Land Zoroastrianism, Manicheanism, Nestorianism, Islam Cultural expansion Essayists: Han Yü, Liu Tsung-ch'üan Poets: Li Po, Tu Fu, Po Chü-yi Painters: Li Ssu-hsün, Wu Tao-tzu, Wang Wei Dance and music
Foot binding introduced	Printing of Confucian classics Li Yü

Dynasties	*Government and Politics*
Sung (960–1279)	Chao K'uang-yin (Sung T'ai-tsu)
	"Disarmament beside the wine
North Sung, 960–1126	cups"
South Sung, 1127–1279	Agreement of River Shan
Liao, 907–1125	The Tangut War
West Hsia, 990–1227	Sung Shen-tsung
Chin, 1115–1234	Fang La rebellion
	Fall of Kaifeng, 1126
	Sung Kao-tsung
	Yo Fei
	Rise of the Mongols
Yüan (1260–1368)	Genghis Khan
	Ogodei
	Yeh-lü Ch'u-ts'ai
	Kublai Khan
	Corruption of Mongol princes
Ming (1368–1644)	Chu Yüan-chang (Ming T'ai-tsu)
	Yung-lo (Ming Ch'eng-tsu)
	Seven Voyages to the "Western"
	Ocean
	The tribute system
	Japanese pirates
	Eunuchs: Wei Chung-hsien
	Chang Hsien-chung, Li Tzu-ch'eng
Ch'ing (1644–1912)	K'ang-hsi, Ch'ien-lung, Yung-cheng,
	Chia-ch'ing
	Secret societies
	Opium War
	Taiping rebellion

Note: For listings that are not discussed in this book the reader may wish to consult Dun J. Li, *The Ageless Chinese: A History* (New York: Scribners, 1971), 2nd edition.

Socioeconomic Development	Culture

Wang An-shih's reforms
Decline of women's status
Paper currency
	Four Colleges
	Movable type
	Philosophers: Chou Tun-yi, Chu Hsi,
	   Lu Chiu-yüan
	Tz'u poets: Liu Yung, Li Ch'ing-
	   chao, Hsin Ch'i-chi
	Essayist: Su Shih
	Historians: Ou-yang Hsiu, Ssu-ma
	   Kuang
	Painting: Mi Fei
	Vernacular tales

Caste system
Corporal punishment
	Lamaism
	Road construction; Grand Canal
	Music drama: *The Romance of the
	   West Chamber*
	The Marsh Heroes
	*The Romance of the Three King-
	   doms*

Plantations Commercial expansion Gentry Deterioration of peasantry	*Yung-lo Encyclopedia* Wang Shou-jen T'ang Yin and Tung Ch'i-ch'ang School system "Eight-legged" essays Ku Yen-wu, Huang Tsung-hsi Jesuits *Flowering Plum in a Golden Vase*
Population increase Opium addiction Taiping's social and economic re- forms Introduction of modern industries	The Han and Sung schools *Four Treasuries* Introduction of Western culture Christianity Yen Yüan *The Dream of the Red Chamber* *An Unofficial History of the Literati* *Six Chapters of a Floating Life*

INDEX

Note: In order to facilitate the location of an entry, the index is compiled in such a way as to ignore the presence or absence of apostrophe, hyphen, or umlaut.